Temperance Torchlights

By MATILDA ERICKSON

Studies, Stories, Songs, Poems, and useful information on Temperance Topics; for the use of Individuals, Churches, Schools, Temperance and Young People's Societies

---

The honor of God, the stability of the nation, the well-being of the community, of the home, and of the individual, demand that every possible effort be made in arousing the people to the evils of intemperance.—*Mrs. E. G. White*

Wipf & Stock
PUBLISHERS
Eugene, Oregon

ACKNOWLEDGMENT

It is a pleasure to acknowledge my indebtedness to those who by their encouragement and practical assistance have made the preparation of this book possible. Elder W. A. Colcord and Prof. M. E. Kern have rendered valuable service by their counsel and in the selection of statistics and other material. Drs. G. H. Heald, W. A. George, David Paulson, and H. F. Rand, and Mrs. Fannie D. Chase have kindly read the manuscript and made very helpful suggestions.

Wipf and Stock Publishers
199 W 8th Ave, Suite 3
Eugene, OR 97401

Temperance Torchlights
By Erickson, Matilda
ISBN 13: 978-1-59752-812-2
ISBN: 1-59752-812-9
Publication date 7/5/2006
Previously published by Review and Herald Pub. Assn., 1920

CONTENTS

A World-Wide Evil

INTEMPERANCE	9–12

The Curse of the Cup

THE LIQUOR TRAFFIC	15–20
SOME FACTS AND FIGURES	21–30
A FEW WORDS FROM LIQUOR DEALERS	31–33
WHAT SCIENCE SAYS ABOUT ALCOHOL	34–42
WHAT SOME PEOPLE SAY ABOUT LIQUOR	43–45
FLASHLIGHTS ON THE EVILS OF INTEMPERANCE	46–57
POEMS AND SONGS	58–68

An Ally of the Liquor Traffic

TOBACCO	71–76
SOME IMPORTANT FACTS	77–81
AS OTHERS SEE IT	82–84
THOUGHTS FOR MEDITATION	85–91
POEMS	92–98

The Great American Fraud

PLEASE DO NOT ASK US	100
PATENT MEDICINES AND DRUGS	101–109
SPARKS FROM THE ANVIL	110–112

The Temperance Movement

TEMPERANCE IN AMERICA	115–122
TEMPERANCE IN OTHER LANDS	123–126

Beacon Lights in the Temperance Movement

SHORT BIOGRAPHIES	129–138

The Law and the Liquor Traffic

PROHIBITION	141–149
SOME RESULTS OF PROHIBITION	150, 151
"THE TIDE HEAVES ONWARD"	152–155
WHY WE FAVOR PROHIBITION	156, 157
READING WORTH WHILE	158–169
THE STORY IN RHYME	170–176

The Corner-Stone of Temperance

BIBLE READING ON TEMPERANCE	178
CHRISTIAN TEMPERANCE	179–184
ALLIES OF INTEMPERANCE	185, 186
THE CURE FOR NATIONAL INTEMPERANCE	187–190
FOUR LESSONS ON TEMPERANCE	191–197
SHORT SELECTIONS	198–202

Temperance Evangelism

WHAT THE TIMES DEMAND	204
OUR DUTY AND RESPONSIBILITY	205–214
HINTS FOR TEMPERANCE WORKERS	215, 216
THE TEMPERANCE PLEDGE	217
TOTAL ABSTINENCE	218, 219
SIGNAL LIGHTS	220–227
RECITATIONS	228–230

Temperance Meetings

WHAT TEMPERANCE WORKERS SHOULD TEACH	232
SUGGESTIONS FOR PROGRAMS	233–235
SUGGESTIONS FOR A YOUNG PEOPLE'S TEMPERANCE RALLY	236
TEMPERANCE RALLIES AT CAMP-MEETINGS	237, 238
THIRTY TOPICS FOR TEMPERANCE PAPERS, ESSAYS, OR TALKS	239
SIMPLE EXPERIMENTS	240–242
SAMPLE PROGRAMS AND PLEDGES	243, 244
BIBLIOGRAPHY	245–248
SONGS WITH MUSIC	68, 128, 176

INTRODUCTION

INTEMPERANCE is the greatest foe of the human family. It is no respecter of persons. It lays its traps and pitfalls for good and bad, strong and weak, great and small, alike. In its milder form it impairs both body and mind, disqualifying them for the highest and best service of life. In its worst form it stamps a curse upon children before their birth, and robs them of food, clothing, love, and education during their helpless years. It lures the young into dens of vice, ruins them for life, and breaks the hearts of their parents. It fills courts with criminal cases, prisons with convicts, and asylums with maniacs. No indictment too terrible could be brought against this gigantic evil.

One of the saddest and most appalling features of the curse of intemperance is the fact that it looks to the boys and girls approaching maturity for its recruits. Upon these it lives and thrives. Intemperance cuts its victims down so fast, that were it not for the fresh recruits from among the innocent youth, its race would soon be run. But the young are taken in its snares, and so the great river of human wrecks flows on forever.

This book is a valuable contribution to the cause of temperance. It is one more keen weapon placed in the hands of the "temperance army." The fund of information it contains will inspire the advocates of temperance to work with greater zeal, and it will lead many who are now halting and indifferent to take a firm stand for the temperance cause. The testimony it gives from many of the world's greatest physicians, statesmen, prison officials, and ministers of the gospel is of great value, and can not fail to make a profound impression upon those into whose hands the book may fall. The statistics, poems, songs, and suggestions relating to temperance meetings will be very helpful to those whose hearts yearn to do something to advance the cause of true temperance.

The century that has passed since Dr. Clark organized the first temperance society in America has been one of marvelous progress and victory for the cause of temperance. The organized movement that has grown out of Dr. Clark's small society has encircled the world. The governments of many nations have felt the power of this movement, and have done much to lessen the evils of intemperance.

What has been accomplished is cheering evidence that the earnest prayers and endeavors of devoted, self-sacrificing temperance workers have not been in vain. But a great work remains to be done. The pressing needs of the suffering, sorrowing, hopeless millions who have already become the prey of this terrible foe, and the welfare of the innocent youth who will surely be taken next unless they receive immediate help, call for the continuation of the earnest endeavors of all who value the blessings and triumphs of the temperance cause.

A. G. DANIELLS.

A WORLD-WIDE EVIL

"Intemperance lies at the foundation of the moral depravity of the world."

RESCUE THE FALLEN

INTEMPERANCE

The Half Has Never Been Told

Before Columbus discovered America, before Titus demolished Jerusalem, and before Joshua marched up to Jericho, intemperance was making havoc of human destinies. Away back to the first lack of self-control amid the glories of Eden, intemperance traces its ancestry. God gave our first parents an opportunity to learn the lesson of self-control. The prohibition under which he placed them stimulated the higher motives, and obedience would have brought increased moral strength, and saved the world its many woes.

But one day the tempter came to the Edenic home. It was an ideal home. Sorrow had never crossed its threshold; poverty had never entered its door; it knew nothing of trouble and sickness. Day by day the sun rose and set on that happy, peaceful home. But after the tempter's visit all was changed. His pleasing arguments and well-sounding promises received consideration. Had he only reminded the happy home of the other side of his story — the dark side! Had he only reminded the dwellers in Eden that his plan for self-indulgence would bring them self-destruction! that it would rob them of their purity and of their keen appetite for the true and beautiful! that it would bring sorrow and suffering into their home, and cause peace and happiness to flee away! But no; filling the listening minds with pleasant and curious anticipations, he led his victims on to eat the bitter fruits of self-indulgence.

For six thousand years he has been using that same scheme of self-indulgence for luring humanity on to ruin. Blinding the eyes of the sons and daughters of men to the awful results of sin, he holds before them the temporary pleasures it brings; and earth's disappointed, sorrowful masses testify to the success of his plan for destroying the children of men. Down through the ages its records tell of naught but earth's deepest suffering, greatest woes, and most flagrant sins. Intemperance in eating and drinking was one of the prevailing sins of Sodom, and the fundamental cause of the moral corruption of the world in Noah's day. It was intemperance that hurled Belshazzar from the Babylonian throne, and later brought to a sudden close Alexander's career as emperor of the world. That same sin was the prime cause of the fall of the great Roman empire. It overthrew the house of Orleans, and sent the royal family of France into exile. To nations and to individuals it has ever been the mortal enemy of peace, prosperity, and happiness. It has dug more graves, and sent more people into eternity, than have all the pestilences and wars that have wasted life since the world began. Of the sorrow, the shame, and the woe it has caused, the half has never been told.

The Outlook To-day

The sequel to intemperance is found in most of the miseries that abound in both civilized and uncivilized nations. Look at China under the opium curse, which is still robbing the Celestial Kingdom of her manly men. Hear the cries from the liquor-stricken districts of Africa. "We beg of you to send us more gospel and less rum," pleads the Kongo native; but still, with the tidings of peace to the poor heathen, goes the weapon for their present and eternal destruction. Everywhere tobacco in its various forms is barring children and youth from their highest possibilities, and robbing the world of its best assets. Patent medicines, drugs, and many popular drinks are parasites of public health and public wealth. Many homes, disregarding the principles of healthful living, are giving to their children the first lessons in intemperance.

A World-Wide Evil

Every year millions upon millions of dollars are consumed in buying wretchedness, poverty, disease, degradation, lust, crime, and death. Each year intemperance is crowding more and more unfortunate beings into houses of prostitution, dens of vice, criminal courts, prisons, almshouses, insane asylums, and hospitals. But nowhere is the curse felt more bitterly than in the home. It is there the burning tears flow, and the agonizing cries escape the lips. "Mary," said a poor drunkard to his pale-faced wife, "you should have married a better man." "I did, John," she replied, softly, lifting her tear-dimmed eyes. This is only one of the marred marriages, only one of the shipwrecked husbands, only one of the broken-hearted wives, only one of the ruined homes.

Hope for the Tempted

Can this tide of evil ever be rolled back? Must intemperance forever rest like a blight upon Christian lands? Must it every year sweep like a devouring fire over our happy homes? Have all the efforts of temperance workers been in vain?

> "Sometimes we are almost discouraged,
>   The way is so cumbered and steep;
> Sometimes though we're spent with sowing,
>   There cometh no harvest to reap,
> And we faint on the road and falter,
>   As our faith and our courage are gone,
> Till a Voice, as we kneel at the altar,
>   Commands us, 'Take heart and go on.'"

God still holds the helm of the universe; and though the instigator of intemperance claims this world, God says to the tempted one, "Be . . . strong, and show thyself a man." And by the grace of him who overcame the world, the weak and tempted can withstand the tempter's power. But some one must help the weak to lay hold on the only arm that can save. "The honor of God, the stability of the nation, the well-being of the community, of the home, and of the individual demand that every possible effort be made in arousing the people to the evil of intemperance." There is a place in this temperance cause for every young man and woman on God's earth; first, in Christ, to become more than conquerors, and then to go forth with the motto, "No compromise and no cessation of efforts till victory is gained."

> "Freighted with love, our temperance ship
> Around the world shall sail;
> Take heart and hope, dear mariners,
> God's errands never fail."

One of the oldest Egyptian papyri belonging to the fifth Egyptian dynasty contains the following warning against drinking in wine shops: "My son, do not linger in the wine shop, or drink too much wine. It causeth thee to utter words against thy neighbors that thou rememberest not. Thou fallest upon the ground, thy limbs become weak as those of a child. One cometh to do trade with thee, and findeth thee so. Then say they, 'Take away the fellow, for he is drunk.'" — *Dr. W. L. Brown.*

The oldest known tombs in the historic period constantly contain references to wine and beer as among the offerings to the dead. Discoveries made during the past few years have brought to light tombs of the kings of the first three dynasties. Curiously enough, some of the things found therein are the clay sealings with the king's name on wine jars. (See Petrie's "History of Egypt," Vol. I, fourth edition, 1899.) — *Dr. A. F. R. Platt.*

Intemperance is the mightiest of all the forces that clog the progress of good. — *Buxton.*

Intemperance is the voluntary extinction of reason. — *Channing.*

THE CURSE OF THE CUP

"Alcohol is the one evil genius, whether in wine or ale or whisky, and is killing the race of men."

"What is alcohol? — A poison — a brain poison — a soul poison — a poison of virtues, of morals and religion — the cause of more sin than all the other causes combined."

There was an old decanter, and its mouth was gapping wide; the rosy wine had ebbed away and left its crystal side; and the wind went humming, humming; up and down the sides it flew; and through the reed-like hollow neck, the wildest notes it blew. I placed it in the window where the breeze was blowing free, and fancied that its pale mouth sang in queerest strains to me: "They tell me —puny conquerors!—the Plague has slain his ten, and War his hundred thousands of the very best of men! but I"'twas thus the bottle spoke— "But I have conquered more than all your famous warriors and maidens fair by far. Come drink from out my cup the beverage that dulls the brain and burns the spirit up; that puts to shame the conquerors that lay their thousands low; for this has deluged millions with a lava tide of woe. Though in the path of battle darkest waves of blood may roll, I, while I slew the body, have also slain the soul. Nor want nor sword, nor ghastly plague, such havoc ever wrought as I in rage, or sheerest sport on the innocent have brought. And still I breathe upon them and they wilt beneath my breath, and year by year my victims tread the dismal road to death.

THE OLD DECANTER

THE LIQUOR TRAFFIC

In Some Heathen Lands

The liquor traffic is a curse wherever it goes. As a Japanese proverb says, "First the man takes a drink, then the drink takes a drink, then the drink takes the man." That is exactly what intemperance has done for some of the Pacific islanders. The American saloon is considered the Philippines' greatest curse. Drinking has not only made the Hawaiians an aimless people, but it is also hastening their extinction. "The Maoris of New Zealand, once probably the noblest race with which civilization has been brought in contact, are now a lazy, drunken, immoral people;" and the chief justice of New Zealand says that if drinking continues, the Maoris will soon be exterminated. Similar conditions exist in Fiji, Samoa, Tonga, and other island groups, as well as in the larger islands near the continents. The Bushmen of Australia, once strong and robust, have been destroyed by the white man's whisky. When the traffic entered Madagascar, it produced frightful havoc there. "The crime of the island rose in one short year by leaps and bounds too fearful to record." To Africa in many respects civilization proved to be an "apostle of vice." Sir Richard Burton, discoverer of Tanganyika, says, "It is my sincere belief that if the slave-trade were revived with all its horrors, and Africa could get rid of the white man, with the gunpowder and rum which he has introduced, Africa would be a gainer of happiness by the exchange." These are some of the records which are rolling a humiliating reproach unto civilized lands, in showing that the liquor curse was brought to the poor heathen by his more enlightened brother.

In Europe and America

The same spirit of commercialism which has introduced the liquor traffic into heathen lands, fosters it in civilized countries. In these the curse has long continued to spread, and is speedily making the larger cities sinks of corruption. While it is impossible to obtain statistics showing fully the ravages of this world-wide curse, a few figures will help us to sense its enormity. In fifty-five years the drink bill in the United States increased fivefold per capita; in France, since 1880, it has increased from 2.32 liters per capita to 4.35 liters. Great Britain destroys ninety million bushels of grain yearly in the manufacture of beer. That grain would make about five billion four hundred million pounds of bread. Each year the fair land of the "stars and stripes" spends about one billion six hundred million dollars for intoxicants. The saloons within her borders, allowing eleven feet frontage for each, would line both sides of a street reaching from Washington, D. C., to Kansas City, Missouri. Chicago alone is said to spend four hundred thousand dollars a day for liquor. In Boston, it is said, over one hundred thousand persons pat-

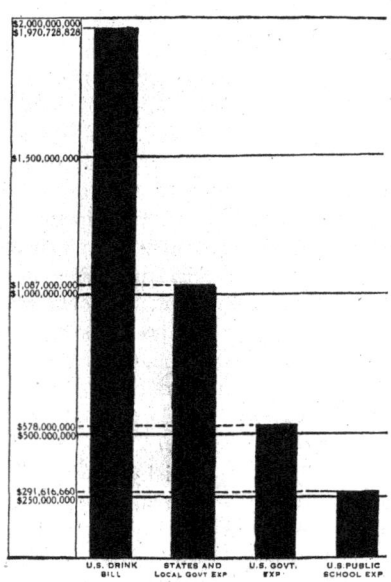

UNITED STATES DRINK BILL

The Curse of the Cup

ronize the saloons every day, and $22,675 are passed over the bars. The kegs which the nations fill yearly with beer would belt the world at the equator seven times.

The Returns

Vast sums of money are consumed in the liquor traffic. But it does not stop there. Far more deplorable is the suffering and woe for which it is responsible. The great cause of poverty, of disease, of crime, and of sorrow — is drink.

From each bushel of corn turned over to the liquor traffic —

The distiller gets four gallons of whisky, which retails at	$17.00
The farmer gets	.45
The government gets	4.40
The railroad company gets	1.00
The manufacturer gets	4.00
The drayman gets	.15
The retailer gets	7.00
The consumer gets	drunk
The wife gets	hunger
The children get	rags

It is almost impossible to read of a crime for which liquor is not in some way responsible. The dividend which the traffic pays to the United States is twenty-five per cent of all the poverty that seeks public relief, fifty per cent of insane cases, seventy-five per cent of the murders committed, and eighty-six per cent of all crimes. In 1908 there were 8,952 murders in the United States, and 10,852 suicides; and each year about fifty thousand persons become insane. Yearly the liquor traffic in this country causes one hundred thousand men to reel into drunkards' graves. Nor does it curse the drinker alone. It bequeaths to his posterity diseased bodies and weakened constitutions; to his home it brings strife, poverty, and sorrow; it threatens the public safety of his community; and it robs his country of her nobility.

It does more; for the saloon never comes alone. It always brings with it the gambling booth, the dancing hall, and other dens of pollution. "The worst and most prolific source of ungovernable lust in the world is the saloon." From its darkened windows and screened doors, it sends forth sensational music to captivate those whose feet have not yet crossed the cursed threshold. The cheap talk of the saloon, the filthy stories, the obscene pictures, the suggestive songs, all are a part of its machinery for putting "the beast within men on the throne." An association in Chicago says that in one year nineteen hundred permits to sell liquor were granted to dance halls, making them, more than ever, schools of infamy. But here the heart-rending results of the liquor traffic stifle statistics. Figures never can measure the sorrow and agony of young men and women who have entered the door "where virtue, once entered, is virtue no more."

Saloon Wants

Yet in the face of such facts, hundreds of thousands are to-day going toward drunkards' graves. Vacancies in the drunkards' line are soon filled. Volunteers crowd it continually.

> "'Tis somebody's boy who will fill the place,
> Somebody's boy with his fair young face;
> 'Tis somebody's boy — is it yours or mine? —
> That will fill the place in the drunkards' line."

Just as the sawmill needs wood, and the flour-mill needs grain, to make the business profitable; so the liquor dealers need boys — and they plan to get them. Should the saloon in your community put forth a truthful and an unmasked advertisement, it would read something like this: —

"Wanted, one hundred boys for new customers; old

ones dropping off,— ten committed suicide; twenty in jail; fifteen sent to poorhouse; five sent to insane asylum."

A Los Angeles paper speaks of clubs organized to prepare boys to become patrons of saloons and gambling halls.

HOW MY BOY WENT DOWN

In some towns tickets, signed by brewing companies, have been distributed among boys. These tickets read: "To Shipping Room. Give bearer —— glasses of beer." Such snares are laid for the youth. Let us save them from the first taste. That first glass is the devil's ironclad mortgage on them.

During the temperance campaign preceding election in a certain city, a banner floated across the street, on which were these words: "The saloon wants your boy. Can you spare him?" It is noble to cast out the life-line to those struggling in the sea of intemperance, but far better to light some beacon to guide the youthful feet aright.

The Saloon Problem

But this foe, with which every temperance worker must reckon, has ensconced himself in a fortress whose walls of appetite, avarice, politics, and of social customs, are well-nigh impregnable. On the side of appetite stand those who are slaves of the cup; on the side of avarice are lined up the liquor forces whose bank accounts depend upon the success of the traffic; on the side of politics stands the government with uplifted shield; and on the side of custom is "the social drinking cup" of the Anglo-Saxon races, which has for centuries been planting in nations the fatal passion of drink.

Thus the traffic is guarded. And this guard is often re-enforced. The saloons, being the main point of contact between the liquor dealers and the public, are the real recruiting stations of the traffic. Everywhere these "schools of crime" are educating people to wrong ideals of life. Taking New York City as a whole, there are ten saloons to every place of public worship, and a certain district of that city which has one hundred eleven churches, chapels, and missions, contains four thousand sixty-five saloons. Chicago has one thousand places of public worship; she has seven thousand two hundred saloons. "The saloon is a day-school, a night-school, a vacation school, a Sunday-school, a kindergarten, a college, and a university, all in one. It runs without term-ends, vacations, or holidays." Such is the diligence of the enemy in the fortress. That enemy is the most formidable agent of degeneration, and lurks as a foe at the foundation of all social and political reform.

The life insurance companies make a business of estimating men's lives, and can only make money by making correct estimates of whatever influences life. Now they expect that a man, otherwise healthy, who is addicted to beer drinking, will have his life shortened from forty to sixty per cent. For instance, if he is twenty years old and does not drink beer, he may reasonably expect to live until he is sixty-one. If he is a beer drinker, he will probably drop off somewhere between forty and forty-five instead of living to sixty-four, as he should. There is no sentiment, prejudice, or assertion about these figures.— *Dr. S. S. Thorn, Toledo, Ohio, in U. S. Senate Document published in 1901.*

SOME FACTS AND FIGURES

Dr. E. Kurz, of Heidelberg, Germany, found that out of one thousand one hundred fifteen criminal assaults committed in one judicial district, seventy per cent were committed in the saloon, and less than ten per cent in any other one place.

Three presidents of the United States — Lincoln, Garfield, and McKinley — were assassinated by men on fire with whisky. The murderer of McKinley was born in a saloon, spent fourteen years of his life in the saloon, and when he went to Buffalo to do his awful work, stayed in a saloon.

A lord chief justice of England said: " Judges weary with calling attention to drink as the principal cause of crime. But I can not refrain from saying that if they could make England sober, they would shut up nine tenths of the prisons."

A judge of Philadelphia says: " We can trace four fifths of the crimes that are committed to the influence of rum. There is not one case in twenty where a man is tried for his life, in which rum is not the direct or indirect cause of the murder. Rum and blood, I mean the shedding of blood, go hand in hand."

A Boston district attorney says: " Ninety-nine out of one hundred of the crimes in our commonwealth are produced by intoxicating liquors."

From the testimony of physicians, it is proved that " one hundred thousand persons die annually in the United States as the result of drink."

In one year over one million dollars' worth of property was destroyed by the failures of beer-drinking engineers and switchmen.

Of six hundred eleven paupers in the Edinburgh poorhouse, not one was a total abstainer; four hundred seven of them admitted that their poverty was due to intemperance.

"Out of every one hundred patients that I have charge of at the London Hospital," says Sir Andrew Clark, M. D., "seventy owe their ill health to alcohol."

Sixty thousand drunkards die every year in Great Britain, and at least one hundred twenty thousand lose their lives from alcoholic excesses.

Some one has estimated that all the widows and orphans left behind by drunkards, if standing hand in hand, would belt the globe three times.

"Less money is expended for food and clothing by all the people in the United States than is spent for drink by one third of the people."

The United States drink bill is nearly two hundred times as much as is given by all denominations for foreign missions, and more than twice the amount spent for bread.

The annual police expenditure in the United States is twenty-five million dollars, almost all of which is chargeable to intemperance. There are seventy thousand criminals in the land, involving an expenditure of one hundred twenty-five million dollars a year, and a total loss to the country of more than six hundred million dollars annually. Of the thirty-five thousand tramps abroad in the land, eighty per cent are brought to their present condition through drink.

Hundreds of fine vessels are lost annually because of drunken officers, and over fifty per cent of all accidents occurring on German railroads, declares Dr. Ennis, of the University of Heidelberg, are due to the bewilderment of the operatives who have used stimulants.

More money is spent annually in the United States for whisky, tobacco, and opium than would be required to pay off the national debt.

The "blind tiger" does not confine itself to prohibition territory. Chicago, with its seven thousand licensed saloons, has two thousand five hundred "blind tigers."

The silver dollars used yearly for liquor in the United States, when laid one on top of the other, would make a column 2,992 miles high.

If all the money in the United States were equally divided among the eighty million inhabitants, each would have $33.46, of which $17.15, as now expended, would be spent annually for drink.

The money spent for drink would meet all the net expenses of the government, and not only pension the disabled soldiers, and give an old-age pension of twenty dollars a month to all persons over sixty years of age, but would also provide for the education of each child in the United States from five to eighteen years of age.

For every one thousand killed in battle, rum has dug the grave for twelve thousand.

A Massachusetts manufacturer, in payment of his seven hundred operatives, gave each one a crisp, new ten-dollar bill on Saturday night. Each bill was marked so that it could be recognized. By the Tuesday following, it was found that *four hundred ten* of these seven hundred bills had been deposited in the banks by saloon-keepers.

We have one hundred seventy thousand insane persons in our asylums, fourteen per cent of whom are the immediate victims of strong drink, and many more the indirect victims.

Thirty-seven per cent of the poverty found in almshouses is due to liquor. Forty-five per cent of the destitute children are in that condition because of the liquor habit.

Chief Justice Noah Davis, of New York, recently said: " There is an average of more than two persons murdered in New York City weekly, and there are sixty-seven thousand persons arrested annually for crime, and *nine tenths* of the crimes committed are traced directly to the grogshops." He says, further: " I have sat in the bench twenty-six years, and have sentenced to death many, and the poor wretches had no other excuse but, ' I was drunk.' Our laws make that an aggravation of the crime, while they legalize the drunkard-making. 'How long, O Lord, how long!' until the drunkard-makers, the crime-manufacturers, are brought to judgment!"

A prominent secretary in the Young Men's Christian Association says: "On Sunday evening, Feb. 26, 1899, a

THE REAL BLACK HAND.

careful count was made of the men in a Madison Street saloon (in Chicago) at seven o'clock. The number was five hundred twenty-four, and during the next two hours, four hundred eighty more men entered. At one of the billiard tables young men, six deep on all sides, were engaged in open gambling. Private stairways connect this saloon with the vilest theater in the city. There are three thousand billiard and pool rooms in the city, generally adjacent to, or a part of, a saloon."

Within a brief period in New York City six boys, aged seven, nine, ten, eleven, twelve, and fourteen respectively, were convicted of burglary, three of them having developed a shrewd plan to rob sixty houses. Two boys, fifteen and seventeen years old, were found guilty of assault and highway robbery. Three boys, ten, fourteen, and sixteen years of age, were convicted of murder. In each of these instances alcohol bore a conspicuous part in the family history. Hardly a day passes without its record of juvenile crime.— *Dr. T. A. MacNicholl.*

The population of the British Isles is about the same as of Japan. Their pauper laws are about the same, yet while Japan has only twenty-five thousand paupers, Great Britain has one hundred thousand.

A leading English physician recently declared that the use of alcoholic liquor caused one hundred forty thousand deaths in Great Britain annually.

According to official statistics for Germany in 1900, in Berlin alone eight hundred persons are treated annually by medical men for delirium tremens, while throughout Germany twelve thousand are treated annually for the same disease. Fourteen thousand drunkards are confined in prison, and six thousand in lunatic asylums.

In Leipsic it was found that out of forty-two boys, whose ages averaged seven years, fourteen confessed to having been drunk, twenty-four to having habitually tasted brandy, and seventeen to daily drinking.

In 1903 drink caused more than fifteen thousand divorces in the United States.

"President Schurman, of Cornell University, who was at the head of the Philippine Commission, said: "I regret that the Americans let the saloon get a foothold in the islands. It has hurt the Americans more than anything else, and the spectacle of Americans drunk awakens disgust in the Filipinos. We suppressed the cock-fights there, but left the saloon to flourish. One emphasized the Filipino frailty, and the other the American vice. I have never seen a Filipino drunkard."

The rum tragedy in Manila and throughout the Philippine Islands is the great disgrace in connection with our recent era of expansion. An advance agent of a certain American brewery was in the first ranks of Dewey's force, and ship-loads of beer were following close after the fleet. —*Harry Warner, Secretary of the Intercollegiate Prohibition Association.*

Many a man who calls himself a moderate drinker is in danger of leaving upon society a greater burden than if he rapidly ruined himself through excess, and threw himself directly upon its support.—*Harry Warner.*

Liquor Drinking in the United States

That liquor drinking has been steadily increasing in the United States despite all efforts to lessen the evil, will appear from the following table, only 1908 showing a slight decrease:—

1840	4	gallons per capita
1850	4	" " "
1860	5 1/3	" " "
1870	7 2/3	" " "
1880	10	" " "
1882	12	" " "
1884	12 1/2	" " "
1887	13 2/3	" " "
1888	14 1/3	" " "
1890	15 1/2	" " "
1900	17 2/3	" " "
1906	21	" " "
1907	23 1/2	" " "
1908	23	" " "

The Curse of the Cup

England's Drink Bill

Speaking on the extent of "Great Britain's drink bill," the *English Watchword* has this to say: —

"Thanks to our brewers and publicans, and the co-operation of the magistrates who license them, and the consent of the Christian church which permits the liquor traffic to continue, we have: —

"1,000,000 *paupers* on the rates through *drink*.

100,000 *criminals* in jail through *drink*.

50,000 *lunatics* in asylums through *drink*.

60,000 *deaths* annually through *drink*, and a standing army of —

60,000 confirmed *drunkards*."

The World's Output of Beer

The enormous extent of the beer industry may be gauged by the following table of the world's output, for the year 1903, of the chief beer-drinking countries of the world, compiled by Gambrinus (Vienna): —

	NO. OF BREWERIES
Germany	18,230
United Kingdom	5,547
America and Australia	2,210
Austria-Hungary	1,436
Belgium	3,319
France	3,360
Russia	920
Sweden	250
Denmark	370
Switzerland	228
Holland	372
Other countries	260
Total	36,502

The beer produced by these 36,502 breweries is estimated at 262,708,000 hectoliters, considerably over 150,000,000 barrels. The materials used involved 7,700,000 tons of malt or malt equivalents, and 2,106,000 hundredweight of hops.

How the United States Uses Money

In 1905 the citizens of this so-called " Christian nation " spent $1,600,000,000 for intoxicants; $600,000,000 for pleasure; $24,000,000 for chewing-gum; $10,000,000 for poodle dogs; and $8,000,000 a day for gambling. The amount contributed to foreign missions was $7,500,000."

How to Pay the Household Bill

It has been estimated that a man who has been accustomed to spend twenty cents a day for drink, can, by saving it, order during one year the following articles: —

3 barrels of flour
200 pounds granulated sugar
29 pounds corn-starch
125 pounds macaroni
60 pounds white beans
1 dozen scrubbing-brushes
20 pounds rice
1 barrel crackers
100 pounds hominy
25 cans tomatoes
1 ream note-paper
500 envelopes
6 pounds of currants
5 gallons of olives
20 pounds of cereal coffee
32 pounds of nut foods
20 pounds dried peaches
50 pounds best raisins
1 dozen packages herbs
40 pounds oatmeal
1 dozen brooms
12 bottles machine-oil
24 cans green peas
20 pounds dried apples
25 pounds prunes
10 pounds laundry starch
26 pounds table salt
12 bottles maple sirup
100 bars soap
25 pounds of cooking oil
12 dozen lemons
2 periodicals

Alcohol in Different Countries

The following table gives the relative amount of alcohol consumed per capita in different countries. The statistics are obtained by adding the percentage of alcohol contained in the various beverages consumed: —

The Curse of the Cup

COUNTRY	QUARTS PER CAPITA	COUNTRY	QUARTS PER CAPITA
Belgium	12.58	Great Britain	8.17
France	12.57	Austria	7.99
Spain	12.05	United States	7.95
Denmark	10.87	Holland	6.30
Switzerland	10.73	Russia	5.21
Italy	10.35	Sweden	4.43
Portugal	10.10	Canada	3.32
Rumania	9.74	Norway	2.66
Germany	9.25	Finland	1.84
	Servia	8.46	

Chicago's Wasted Resources

There are, in round numbers, seven thousand licensed saloons in Chicago. Estimating the average income of these at thirty dollars a day (a low estimate), it amounts to $67,287,750 a year. This money, if turned into channels of usefulness, could, according to the Chicago *Record,* be made to produce the following result: —

Employ 10,000 men cleaning streets and on public improvements, at $1.50 a day	$ 4,695,000
Employ 2,000 teams and men cleaning alleys and streets, at $4 a day	2,504,000
Give each of 60,000 poor families in the city of Chicago $1 a day	18,780,000
Pay the car-fare for 250,000 working people to and from work	7,825,000
Pay for lunch of 250,000 working people, at 20 cents each	15,475,000
Buy one $20 suit of clothes for each of the 250,000 working people	5,000,000
Buy one $4 pair of shoes for each of the 250,000 working people	1,000,000
Buy one $25 suit of clothes for the father of each poor family	1,500,000

Buy one $3 pair of shoes for the mother of each poor family	$ 180,000
Buy one $10 dress for each of these mothers	600,000
Buy two tons of coal for each poor family, at $6.50 a ton	780,000
Buy one barrel of flour for each poor family, at $4 a barrel	240,000
Buy one $4 suit of clothes for every boy and girl in the public schools	723,564
Establish one free library and museum in each division of the city, at $1,000,000 each	3,000,000
Build 30 new schoolhouses, at $100,000 each	3,000,000
Build 36 new churches, at $50,000 each	1,800,000
Give to the Fresh Air fund for poor children	75,000
Give to the various hospitals of the city	100,000
Total	$67,277,564
A balance to begin the new year with	10,186

One Divorce in Five Due to Drink

One of the most striking arguments for temperance reform, says Mr. L. A. Brady, is to be found in certain cold, dispassionate statistics issued by the United States Census Bureau. These figures show that intemperance, as either a direct or a contributing cause, was responsible for more than nineteen per cent — practically one fifth — of all divorces granted in the United States during the twenty years between 1887 and 1906 inclusive. Since at the present rate at least every twelfth marriage ends in divorce, we get a proportion of one home in every sixty-one wrecked by drink. Moreover, the census authorities themselves, according to Mr. Brady, admit that these figures represent only the most flagrant and palpable instances of the part which intemperance plays in divorce, and that greater percentages than those actually given would be nearer the truth.— *Literary Digest, July 17, 1909.*

A FEW WORDS FROM LIQUOR DEALERS

In an address at the liquor men's convention held in Columbus, Ohio, one speaker said: " The success of our business is dependent largely upon the creation of appetite for drink. Men who drink liquor, like others, will die; and *if there is no new appetite created, our counters will be empty, as well as our coffers.* Our children will go hungry, or we must change our business to that of some other more remunerative.

"The open field for the creation of appetite is among the boys. After men have grown, and their habits are formed, they seldom change in this regard, and I make the suggestion, gentlemen, that *nickels expended in treats to the boys now will return in dollars to your tills after the appetite has been formed."*

Mr. McCarthy, a representative of the Bartenders' League, in speaking against the prohibition of liquor sales in the District of Columbia, according to the Washington *Times* of May 6, 1908, said: —

"The American saloon is the poor man's club. It is the nearest approach to absolute democracy in this country. The saloon is the greatest college, without books, in the United States. There is more good in the saloon than is dreamed of in our philosophy. Its ultimate goal is true temperance "

W. H. Hull, general manager of a Peoria, Illinois, distillery, said, as reported in the Washington *Evening Star* of March 28, 1908: —

"I have now forty lecturers in the field. In the coming week they will make three hundred speeches in the principal towns of the State. We think that if the people get a fair idea of what prohibition fanaticism is doing to us, they will give the liquor dealers a square deal.

"We are not fighting temperance, but prohibition.

"The demand for stimulating drinks is world-old, and I say it is much more profitable for a community to have saloons which pay a large revenue than that the liquor should be dealt out by stealth."

Declaration of Principles

The following declaration of principles was adopted, without a dissenting voice, at the forty-eighth annual convention of the United States Brewers' Association held in Milwaukee in June, 1908: —

"The United States Brewers' Association, in convention assembled, presents the following declaration of principles, and declares its sympathy with, and offers its co-operation to, any movement looking to *the promotion of habits of temperance in the use of fermented beverages.* By temperance is meant temperate use — neither abuse nor disuse. We believe that the temperate use of beer promotes health and happiness, which are the underlying conditions of morality and social order, and in this belief we are supported by the vast preponderance of educated as well as popular opinion all over the world."

As Brewers See It

Of course, bills designed to render State prohibition effective by federal legislation have always loomed up at one period or another during the progress of the movement, but it is only of the years that they have been taken so seriously as to bring their enactment within the range of probability.

There are few signs that the prohibition wave which has swept up from the South is about to recede. Only those who are ignorant of the history of the past will dare predict that the wave has already reached its highest point. Like all previous emotional movements, the present one is transitory, of course. But it has been a long time in gathering momentum, and is not likely to disappear of a sudden, although it may undergo some changes. The first temperance movement in the United States required more than ten years to reach a climax. That was in the twenties of the last century. Its successor, in the fifties, also lasted many years. All these movements bear a strong resemblance to each other. The propelling power, then as now, has chiefly been emotion backed by religious sentiment.— *1909 Year Book of United States Brewers' Association.*

The Saloon According to the Saloon-Keeper

A missionary worker, with the hope of sowing some seeds of truth in the hearts of those to whom he might obtain access, visited a number of saloons in a certain city, to secure, if possible, the use of one for holding a Christian meeting. Entering first the saloon nearest his own church, the following conversation occurred: —

" Are you the proprietor? "

" Yes; what do you want? "

" I want to get this room for a meeting to-morrow afternoon at four o'clock."

" What kind of meeting? "

" A Christian meeting."

" You can't have it. Are you just off the island? "

" You'd get some money."

" Don't want your money. I've got so much money now I don't know what to do with it. See that gold? See these bills? "

" Will you come to a four-o'clock meeting in the church, and tell your experience, how you got into this business, what keeps you in it, and how it works? "

" No; that church stands for getting people to heaven; this business gets people to hell."

WHAT SCIENCE SAYS ABOUT ALCOHOL

It is false that alcohol aids digestion.— *F. R. Lees, M. D.*

I have come to the conclusion that alcohol as a medicine can be wholly dispensed with, and more speedy and thorough restoration of health and the prolongation of life be insured. — *John H. Griscomb, M. D.*

Good health will, in my opinion, always be injured by even small doses of alcohol. Even in small doses it will take the bloom from, and injure the perfection and loveliness of, health, both mental and moral.— *Sir Andrew Clark, M. D.*

I hardly know any more potent cause of disease than alcohol.— *Sir William Gull, M. D.*

People say that ardent spirits keep the cold out. I say, they let it in. Few seamen have been in the cold more than I have, and I know that spirits do harm.— *Captain Peary.*

The common notion that some form of alcoholic beverage is necessary in tropical climates is, I firmly believe, a mischievous delusion.— *Dr. Parkes.*

It is often thought that wine and beer and spirits give strength to a man; that they make the muscles contract with more force, and sustain the action. I have put this matter to test by means of experiments, and I have found that the idea of alcohol giving force and activity to the muscles is entirely false.— *B. W. Richardson, M. D.*

Whoever wants, by a short and easy method, to divest his thinking of all clearness and balance, let him apply the bottle.— *John Guthrie, M. A., D. D.*

Six thousand persons in the State of New York alone, owe their insanity to alcohol.— *Dr. Frederick Pellesan, of Columbia University.*

It is an absolute scientific fact that alcoholic drinks, more than any other factor, injure our national life, diminish the physical and intellectual forces of our race, impregnate them with hereditary diseases, and lead to degeneracy.— *A German Scientist*.

Dr. Bollinger, of Munich, said that as a result of excessive beer drinking, it is very rare to find a normal heart and normal kidneys in an adult resident of the city of Munich.

It is estimated that nearly one half of the young men in Germany, between the ages of eighteen and twenty-two, are incapable of bearing arms, the prevalence of heart-disease having increased among them by three hundred per cent within the last twenty years. Beer drinking is considered one of the principal causes of this degeneracy.

From fifty-five to seventy-seven per cent of the descendants of drinking parents are dullards, but only from four to ten per cent of the descendants of abstainers.

The Heritage of Intemperance

In my study of thirty thousand children, taken from the schools attended by the wage-earning classes in New York, I have found conditions apparently incredible in a civilized country. Laboring under the functional trait, inherited from drinking parents, we found that seventy per cent of the children have managed to secure alcoholic beverages in some form, ranging from a glass of beer a week to five glasses a day. Twenty per cent drink wine or spirits.

Of the children found to have parents addicted to the use of alcohol, seventy-one per cent are afflicted with functional or organic disorders directly traceable to their inherited weakness from alcoholic parents, and the trail leads even to the grandchildren of moderate or more regular users of alcoholic beverages.— *Dr. T. Alexander MacNicholl*.

Innocent Sufferers

Dr. Osler, formerly of Johns Hopkins University, has shown that alcoholism and infectious diseases, like tuberculosis, are visited upon the children even " unto the third and fourth generation." In a record of ten families, where the parents were moderate drinkers, it was recently found that out of the fifty-seven children born of the unions, twenty-three died in the first few weeks, six were idiots, five undergrown, five had epilepsy, five suffered from lesser diseases which could be traced to the influence of alcohol, and of the whole number only eleven were considered normal. In the same locality a similar record was made of ten families in which both parents were temperate. Here it was found that . . . the large proportion of fifty out of sixty-one were normal.— *Cosmopolitan, September, 1909.*

Antitheses Between Food and Alcohol

FOOD	ALCOHOL
1. A certain quantity will produce a certain effect at first, and the same quantity will always produce the same effect in the healthy body.	1. A certain quantity will produce a certain effect at first, but it requires more and more to produce the same effect when the drug is used habitually.
2. The habitual use never induces an uncontrollable desire for it, in ever-increasing amounts.	2. The habitual use is likely to induce an uncontrollable desire for more, in ever-increasing amounts.
3. After habitual use, a sudden total abstinence never causes any derangement of the central nervous system.	3. After habitual use, a sudden total abstinence is likely to cause serious derangement of the central nervous system.
4. Is oxidized slowly in the body.	4. Is oxidized rapidly in the body.
5. Being useful, is stored in the body.	5. Not being useful, is not stored in the body.
6. Is the product of constructive activity of protoplasm in the presence of abundant oxygen.	6. Is a product of decomposition of food in the presence of a scarcity of oxygen.

7. Is formed in nature for nourishment of living organisms, and is, therefore, inherently wholesome.

8. The regular ingestion of food is beneficial to the healthy body, but may be deleterious to the sick.

9. The use is followed by no reaction.

10. The use is followed by an increased activity of the muscle cells and brain cells.

11. The use is followed by an increase in the excretion of carbon dioxide.

12. The use may be followed by an accumulation of fat, notwithstanding increased activity.

13. The use is followed by a rise in body temperature.

14. The use strengthens and steadies the muscles.

15. The use makes the brain more active and accurate.

7. Is formed in nature only as an excretion; it is, therefore, in common with all excretions, inherently poisonous.

8. The regular ingestion of alcohol is deleterious to the healthy body, but may be beneficial to the sick (through its drug action).[1]

9. The use, in common with narcotics in general, is followed by a reaction.

10. The use is followed by a decrease in the activity of the muscle cells and brain cells.

11. The use is followed by a decrease in the excretion of carbon dioxide.

12. The use is usually followed by an accumulation of fat through decreased activity.

13. The use may be followed by a fall in body temperature.

14. The use weakens and unsteadies the muscles.

15. The use makes the brain less active and accurate.

— *Dr. Winfield S. Hall.*

---

[1] Excellent physicians, among them the father of the American Medical Association, believe that alcohol is absolutely unnecessary as a medicine.

How Shall We Use God's Gifts?

WHAT BREAD AND BEER DO

Bread increases a man's muscle.

Beer changes muscle to fat.

Grain, made into bread, builds up the man. The strong man builds up his community, helps build the schools and churches, aids in the growth of industries and commerce. He makes all life happier because he uses God's gifts as God intended them to be used.

Grain made into beer, or fruits made into wine or cider or any form of alcoholic drink, break down a man. And the man who takes them, instead of helping to build up a community, is a menace to it. Such men help to fill our jails, penitentiaries, almshouses, and asylums. They bring great expense to a community, because they necessitate having many policemen, hospitals, and places of reform.

Mrs. Winfield S. Hall, a former teacher of physiology, has given us the following clear table of the results of using God's gifts in two different ways: —

                      Happiness

                  Development

              Strength

           Muscle

         Bread

     Grain

         Beer

           Fat

              Weakness

                Decay

                  Sorrow

How, then, shall we use God's gifts?— *Mrs. Edith Smith Davis, Superintendent of Department of Scientific Temperance Instruction of World's W. C. T. U.*

The Facts Plainly Stated

The fact that beer produces body weight is no evidence that it is a food, for morphine, phosphorus, and other deadly poisons do the same. These poisons interfere with normal cell activity, which results in a retention of waste material and fatty degeneration of the tissues. Professor Von Bunge says: "Of all alcoholic drinks, beer is the most injurious." While it produces a species of degeneration of all the organs of the body, it chiefly affects the heart, the liver, and the kidneys.

Any physician who cares to take the time, will tell you that the beer drinker seems incapable of recovering from mild disorders and injuries not usually regarded as of a grave character. Pneumonia, pleurisy, fevers, etc., seem to have a first mortgage on him, which they foreclose remorselessly at an early opportunity. When a beer drinker gets into trouble, it seems almost as if you have to re-create the man before you can do anything for him.

Alcohol diminishes cell activity, and causes fatty degeneration of the heart and other tissues; in appearance, therefore, the user of alcohol may be a picture of health, but in reality he is a degenerate. He has an abundance of flesh, but it is of an inferior quality. The lowered vitality of his tissues renders him incapable of resisting germ diseases. If he does not die of heart-disease or apoplexy, he is almost certain to succumb when stricken down with pneumonia, cholera, or other germ diseases. Cirrhosis of the liver, a condition in which the liver cells are gradually destroyed and replaced by an overgrowth of connective tissue, frequently results from the irritation produced by alcohol.

Children begotten by drinking parents are usually weaklings and defective in both body and mind. Mortality among such in infancy is great. If they survive infancy and reach the age of youth, they are apt to succumb to tuberculosis. Weakened heredity from drinking parents is one cause of the prevalence of this disease among our youth.

The degeneration evinced by the declining birth-rate, which in most of the European countries made necessary the appointment of commissions to investigate its causes, may be attributed partly to the free use of alcoholic beverages; for the more temperate Mongolians and Mohammedans, instead of having a diminishing birth-rate, as is the case in America and in European countries, show a constantly increasing birth-rate. Degeneracy among them is not nearly so marked, and the diseases which prevail in America, such as heart-disease, pneumonia, cerebral hemorrhages, and heat-stroke are very uncommon among them.
D. H. KRESS, M. D.

A Visit to the Hospital

A worker, on a recent visit to Bellevue Hospital, says: "As we entered the ward, the first sight opposite the door was a surgeon dressing a gangrenous arm. His words to the patient, as we caught them, were, ' No, I shall not let you go out; you would get a glass of beer, and that would kill you!' " She continues: " A boy in another bed, motherless, friendless, a stranger in a strange land, speaking no word of ours, had received a slight wound, which pure blood would have thrown off; but he was a beer victim, and his hurt, with his poisoned blood, produced erysipelas. Another had scratched his finger, and his hand is in danger of amputation. And so we went through the list, receiving testimony unexpected to us, almost unasked by us, and almost unconsciously given, that systems clogged with effete matter which beer had prevented passing off were incapable of resisting injury and disease."

Some, if not all of these, no doubt, had thought the beer was doing good. Many boast of the good it does them, or of their being strong in spite of beer. " I have drunk a gallon of beer every day for the last thirty years," said a brewer's drayman, " and I was never in better health than at this moment." Yet the very next day he died in a fit

of apoplexy. The beer told him that lie, and he believed it.
— *Selected.*

Food or Poison — Which?

Some one has said that a lie will travel seven times around the world while truth is putting on its boots. Whether that is really so or not, it is certainly true that many students actually know more about the alcohol-food delusion than they do of the hard, cold scientific facts that show beyond a doubt that alcohol is a poison in any and all quantities. Whence came, then, the " alcohol as a food " notion? That is easily answered.

It has been known for years that a moderate amount of alcohol, while poisoning the body, was at the same time being burned up or oxidized, and to that extent furnished heat and energy, just as a charge of gunpowder, if put into a stove, would burn there and furnish heat, while at the same time it would blast the stove, and perhaps ruin the entire house.

The promoters of the liquor interests, who have so persistently dinned into our ears the fact that two ounces of alcohol could actually be burned up in the system in twenty-four hours, have been very careful to refrain from stating in the same connection that this is true of nearly all poisons when introduced into the body. They have also purposely forgotten to tell us the great truth which Professor Kreapelin of Heidelberg, Germany, has demonstrated by such a vast array of accurate experiments that the whole scientific world has fully accepted his conclusions; namely, that as small a quantity as one third of an ounce of alcohol always produces paralyzing effects on brain activity, nerve sensations, ability to lift, feel, see think, etc., which can be measured by those remarkable instruments of precision with which he works.

So this is what the alcohol-food idea amounts to when it is all boiled down. While the alcohol is burning up in the system, it does furnish a small amount of available heat and energy, but at the same time it is charging such an enormous toll by its paralyzing influences on the entire man, that it is sheer lunacy for any person who is acquainted with the real scientific facts to talk about alcohol being a serviceable food any more than any one of the many well-recognized poisons. DAVID PAULSON, M. D.

Uses of Alcohol

It has been a common practise to condemn alcohol, but it is not the thing itself that should be condemned, but the application to which it is put. The fact that alcohol has wide and varied uses in the arts, sciences, and manufactures, at once shows us that in the service of man, it fills an important and useful place. It is the use of alcohol in the form of intoxicating beverages that should be condemned. The following list of some of the things for which alcohol is necessary shows the important place it fills: —

Aniline colors
Blacking
Burial caskets
Celluloid and zylonite
Chemicals and colors
Chloroform
Dental goods
Dyes
Electrical apparatus
Finishing of carriages and cars, and cabinet work.
Fuel for motors
Fulminating powders
Hats, both straw and felt
Laboratory uses
Lacquers
Methylated spirits
Moldings and picture-frames
Organic analysis
Perfumery
Photographic materials
Preservation of anatomical and other specimens
Quick-drying paints
Rattan goods
Silver plating
Smokeless powder
Shellac
Sulphuric ether
Transparent soap
Thermometers
Tinctures
Varnishes
Vegetable alkaloids

WHAT SOME PEOPLE SAY ABOUT LIQUOR

Wine is a mocker.— *Solomon.*

A curse.— *Queen Victoria.*

A scandal and a shame.— *Wm. E. Gladstone.*

A trap for workingmen.— *Earl Cairnes.*

Stupefies and besots.— *Bismarck.*

The devil in solution.— *Sir Wilfred Lawson.*

Liquid fire and distilled damnation.— *Robert Hall.*

The mother of want and the nurse of crime.— *Lord Brougham.*

Drunkenness is the ripe fruit of moderate drinking.— *Frances E. Willard.*

I never use it; I am more afraid of it than of Yankee bullets.— *Stonewall Jackson.*

O! that men would put an enemy in their mouths, to steal away their brains!— *Shakespeare.*

Intemperance is not the only sin in the world, but it is one of the most prevalent and dangerous.— *Anon.*

Wine has drowned more men than the sea.— *Plebeus Syrus.*

If temperance prevails, then education can prevail; if temperance fails, then education must fail.— *Horace Mann.*

Every moderate drinker could abandon the cup if he would; every inebriate would if he could.— *John B. Gough.*

The liquor traffic is a cancer in society. It must be eradicated; not a root must be left behind.— *Abraham Lincoln.*

Only one shop manufactures paupers and criminals — the drink shop.— *Rev. C. Garrett.*

The saloon men themselves are ashamed of their business; they are not proud of their finished product — a drunkard down in the gutter.— *Anon.*

The use of strong drink produces more idleness, crime,

disease, want, misery, than all other causes put together.— *Editor London Times.*

Grape juice has killed more than grape shot.— *Spurgeon.*

Strong drink is not only the devil's way into a man, but a man's way to the devil.— *Adam Clarke.*

I oppose drink because it opposes me. The work I try to do it undoes.— *Lord Brougham.*

Alcohol nowadays is responsible for more ravages than pestilence, famine, or war.— *Gladstone.*

Alcohol is no more a digester than an appetizer. In whatever shape it presents itself, it is only a poison.— *Fransisque Sarcey.*

Do you know what that man is drinking from the glass which shakes in his trembling hand? — He is drinking the tears and the blood and the life of his wife and children.— *Lamonnais.*

Alcohol gives neither health nor strength nor warmth nor happiness. It does nothing but harm.— *Tolstoi, in Alliance News, London.*

I do not forget the new doctrine that alcohol is "food." It is food for lust, and lies, and idleness, and dishonesty, and every "slug" and "scale" and parasite of character. But from Noah's time to the fourth year of William IV, it never fed a virtue in any man.— *John G. Woolley.*

An Indian chief thus summed up the effects of "firewater" upon his people: "Once we were powerful; we were a great nation; our young men were many; our lodges were full of children; our enemies feared us. . . . Now we are very poor; we are weak; nobody fears us; our lodges are empty; our hunting-grounds deserted; our council fires are gone out."

Men dread cholera, the yellow fever, the smallpox, and take expensive precautions against them, while the ravages of all of them in a year do not produce the mischief that intemperance does in a month.— *J. G. Holland.*

The curse of drink is the cause of more failures in life

than anything else. You can surmount every other fault and habit, but the man who is a confirmed drinker has not one chance in a million of success in life.—*Andrew Carnegie.*

"Phil," asked the general, "if you could choose for your little son from all the temptations which will beset him, the one most to be feared, what would it be?" General Sheridan leaned his head against the doorway, and said, soberly, "It would be the curse of strong drink."

The worst feature of the domestic phase is that the passion to drink ruins affections, breaks family ties, and makes men callous to the anguish of wife, children, and friends. The frequency of divorce is one of the danger-signals. There were in 1903 twenty-three thousand divorces granted in the United States alone. According to the deliberate testimony of the judges who legally sever the matrimonial band in the courts, "more than two thirds of the divorces are occasioned by the use of intoxicants.—*John Marshall Barker, Ph. D.*

At the twelfth International Congress on Alcoholism, held in London, June, 1909, Sir Thomas Whittaker, a member of the British Parliament, said: "Do the people of this country realize that the working men of England alone swallow every year the value of every inch of land within the seas surrounding these islands? I do not mean agricultural land only, but cities, the city of London, and the land on which stands the Bank of England. The working men of this country spend on an average seventy-five dollars each a year for alcohol. Whatever may be the case in other places, working men can not afford this expenditure. It is all waste."

FLASHLIGHTS ON THE EVILS OF INTEMPERANCE

Baby's Shoes

A touching conversation once took place on the train as the writer was on the way for a visit among friends in the East, as follows: —

"No, I won't drink with you to-day, boys!" said a drummer to his companions, as they settled down in a smoking-car and passed the bottle. "The fact is, boys, I have quit drinking; I've sworn off."

"What's the matter with you, old boy?" sung out one. "If you've quit drinking, something's up. What is it?"

"Well, boys, I will tell you. Yesterday I was in Chicago. Down on Clark Street a customer of mine keeps a pawn-shop, in connection with other business. I called on him, and while I was there, a young man, not more than twenty-five, wearing threadbare clothes, and looking as hard as if he hadn't seen a sober day for a month, came in with a little package in his hand. He unwrapped it, and handed the article to the pawnbroker, saying, 'Give me ten cents.' And, boys, what do you suppose it was? A pair of baby's shoes — little things, with the buttons only a trifle soiled, as if they had been worn only once or twice. 'Where did you get these?' asked the pawnbroker. 'Got 'em at home,' replied the man, who had an intelligent look and the manner of a gentleman, despite his sad condition. 'My wife bought 'em for our baby. Give me ten cents for 'em — I want a drink.' 'You had better take the shoes back to your wife; the baby will need them,' said the pawnbroker. 'No, s-she won't, because she's dead. She's lyin' at home now — died last night.' As he said this, the poor fellow broke down, bowed his head on the show-case, and cried like a child. Boys," continued the drummer, " you may laugh if you please, but I — I have a baby at home, and I swear I'll never take another drink."— *National Temperance Advocate.*

Saloon Catechism

What curses the unborn babe? — *The saloon.*

What robs the little child of clothing, food, and love? — *The saloon.*

What takes the tender youth out of school, sending him to work? — *The saloon.*

What causes the manly boy to blush for his father? — *The saloon.*

What lures young girls into its dens of vice? — *The saloon.*

What thief takes pictures, furniture, and comforts from the home? — *The saloon.*

What sends a mother out to scrub? — *The saloon.*

What turns a deaf ear to a pleading wife? — *The saloon.*

What impoverishes but never helps? — *The saloon.*

What gives " free lunches " and so-called " charity " to increase trade? — *The saloon.*

What is the only business built up by debauchery? — *The saloon.*

What fills the jails, reformatories, and prisons? — *The saloon.*

What constantly defies the law? — *The saloon.*

What costs the county, city, and State more than all other things? — *The saloon.*

What backs up dance halls and houses of ill fame? — *The saloon.*

What bribes legislatures, cities, and corporations? — *The saloon.*

What furnishes free drinks for the police? — *The saloon.*

What fills the courts with criminals, young and old? — *The saloon.*

What ruins body, mind, and soul? — *The saloon.*
What makes a man a demon in private? — *The saloon.*
What fools the citizens by talk of revenue? — *The saloon.*
Who owns the most stock in a saloon? — *The devil.*

What would reduce our taxes and replenish pocketbooks and banks? — *The abolishment of the saloon.— Rev. W. A. Bartlett.*

When the Saloon Is Respectable

During a lively discussion on the subject of temperance in an Alleghany Mountain stage, one of the company who had hitherto remained silent said: "Gentlemen, I want you to understand that I am a liquor dealer. I keep a public house at ——, but I would have you know that I have a license, and keep a decent house. I don't keep loafers and loungers about my place, and when a man has enough, he can't get any more at my bar. I sell to decent people, and do a respectable business." "Friend," replied a Quaker, "that is the most damnable part of thy business. If thee would sell to drunkards and loafers, thee would help to kill off the race, and society would be rid of them. But

SPEAKING OF VICE —

thee-takes the young, the poor, the innocent, and the unsuspecting, making drunkards and loafers of them. When their character and money are all gone, thee kicks them out, and turns them over to other shops to finish off, and thee ensnares others and sends them on the same road to ruin."
— *Minnie K. Hoffmann, in Sunday School Times, March 13, 1909.*

Saloon Reform

The Chicago Liquor Dealers' Association, following suggestions made at national conventions of men engaged in the liquor trade, has decided to take steps to offset the effect of the prohibition movement by requiring saloon-keepers to live up to the law. In carrying out this policy, the association has adopted the following interesting set of rules: —

To obey all ordinances.

To cease serving drinks to women at public bars.

To stop all forms of gambling whatever on saloon premises.

To exclude all indecent pictures or advertisements from saloons.

To drive away all disorderly persons or loafers.

To refuse to sell drinks to intoxicated persons, or to known inebriates, or to minors.

These rules are interesting as a confession, but that is all. They admit practically all that temperance workers have ever charged against the saloon. They concede that the laws are not now obeyed, that drinks are served to women, that gambling is permitted on saloon premises, that indecent pictures and advertisements are displayed in public drinking places, that disorderly persons and loafers are allowed to make saloons their headquarters, and that drinks are sold to intoxicated persons, to known inebriates, and to children. If honest confession is really good for the soul, Chicago's saloon-keepers' souls must be feeling particularly well satisfied with themselves since the promulgation of these new rules.

But does any one believe that they will do that? And if they should do it, does any one believe that the saloon, morally, would be any less obnoxious than it now is? — *Woman's National Daily, July 20, 1909.*

The "Melican Heathen"

A Chinaman applied for the position of cook in a family which belonged to a fashionable church. The lady asked him: —

"Do you drink whisky?"

"No, I Clistian man."

"Do you play cards?"

"No, I Clistian man."

He was engaged, and was found honest and capable. By and by the lady gave a progressive euchre party, with wine accompaniments. John did his part acceptably, but the next morning he appeared before his mistress, and said: —

"I want quit."

"Why, what is the matter?"

"I a Clistian man; I told you so before. No workee for Melican [American] heathen!'"— *Selected.*

Beer or Bride, Which?

An incident which occurred in Massachusetts not long ago, suggests the question whether a young man who thinks more of his beer than of his bride is worthy of a bride.

A young couple were married at two o'clock in the afternoon. Arriving at a certain place at eight o'clock in the evening, as they were passing a hotel café, the young man said: "I'm going in to have a glass of beer. Wait a minute, will you?"

"No, I won't," responded the bride. "You take me or the beer right now."

"I'll take the beer," said the young man.

The bride of only six hours wheeled about, and started for the union station, leaving the young man on the spot.

W. A. COLCORD.

Opened His Eyes

A young man entered the barroom of a village tavern, and called for a drink.

"No," said the landlord. "You have had too much already. You have had delirium tremens once, and I can not sell you any more."

A TIMELY WARNING

He stepped aside for two young men who entered, and the landlord waited upon them very politely. The other stood silent and sullen. When they had finished, he walked up to the landlord, and addressed him as follows: —

"Six years ago, at their age, I stood where these young men are. I was a man with fair prospects. Now, at the age of twenty-eight, I am a wreck, body and mind. You led me to drink. In this room I formed the habit that has been my ruin. Now sell me a few glasses, and your work will be done. I shall soon be out of the way; there is no hope for me. They can be saved; they may be men again. Don't sell it to them. Sell it to me, and let me die, and the world will be rid of me; but for heaven's sake sell no more to them."

The landlord listened, pale and trembling. Setting down his decanter, he exclaimed, "God helping me, that is the last drop I will sell to any one." And he kept his word.—*Selected.*

Saloon-Keeper's Sign

"Your sign is down, mister," said little Johnnie, boldly. The barkeeper looked surprised, wiped his hands, and came out from behind the bar.

"Come on," he said, "we'll see."

When they came outside, he looked up at the big brass signs on each side of the door, all brightly polished and safe, and then turned to the lad, and said, gruffly, "What are you talking about, boy? My signs aren't down."

He talked so loud that several persons stopped to listen, and then Johnnie said, pointing to the miserable drunkard in the gutter, whom the saloon-keeper had overlooked, "*There's your sign, mister.*"

To the discomfiture of the saloon-keeper, a spectator replied, heartily, "You're right, sonny!"—*J. George Frederick.*

You Did It

Little Bessie was dying. Her father had come home crazed by drink, and had struck her a terrible blow on the spine. There was great grief in the home.

Among those of the neighbors who had gathered in amid the excitement was the saloon-keeper, who had been selling the poisonous liquor in that neighborhood for years. He drew near the death-bed, and heard the mother say, "That blow has killed our darling."

Little Bessie caught the whisper, and raising her eyes, which were growing large in death, she fixed a dying gaze on the saloon-keeper, and said, "*You did it!*" In a few moments she died. Bessie's dying words were never forgotten by the man who had sold her father the whisky. Over and over again he could hear the child say, "You did it!"

Bessie was dead! Who do you think killed her?—*Selected.*

The Curse of the Cup

The Artist Astonished

When Leonardo da Vinci was painting his masterpiece, "The Last Supper," it is said he chose a young man to sit for the character of the Saviour who was a chorister in the beautiful Milan cathedral. Years passed before the

AS I AM NOW

picture was completed. The artist left the character representing Judas to the last, and one day, while in the city of Rome, he noticed a man in the streets of that city whom he selected as his model. With bent shoulders, and an evil, cold, and hardened expression, the man came terribly near to the artist's conception of the Lord's betrayer. After entering the studio, the man began to look around, and finally said to Da Vinci, "Maestro, I was in this room twenty-five years ago. I then sat for Christ." Such is one effect of the sin of intemperance.

The Model Saloon

"FRIENDS AND NEIGHBORS: I am grateful for past favors; and having supplied my store with a fine line of choice wines and liquors, allow me to inform you that I shall continue to make drunkards, paupers, and beggars, for the sober, industrious, respectable members of the community to support. My liquors will excite riot, robbery, and bloodshed.

"They will diminish your comforts, increase your expenses, and shorten life. I shall confidently recommend them as sure to multiply fatal accidents and incurable diseases.

"They will deprive some of life, others of reason, and all of peace. They will make fathers fiends, wives widows, children orphans, and all poor. I will train your sons in infidelity, ignorance, lewdness, and every other vice. I will thus 'accommodate the public;' it may be at the loss of my soul. But I have a family to support. The business pays — and the public encourages it.

"I have paid my license, and the traffic is lawful, and if I don't sell liquor, some one else will. I know the Bible says, 'Thou shalt not kill,' and that no drunkard shall inherit the kingdom of God, and I do not expect the drunkard-maker to fare any better, but I want an easy living, and I have resolved to gather the wages of iniquity, and fatten on the ruin of my species.

"If you doubt my ability, I refer you to the pawn-shop, the poorhouse, the police court, the hospital, the penitentiary, and the gallows, where you will find many of my best customers have gone. The sight of them will convince you that I can do what I say."— *Selected*.

Two Kinds of Bars

There are two kinds of bars connected with the saloon business — the kind over which men pass their money, and receive in exchange the poisoning of body and soul, the filching of their reason, the disgrace, sorrow, and poverty of themselves and their families; and the kind behind which men are shut away from the rest of humanity when drink has driven them to crime. He who passes his earnings over the one tempts the devil to put him behind the other. Abolish the first kind, and we can dispense with more than three fourths of the latter.

We can do more than that,— we can stop a river of sorrow, and wipe out a sea of tears; we can put peace and happiness in the place of turmoil, abuse, and wretched poverty; we can build parks for tenement children to play in, instead of prisons for their fathers and brothers to be shut away in; we can build houses for the families of the poor, in the place of scaffolds on which to hang the head of the household when drink has made him the murderer of his own flesh and blood; we can prepare the children of the poor to do honest battle with adversity, instead of sending them to sweat-shops to grow up to manhood with a handicap of ignorance and a predilection for crime; we can write, "Vacant — for Rent," over the gates of our poor-farms and almshouses, and stop a great portion of the turbid stream that is flowing into our asylums; we can close two thirds of the brothels, put the procurer and procuress largely out of business, and feel that the dangers threatening our daughters from that source are reduced in like ratio. We can do all that, and more, when we have closed that kind of bar over which money is exchanged for liquor, character for appetite, peace for misery, honor for disgrace, hope for despair, and the possibility of heaven for the certainty of hell.   C. M. SNOW.

Expensive Mortgages

God does not often honor with old age those who have in early life sacrificed swine on the altar of the bodily temple. Trembling and staggering along these streets to-day, are men all bent and decayed and prematurely old, for the reason that they are paying for the liens that they put upon their physical estate before they were thirty. By early dissipation they put upon their body a first mortgage, a second, a third mortgage; and 'those mortgages are now being foreclosed, and all that remains of their earthly estate the undertaker will soon put out of sight. " I promise to pay my life, thirty years from date, at the bank of the grave," says every infraction of the laws of your physical being.— *T. De Witt Talmage.*

Moderate Drinking

As a rule, all habitual drinkers were once moderate drinkers. There may be instances where men have plunged suddenly into violent excess with suicidal intent, but such exceptions are rare. The rule is that the habit starts from the first glass, and in some cases its course is run more rapidly than in others. . . . There is only one safe and certain way, and that is, Avoid the use of alcoholic beverages in moderation, and you will never use them to excess.— *From " The Moderate Drinker," by L. D. Mason, M. D.*

No Match for Alcohol

When a boy, I heard a drunkard boasting that no man had ever been able to throw him in a wrestling match. Said a bystander, "There is one that has thrown you many times." "Who?" demanded the boaster. "Hall," was the reply. "What Hall?" said the boaster. "Alco-Hol," was the response.

Of course the joke created a laugh; but what a suggestion was in it! Alcohol has not only thrown but slain his thousands. All along the stream of time lie the wrecks of life. Human caricatures, man-made brutes, tears of wives, cries of children, ruined homes, paupers' graves, and mountains of crime mark the pathway of the ravages of this hydra-headed, Briarean-handed, stony-hearted giant.— *Signs of the Times.*

A Universal Peril

It is not the drunkard and his family alone who are imperiled by the work of the liquor seller, nor is the burden of taxation the chief evil which his traffic brings on the community. We are all woven together in the web of humanity. The evil that befalls any part of the great human brotherhood brings peril to all.

Many a man who through love of gain or ease would have nothing to do with restricting the liquor traffic, has found, too late, that the traffic had to do with him. He has seen his own children besotted and ruined. Lawlessness runs riot. Property is in danger. Life is unsafe. Accidents by sea and by land multiply. Diseases that breed in the haunts of filth and wretchedness make their way to lordly and luxurious homes. Vice fostered by the children of debauchery and crime infect the sons and daughters of refined and cultured households.

There is no man whose interests the liquor traffic does not imperil. There is no man who for his own safeguard should not set himself to destroy it.

Above all other places having to do with secular interests only, legislative halls and courts of justice should be free from the curse of intemperance. Governors, senators, representatives, judges, men who enact and administer a nation's laws, men who hold in their hands the lives, the fair fame, the possessions, of their fellows, should be men of strict temperance. Only thus can their minds be clear to discriminate between right and wrong. Only thus can they possess firmness of principle, and wisdom to administer justice and to show mercy.— *Mrs. E. G. White.*

POEMS AND SONGS

What a Barrel of Whisky Contains

A barrel of headaches, of heartaches, of woes,
A barrel of curses, a barrel of blows;
A barrel of sorrow for a loving, weary wife,
A barrel of care, a barrel of strife;
A barrel of unavailing regret,
A barrel of cares, a barrel of debt;
A barrel of hunger, of poison, of pain,
A barrel of hopes all blasted and vain;
A barrel of poverty, ruin, and blight,
A barrel of tears that run in the night;
A barrel of crime, a barrel of groans,
A barrel of orphans' most pitiful moans;
A barrel of serpents that hiss as they pass,
That glow from the liquor in the bead of the glass;
A barrel of falsehoods, a barrel of cries
That fall from the maniac's lips as he dies!

—*Selected.*

"If"

If you wish a red nose and dim, bleary eyes;
If you wish to be one whom all men despise;
If you wish to be ragged and weary and sad;
If you wish, in a word, to go to the bad;
    Then drink!

If you wish that your life a failure may be;
If you wish to be penniless — out at the knee;
If you wish to be homeless, broken, forlorn;
If you wish to see pointed the finger of scorn;
    Then drink!

If your tastes don't agree with the "if's" as above;
If you'd rather have life full of brightness and love;
If you care not to venture nor find out too soon
That the gateway to hell lies through the saloon,
    Then *don't drink!*

—*Selected.*

The Curse of the Cup

Wanted

Wanted, some bright boys, full of cheer,
To stand at my counter as drinkers of beer,
To fill up the ranks, without further delay,
Of the army of drunkards passing away.
A hundred thousand a year will just supply
The loss to our trade from the drunkards who die.
Send those who can toil, or have wealth to bestow,

For profits are small on old drinkers, you know;
Let them come from the shop, the school, or the home;
We'll welcome them all, whoever may come.
Let mothers surrender their sons to our cause,
And fathers keep voting for good license laws;
For if you vote to keep running the mill,
You must furnish grist, or the wheels will stand still.
— *Selected.*

The Hotel Bar

A bar to heaven, a door to hell,—
Whoever named it, named it well.

A bar to manliness and wealth,
A door to want and broken health;

A bar to honor, pride, and fame,
A door to sin, and grief, and shame;

A bar to hope, a bar to prayer,
A door to darkness and despair;

A bar to honored, useful life,
A door to brawling, senseless strife;

A bar to all that's true and brave,
A door to every drunkard's grave;

A bar to joys that home imparts,
A door to tears and aching hearts;

A bar to heaven, a door to hell,—
Whoever named it, named it well.

— Selected.

A Signboard

I will paint you a sign, rumseller,
 And hang it over your door;
A truer and better signboard
 Than ever you had before.
I will paint with the skill of a master,
 And many shall pause to see
This wonderful piece of painting,
 So like the reality.

I will paint yourself, rumseller,
 As you wait for that fair boy,
Just in the morning of manhood,
 A mother's pride and joy.

The Curse of the Cup

He has no thought of stopping,
  But you greet him with a smile,
And you seem so blithe and friendly,
  That he pauses to chat awhile.

I will paint you again, rumseller,
  I will paint you as you stand
With a foaming glass of liquor
  Extended in your hand.
He wavers, but you urge him,
  " Drink, pledge me just this one!"
And he takes the glass and drains it,
  And the hellish work is done.

And next I will paint a drunkard;
  Only a year has flown,
But into that loathsome creature
  The fair young boy has grown.
The work was sure and rapid,
  I will paint him as he lies,
In a torpid, drunken slumber,
  Under the wintry skies.

I will paint the form of the mother
  As she kneels at her darling's side,
Her beautiful boy that was dearer
  Than all the world beside.
I will paint the shape of a coffin,
  Labeled with one word —" Lost,"
I will paint all this, rumseller,
  And will paint it free of cost.

The sin and the shame and the sorrow,
  The crime and the want and the woe,
That are born there in your workshop,
  No hand can paint, you know.
But I'll paint you a sign, rumseller,
  And many shall pause to view
This wonderful swinging signboard,
  So terribly, fearfully true.

—Selected.

Something to You

"'Tis nothing to me," the beauty said,
With a careless toss of her pretty head;
"The man is weak if he can't refrain
From the cup you say is fraught with pain."

It was something, when, in after-years,
Her eyes were drenched with burning tears,
And she watched in lonely grief and dread,
And startled to hear a staggering tread.

"'Tis nothing to me," the mother said;
"I have no fear that my boy will tread
In the downward path of sin and shame,
And crush my heart and darken his name."

It was something to her when her only son
From the path of right was early won,
And madly cast in the flowing bowl
A ruined body, a sin-wrecked soul.

"'Tis nothing to me," the merchant said,
As over his ledger he bent his head;
"I am busy to-day with tare and tret,
I have no time for fume and fret."

It was something to him when over the wire
A message came from a funeral pyre;
A drunken conductor had wrecked a train,
And his wife and child were among the slain.

"'Tis nothing to me," the voter said,
"The party's loss is my only dread;"
Then he gave his vote to the liquor trade,
Though hearts were crushed and drunkards made.

It was something to him, in after-life;
His daughter became a drunkard's wife,
And her hungry children cried for bread,
And trembled to hear their father's tread.

It is something for us to idly sleep,
While cohorts of death their vigils keep
To gather the young and thoughtless in,
And grind in our midst a grist of sin.

'Tis something, yes all, for us to stand
Clasping by faith the Saviour's hand;
To learn to labor, live, and fight
On the side of God and unchanging right.

—*Selected.*

The Two Glasses

There sat two glasses, filled to the brim,
On a rich man's table, rim to rim:
One was ruddy and red as blood,
And one was as clear as the crystal flood.
Said the Glass of Wine to his paler brother:
"Let us tell tales of the past to each other.

"I can tell of a banquet and revel and mirth,
   Where I was king, for I ruled in might;
And the proudest and grandest souls on earth
   Fell under my touch, as if struck with blight.
From the heads of kings I have torn the crown;
From the heights of fame I have hurled men down.

"I have blasted many an honored name;
I have taken virtue and given shame;
I have-tempted the youth, with a sip, a taste,
That has made his future a barren waste.
Far greater than any king am I,
Or than any army under the sky.

"I have made the arm of the driver fail,
And sent the train from its iron rail;
I have made good ships go down at sea,
And the shrieks of the lost were sweet to me.
Fame, strength, wealth, genius, before me fall,
And my might and power are over all.

"Ho! ho! pale brother," laughed the Wine,
"Can you boast of deeds as great as mine?"
Said the Glass of Water: "I can not boast
Of a king dethroned or a murdered host;
But I can tell of hearts that were sad,
By my crystal drops made light and glad.

"Of thirsts I have quenched, and brows I have laved:
Of hands I have cooled, and souls I have saved.
I have leaped through the valley and dashed down the mountain,
Slept in the sunshine and dripped from the fountain;
I have burst my cloud-fetters, and dropped from the sky,
And everywhere gladdened the landscape and eye.

"I have eased the hot forehead of fever and pain;
I have made the parched meadows grow fertile with grain;
I can tell of the powerful wheel of the mill,
That ground out the flour and turned at my will;
I can tell of manhood, debased by you,
That I have uplifted and crowned anew.

"I cheer, I help, I strengthen and aid,
I gladden the heart of man and maid;
I set the chained wine captive free,
And all are better for knowing me."

These are the tales they told each other —
The glass of wine and its paler brother —
As they sat together, filled to the brim,
On the rich man's table, rim to rim.

— *Selected.*

The License Sacrifice

A mother sits weeping in sorrow and shame;
Her heart-strings are bleeding, her love all aflame;
While the cry from her heart for her long-erring boy
Is, "Where, O, where, is my darling Roy?

The Curse of the Cup

"I rocked his wee cradle, and wheeled the small cart
  That carried my treasure, the joy of my heart;
Then taught his small feet the way they should run,
  And laughed at his innocent, rollicking fun.

"I sang with my bonnie, and heard his sweet prayer,
  Then asked the dear Father to lead him with care;
While up toward the stature of manhood he grew,
  The boy of my heart, so honest and true.

"He grew to full manhood, tall, stately, and true,
  With smile still as sweet and eye still as blue;
Then out in the world he went from our hearts,
  To the battle of life in the world's busy marts.

"He went, but he came not; O, how can I tell
Of his fall from our heaven to the world's deepest hell!
Down, down from the teachings of mother and home,
  To the vileness and sin of a licensed saloon.

"He breathed of that poison, then entered the door,
  Where virtue, once entered, is virtue no more;
And all of his passions aflame to destroy,
  Went down, like a wreck, my once noble boy.

"O God, reach down and save other boys!
  Let not other hearts be bereft of their joys!
Waken men; rescue manhood; drive rum from all lands;
  O, spare mother hearts by omnipotent hands!

"God, waken the church and waken the state!
  Awaken our people, the rich and the great!
Hurl thunderbolts down, if needed, to stay
This traffic in blood. God, hasten, I pray."

— *Selected.*

Whisky in Its Place

[The following verses were written upon the occasion of hearing a man make the remark that whisky was good in its place.]

    Good in its place! Where is that place?
    Thou fiend that curses the human race,
    Where is that place? O, let me tell;
    For I have learned thy secret well.

    Show me the place where you have been,
    And there's the place where crime is seen;
    Show me the place your presence blights,
    And there's the place for brawls and fights.

    Go see the graves that you have filled,
    Go see the blood that you have spilled;
    Then tell me that there is a place
    Where you should show your demon face.

    Go ask the drunkard's wretched wife
    What's been the terror of her life;
    What turned her raven locks to snow,
    And laid her wretched husband low?

    See how she looks by man forsaken;
    See her by want and sorrow shaken;
    See her hide in deep disgrace,
    Then say no more about your place.

    Go hear the orphan's cry for bread;
    Go hear the widow mourn her dead;
    Go see the drunkard's haggard face,
    And ask of them where is thy place.

    Ask the pauper at the poorhouse door,
    What makes his heavy heart so sore.
    He'll say, while tears run down his face,
    Because he had for you a place.

    Go see the place where demons lurk,
    Go watch them in their devilish work,

As they with knives each other chase,
And there, vile whisky, is thy place.

There's where the gallows finds its food;
There's where the prison gets its brood;
There's where crime and poverty embrace,
While rushing on their headlong race.

— *Selected.*

The Drunkard's Lament

[Words written and sung by John B. Gough]
(Air.—" Long, Long Ago.")

Where are the friends that to me were so dear?
    Long, long ago — long ago.
Where are the hopes that my heart used to cheer?
    Long, long ago — long ago.
Friends that I loved, in the grave are laid low;
Hopes that I cherished are fled from me now;
I am degraded, for *rum* was my *foe,*
    Long, long ago — long ago.

Sadly my wife bowed her beautiful head,
    Long, long ago — long ago.
O, how I wept when I knew she was dead!
    Long, long ago — long ago.
She was an angel, my love and my guide;
Vainly to save me from ruin she tried.
Poor, broken heart! it was well that she died,
    Long, long ago — long ago.

Let me look back on the days of my youth —
    Long, long ago — long ago.
I was no stranger to virtue and truth,
    Long, long ago — long ago.
O for the hopes that were pure as the day!
O for the loves that were purer than they!
O for the hours that I squandered away!
    Long, long ago — long ago.

From "Silver Tones," a 35-cent song book, published by Rev. W. A. Williams, 3012 Richmond St., Philadelphia, Pa.

AN ALLY OF THE LIQUOR TRAFFIC

"Tobacco is a slow, insidious, but most malignant poison. In whatever form it is used, it tells upon the constitution; it is all the more dangerous because its effects are slow, and at first hardly perceptible. It excites and then paralyzes the nerves. It weakens and clouds the brain. Often it affects the nerves in a more powerful manner than does intoxicating drink. It is more subtle, and its effects are difficult to eradicate from the system. Its use excites a thirst for strong drink, and in many cases lays the foundation for the liquor habit."

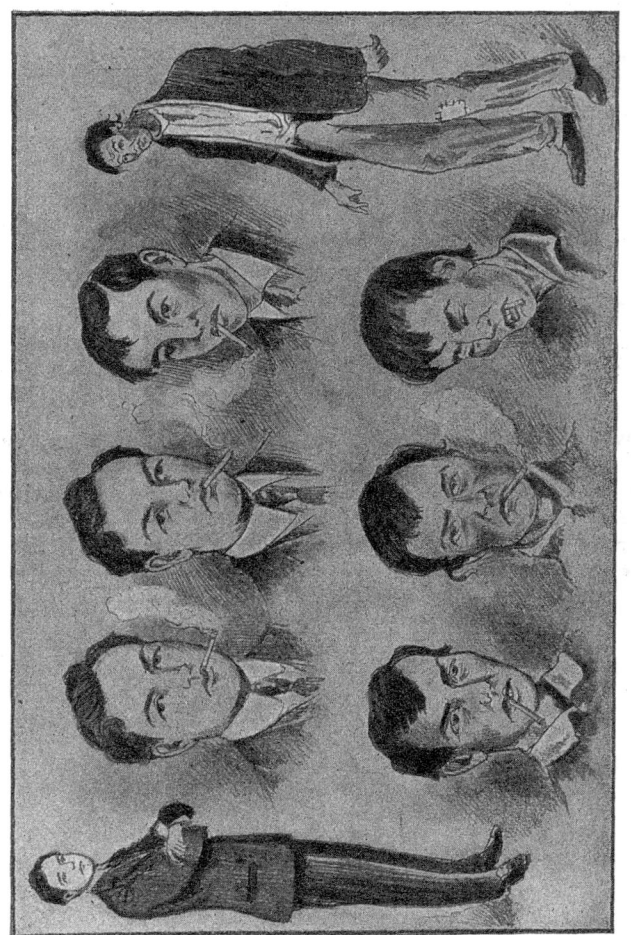

THE CAREER OF A CIGARETTE SMOKER

TOBACCO

Historical Notes

Less than three hundred fifty years ago tobacco was introduced into civilized countries. Since then it has conquered every nationality; and with increased power it is to-day ruining the lives of millions of people. The tobacco habit seems to have originated with the natives of the West Indies and with the Indians of South America. In 1565 it was brought to England by Sir John Hawkins. Other prominent men recommended it, and for some time it was supposed to be a remedy for many ills. However, as the habit became more prevalent, its hurtful influences were apparent.

Efforts were generally made to suppress it. In some countries persons who persisted in using it were obliged to separate themselves from society. The Grand Duke of Moscow forbade his subjects to use it, and made a second offense punishable by death. A similar position was taken by the sultan of Turkey. James I, who sought hard to suppress the filthy custom in England, wrote thus to his subjects: "Now, my good countrymen, let us, I pray you, consider what honor or policy can move us to imitate the barbarous and beastly manners of the wild, godless, and slavish Indians, especially in so wild and filthy a custom? Shall we, I say, that have been so long civil and wealthy in peace, famous and invincible in war, fortunate in both,— shall we, I say with blushing, abase ourselves so far as to imitate these beastly Indians, slaves to the Spaniards, the refuse of the world?"

But regardless of the efforts made against the tobacco habit in its infancy, it has wrought sad havoc upon the human race. "Smoking," says Dr. D. H. Kress, "is at present almost universal among men in all English-speaking countries. It is also prevalent in Polynesia, China, Japan, Siam, etc. In Burma the mother takes the cheroot from her mouth, and puts it to the lips of her nursing babe. In New Zealand the habit is almost universal among the natives, women and children using it the same as do men and boys. The Kafirs of Africa are habitual smokers. Stanley's pygmies of Central Africa are also said to be inveterate users of the weed." In the Eastern hemisphere, tobacco is used more generally than any other narcotic.

Evils of the Tobacco Habit

The argument that the cold world looks pleasanter through the blue haze of tobacco smoke, may be true,— such is the deceitfulness of sin,— but the truthfulness of that argument only increases the danger of the foe. Under friendly pretensions the vice is digging a grave for man's mental, moral, and physical possibilities.

When Napoleon III of France learned that the tobacco-using students in the Polytechnic School at Paris, failed in their examinations, he promptly forbade the practise. At Harvard no tobacco user has stood at the head of his class for fifty years. Like cocaine or morphine, tobacco blunts the moral perception. Sin does not look so sinful through the tobacco veil. Greeley said, "All tobacco users are not horse thieves, but all horse thieves are tobacco users." More than this; the weed is responsible for many diseases. Often obituaries would speak more truthfully if they read, "Tobacco," instead of "heart failure," etc. Nicotine acts directly upon the heart. In 1902, out of sixty-seven applicants for admittance into the United States army, forty-three were rejected because they had "tobacco hearts." It is said that the tobacco habit has made one half of Germany's young men unfit to bear arms. Dr. Grimshaw says: "So insidious are its effects that few have regarded it as swelling the bills of mortality. It is, nevertheless, true that multitudes are carried to the grave every year by tobacco alone."

An Ally of the Liquor Traffic

Rear-Admiral Schroeder tells the story of a man who stole a bunch of tobacco leaves from a Havana dock. Secreting them under his clothes next the skin, he went on with his work. He perspired freely, and suddenly fell unconscious to the floor. Treating him first for sunstroke, his companions soon discovered his plight, but not until he had nearly lost his life. This shows the danger of absorbing the ingredients of the weed. But what is the smoker forcing into his system? According to the analysis given by the authors of the book, "The School of Health," the ingredients of tobacco smoke are: "(1) Prussic acid, a deadly poison, too well known to need description; (2) carbonic acid gas (about five per cent); (3) an oily substance of such deadly character that a drop placed on the tongue of a snake causes immediate death; (4) nicotine, an alkaloid known to be one of the most virulent poisons in existence, one tenth of a grain of which is sufficient to kill a fair-sized dog."

All the while that a man is enjoying his tobacco, it is weakening his brain, his liver, his kidneys, and his heart. He is sinning against himself, those about him, and his posterity. Sir Benjamin Brodie says: "No other evils are so manifestly visited upon the third and fourth generations as are the evils which spring from the use of tobacco." Dr. Trall says: "Many an infant has been killed outright in its cradle by the tobacco smoke with which a thoughtless father filled the room."

Then this habit, when it comes, usually comes to stay. In time it becomes so powerful that it defies the combined strength of the user's will and judgment to throw it off. Worse yet, it seldom stays alone. Liquor is a near relative of tobacco in all forms. The former stimulates the action of the heart; the latter depresses it. Dr. Brewer says: "It can be asserted with great certainty that the boy who begins to use cigarettes at ten, will drink beer and whisky at fourteen, take morphine at twenty-five, and spend the rest of his lifetime alternating between cocaine, spirits, and opium."

Cigarette Smoking

The cigarette made its first appearance in this country in 1876. Spain was perhaps its first home; but to-day it is cosmopolitan. Everywhere it is making inroads upon the health, the morals, and the usefulness of youth.  Governments and commercial corporations are wrestling with it. The British Parliament, in 1906, tried to pass a bill against it. In Norway and in some parts of Germany, laws prohibit boys under sixteen from smoking or buying tobacco. Abyssinian laws forbid its use by the natives. Switzerland, Canada, Japan, Australia, South Africa, and portions of the United States have laws regarding the cigarette.

Some of the largest railroad systems and manufacturing establishments have prohibited the use of it by their employees. Mr. Harriman is credited with saying: "Cigarette smokers are unsafe. I would just as soon get railroad men from an insane asylum as to employ cigarette smokers." A chemical manufacturing company at Lowell, Massachusetts, which employs hundreds of young men and boys, posted the following notice on its door: "Believing that the smoking of cigarettes is injurious to both mind and body, thereby unfitting young men for their work; therefore, after this date [March 1, 1902] we will  not employ any young man under twenty-one years of age who smokes cigarettes." During the Boer War, England rejected eight thousand men out of twelve thousand who offered their services. One cause of their disability was found to be smoking. At that time the Chicago *Herald* received the following cable from South Africa: "The

An Ally of the Liquor Traffic 75

cigarette is playing havoc with the British army; and if something is not done soon, Great Britain will be defended, or rather, undefended, by a collection of weak-minded, weak-bodied youth capable of no real effort of any kind."

Yet, regardless of these facts, hundreds of thousands of youth are selling their birthrights. During the last ten years the cigarette sales have increased one hundred fifty per cent in Great Britain, and more than one thousand per cent in Germany. In England the cigarette causes twenty thousand deaths annually. The money Americans use for cigarettes yearly, would buy a pair of shoes for each child in this country, and provide one hundred thousand small families with the necessities of life. Each year the world spends fifty million dollars more for tobacco and snuff than for bread. Read Isa. 55:2. Dr. W. T. O'Reilly, who laments conditions in New Orleans, says: " Especially among newsboys and street urchins do you see the effects of nicotine most decidedly. Perhaps ninety per cent of them are addicted to the habit, many of them yet in knee trousers." Judge Stubbs, of the juvenile court in Indiana, who in twenty months tried twelve hundred eight boys and girls, says: " By far the most potent cause is the cigarette habit." More than two hundred twenty thousand boys and youth are in jails or reformatories in the United States. Almost without exception these are addicted to cigarette smoking.

Nor is the habit limited to boys. It is humiliating to contemplate that " ladies' cigarettes " now hold a prominent place in many show-cases. Many a girl carries a telltale mark on her index finger, and her future is no brighter than the boy's. Ladies of fashion in Paris no longer apologize for lighting their cigarettes after dinner. The Canal Zone is a cigarette-smoking country. Often women will be smoking a cigarette while preparing the evening meal. In Russia the czarina has forbidden the ladies of her court to smoke; neither will she tolerate those whose clothes or breath are laden with the odor.

Something Must Be Done

No phase of the tobacco habit is more deplorable than the cigarette. Before the judgment is developed, while the foresight is vague, and the power of resistance weak, the vile cigarette seizes the youth and leads them into the very portals of hell. Shall it continue to rob boys of their manhood, girls of their purity, and nations of their truest heritage? Terrible are the consequences of the liquor traffic; yet Frank Swan, secretary of the Anti-Cigarette League, says: "A far greater danger is threatening the rising generation from cigarette smoking than from drink."

But face to face with this impending calamity, many who should be helping the youth are themselves hopelessly addicted to the habit. The public press and the various professional fraternities, generally speaking, are giving only a half-hearted support to the efforts at reform. But there are some who are not idly waiting for popular applause to indorse this cause. Among them are the workers in the Anti-Cigarette League. They are bravely giving the signal of alarm; and hundreds of youth are being saved from the pernicious habit. There is no time for despair. Let Christians prayerfully plan and work for the salvation of those who are standing on the very precipice of destruction, and who are influencing others to follow in their footsteps.

"Cursed be the social wants that sin against the strength of youth;
Cursed be the social ties that warp us from the living truth."

"God wants the boys,—
The merry boys, the noisy boys,
The funny boys, the thoughtless boys.
God wants the boys with all their joys;
His heroes brave he'd have them be,
Fighting for truth and purity:
God wants the boys."

SOME IMPORTANT FACTS

The United States spends six hundred million dollars for tobacco yearly. Chicago burns twenty-four thousand five hundred dollars daily in cigars alone.

In the year ending June, 1908, the United States smoked more than fifty-five billion cigarettes.

Fires caused by cigarettes are said to cost New York City two million five hundred thousand dollars yearly.

Among other things aboard the ships that carried the American fleet under Admiral Evans to the Pacific coast, were twenty-seven thousand packages of cigarettes.

A Philadelphia cigarette dealer states that he sells one hundred fifty thousand cigarettes a month to women, who come in carriages and send footmen to buy.

The consumers of chewing and smoking tobacco in 1908 paid into the United States treasury at the rate of $54,984 a day. They more than paid the salaries of the United States navy.

And the good old " sisters of the chimney-corner " paid tax on snuff at the rate of $3,473 a day. They thus contributed enough money to Uncle Sam's exchequer to maintain the public health and marine hospital service.

The smokers of cigars and cigarettes pay an average of $66,637 a day in tax, or enough to provide for the salary of the Supreme Court of the United States for a whole year.

Eight States have already made an outlaw of the cigarette. The States which have a place on the honor roll are Tennessee, Indiana, Wisconsin, Nebraska, Washington, Arkansas, Oklahoma, and Minnesota. Several other States have made efforts in this direction.

Nine legislatures within the British empire, it is said, have passed laws against juvenile smoking.

The island of St. Helena, where Napoleon was buried, has an anti-cigarette law with this unusual provision: " Boys detected in the act of smoking or in the possession of tobacco or cigarettes, are liable to a fine of five shillings and *twelve strokes with the birch*."

A certain hotel in New York which refused an actress the pleasure of smoking in its café has met with a storm of protests from actresses who smoke.

District Superintendent E. J. Easley, of the Rock Island Railroad, has issued the following notice: " It is noticeable that many of our employees are addicted to the habit of smoking cigarettes. This is not desirable, and hereafter any employee found smoking cigarettes will be dismissed from service."

George Baumhoff, superintendent of the Lindell Railway, St. Louis, Missouri, once said: " Under no circumstances will I hire a man who smokes cigarettes. He is as dangerous at the front end of a motor as the man who drinks; in fact, he is more dangerous."

The poison, nicotine, was so named by Jean Nicot, who introduced tobacco into France.

Homer, Virgil, Dante, Chaucer, and Shakespeare were not users of the " fragrant weed." Sir Isaac Newton and Gladstone were non-smokers. Some of the famous Americans who never smoked are: Benjamin Franklin, George Washington, Thomas Jefferson, Abraham Lincoln, and Theodore Roosevelt.

One cigarette contains enough nicotine to kill two toads.

The medical examiner of the United States navy says that one half of the applicants to the navy are rejected because of weak hearts due to the use of tobacco.

" All the boys in the police court," says Judge Hildreth, of Holyoke, Massachusetts, " are cigarette smokers."

" Of all the juvenile criminals tried in my court," says Judge Baker, of Louisville, Kentucky, " not one for years has been found free from the stain of cigarettes on the thumb and

An Ally of the Liquor Traffic

first two fingers. Of all the lunatics tried in my court, an attempt is made to learn the cause of lunacy, and in more than half cigarette smoking is assigned as the cause."

Ninety per cent of the rejections in the Spanish-American War enlistment were due to the cigarette, producing an irregular pulse and a weak heart, which would not endure the forced marches.

A general freight manager, employing two hundred clerks, says eighty-five per cent of the mistakes are made by thirty-two cigarette smokers.

The *Woman's National Daily* of June 15, 1909, contained the following item: " Mrs. Alice Mullins, of St. Louis, Missouri, an attractive woman of thirty-five, has been sent to the insane asylum by the Madison County court. Physicians say her insanity is due to her incessant use of tobacco, which she chews continuously when not sleeping. She also occasionally smokes, but prefers to chew the weed."

" General Grant was an inveterate lover of the weed, and died of smoker's cancer. Emperor Frederick of Germany is believed to have contracted, through excessive smoking, the throat affection which cut him off in his prime. Carlyle was a slave of tobacco, but chafed under its bondage, and declared the habit irredeemably bad."

The cigarette manufacturer may endow colleges, but he can not wash from his hands the blood of the cigarette suicides, constantly reported in the papers; he may establish an institution to discipline the minds of the unfortunate youths, but he can not restore to normal condition the brains of those whom the physicians report " insane from cigarette smoking." An economic system that coins from the child's life-blood the profits that enrich the capitalists, can not promote the sobriety and moral power of citizenship.— *John Q. A. Henry, in " The Deadly Cigarette."*

"A missionary to the hop-pickers describes a family where the little children not only smoked cigarettes, but chewed tobacco. In the morning these children were little furies, swearing and fighting until their mother had given them either a 'quid' or a cigarette, when they would settle down either to quiet or to picking hops."

Nothing is more certain to lower the physical and moral tone of our nation than this pernicious habit of juvenile smoking.— *Rev. F. B. Meyer, B. A.*

" The cigarette is made, in most cases, of drugged tobacco. Opium is the chief drug used, a fact testified to by all who investigate."

Tobacco in any form is bad, but in a cigarette there are five poisons: There is the oil in the paper, the oil of nicotine, saltpeter to preserve the tobacco, opium to make it mild, and the oil in the flavoring.— *Professor Latlin.*

During 1903 forty-two of the patients treated at the Paisley Royal Victoria Eye Infirmary were partially or totally blind as a result of smoking.— *Dr. N. Gordon Cluckie.*

More young men are led to the opium habit by cigarette smoking than by patent and proprietary medicines. Sixty per cent of all males under forty years of age, treated in a certain institution in 1896 for opium, morphine, or cocaine using, had been smokers of cigarettes, and sixty per cent of these had no other excuse than that they needed some stimulant more than the cigarette furnished them. — *Dr. Broughton.*

Yesterday I had before me thirty-five boy prisoners. Thirty-three of them were confirmed cigarette smokers. The fact that out of thirty-five prisoners thirty-three smoked cigarettes might seem to indicate some direct connection between cigarettes and crime. Ninety-nine out of a hundred boys between the ages of ten and seventeen years who come before me charged with crime, have their fingers disfigured by the yellow cigarette stains.— *A New York Magistrate.*

An Ally of the Liquor Traffic

In 1855 the students of the science and art schools in Paris were divided into smokers and non-smokers by way of investigating the mental worth of the habit. Of the twenty who came out highest in the examination six were smokers and fourteen did not smoke. Of the twenty who stood lowest, seventeen were smokers and three non-smokers. Five years after, the minister of public instruction issued circulars prohibiting smoking in the colleges and schools throughout the nation.— *Rev. Frank Ballard.*

I leave it to others to discuss the moral side of cigarette smoking. I denounce it simply because of its blighting, blasting effect upon one's success in life; because it draws off the energy, saps the vitality and force which ought to be made to tell in one's career; because it blunts the sensibilities and deadens the thinking faculties; because it kills the ambition, the finer instincts, and the more delicate aspirations and perceptions; because it destroys the ability to concentrate one's mind, which is the secret of all achievement.— *O. S. Marden.*

In the case of the women who are employed in the manufacture of tobacco in a certain factory, the rate of mortality among breast-fed children is ninety-nine per cent if the mother returns to her work soon after her confinement, while the average rate of infantile mortality there is fifty-five per cent, and that of the breast-fed children of mothers other than tobacco workers is thirty-nine per cent.— *Dr. Mutrel.*

A well-known young man of Newburyport, Massachusetts, wrote to a cigarette manufacturer that he had smoked two thousand boxes of cigarettes, and had saved the covers, and wanted to know whether they gave premiums the same as some tobacco firms do. The firm replied that they, as yet, had not given premiums, but in his case, they would make an exception, and provided he would smoke one thousand more boxes, would furnish him a fine coffin.— *John Q. A. Henry, in "The Deadly Cigarette."*

AS OTHERS SEE IT

Tobacco is the worst national curse of modern civilization.— *John Ruskin.*

The Southern Pacific needs bright and ambitious young men, but it has no room for boys who vaporize their brains with tobacco or blow smoke through their nostrils.— *Southern Pacific Railroad Official.*

A young man who smokes is a fool, at least in that particular. He ought to take better care of his nerves, and present a cleaner exhibit of himself.— *Chancellor J. R. Day, of Syracuse (New York) University.*

It is painful to contemplate how many promising youths must be enfeebled in their minds and bodies before they arrive at manhood, by the use of tobacco.— *Professor Lizars, of Edinburgh.*

I never knew of but one good use that tobacco was put to, and that was to kill lice on cows.— *Carrie Nation.*

I believe that no one who smokes tobacco before the bodily powers are developed, ever makes a strong, vigorous man.— *Dr. Ferguson.*

I shall not hesitate to pronounce tobacco in young men to be evil, and only evil, physically, mentally, and morally.— *Edward Hitchcock, of Amherst College.*

The cigarette is the devil's device for killing young Americans.— *The Boy Magazine.*

Place the heel of your will upon the neck of the cigarette.— *Lucy P. Gaston.*

A boy who smokes cigarettes is like a cipher with the rim knocked off.— *Robert Burdette.*

Acrolein is one of the most terrible drugs in its effect on the human body. The burning of ordinary cigarette-paper always produces acrolein. That is what makes the

An Ally of the Liquor Traffic

smoke so irritating. I really believe that it often makes boys insane. We sometimes develop acrolein in this laboratory in our experiments with glycerine. One whiff of it from the oven drove one of my assistants out of the building the other day. I can hardly exaggerate the dangerous nature of acrolein, and yet that is what a man or a boy is dealing with every time he smokes an ordinary cigarette. — *Thomas A. Edison.*

Tobacco does more to undermine the success of young men than does any other one factor. Why? — Because it is the entering wedge of two lines of dissipation, either of which may defeat success. The first line is the dissipation of cash for things unnecessary. The second line of dissipation is that of sense-gratification. One uses tobacco partly because of its flavor, and partly for the sedative action which it exerts upon the nervous system. It is just this sedative effect which steals away a young man's vigilance and alertness, and handicaps him in the struggle for success. The use of tobacco paves the way to other dissipation by requiring a compensating stimulant to overcome its sedative effect, and by making the common, wholesome foods taste insipid and flat. A vast majority of drunkards were smokers before they were drinkers.— *Winfield S. Hall, M. D.*

More and more young men are hoisting the sign, "I am a fool," by appearing in public with a cigarette. In our own offices, where we employ a great many young men, a cigarette smoker gets no job, or if he has it, he gets no advancement. The fact that he smokes cigarettes is proof positive that he is weak in the upper story.— *P. M. Sharpless.*

The cigarette is the American abomination. *No cigarette victim can climb to the top of the ladder.*— *Justice David Brewer, of the United States Supreme Court.*

The continual dryness of the mucous membranes of the mouth and pharynx, due to the paralyzing influence of the cigarette on the nerve terminals, a thirst which the drinking of water will not relieve, is readily quenched by alcoholic drinks, and this discovery once made by the cigarette habitué, leads to frequent indulgences in liquor.— *Dr. C. L. Hamilton.*

Horace Greeley once said, "Show me a drunkard that does not use tobacco, and I will show you a white blackbird." There are white blackbirds, and there are men who use liquor that do not use tobacco; but one is almost as rare as the other.— *Mrs. Fannie D. Chase.*

The prodigious increase of cigarette smoking among boys in the last few years is an evil which will tend to deteriorate the race if not checked.— *Dr. R. Bartholomew.*

Personal impurity of the most loathsome kind is often found with the cigarette habit, and the two together cause many sad cases of insanity. A man with his eyes open to the danger said: "If something is not done to check cigarette smoking and the vice that goes with it, we shall not be able to build insane asylums enough for the victims." — *Lucy Page Gaston.*

The cigarette is a maker of invalids, criminals, and fools, but — not of men. To use it means defeat in life.

"I am not much of a mathematician," said the Cigarette, "but I can add to a man's nervous troubles; I can subtract from his physical energy; I can multiply his aches and pains, and divide his mental forces; I can take interest from his work, and discount his chances for success."

One of the very worst habits in boyhood is the cigarette habit. This has long been recognized by all the judges of the courts who deal with young criminals. These judges know that in nearly every case the drunken sots who appear before them, a disgrace to their parents, themselves, and the state, began as boys smoking cigarettes. The cigarette habit not only had a grip upon them in boyhood, but it invited all the other demons of habit to come in and add to the degradation that the cigarette began.— *Hon. Ben B. Lindsey.*

THOUGHTS FOR MEDITATION

Seven Weighty Questions

Each act of life is prompted by some motive, or done simply from habit. What is the motive that prompts the people of the United States to spend annually six hundred million dollars for tobacco? I will ask you, tobacco user, What is your motive in having a part in this immense expenditure? Perhaps the following questions may aid you in determining your motive in using the expensive weed: —

Does your use of tobacco benefit you or your neighbor *spiritually?*

Does it benefit you *morally?*

Does it benefit you *mentally?*

Does it benefit you *physically?*

Does it bring any *financial* returns to you?

Does it increase the happiness of your family or that of your neighbors?

If not, what right then have you to use it?— *Youth's Instructor.*

Not Good for Dogs

At a recent dog show in the United States a large sign was placed over the exhibition room, " No smoking allowed here. It will hurt the dogs." Yes, so it would! Tobacco smoke is a poisonous and loathsome thing. And if animal life needs thus to be protected from its injurious effects, what can be said concerning the claims of human life? Do not forget, fathers, that when you are smoking at home, you are filling your house with the drug, and causing your children to breathe a poison that is dangerous even for dogs! Do not forget, husbands, that when you make your body stink with tobacco, both inside and out, you bring a deadly poison into the company of your wife, which takes the color from her cheeks and the vitality from her life. Do not forget, ye devotees of the weed, that tobacco is bad even for dogs! — *Bible Echo.*

Evils of the Treating Habit

General Frederick Grant says that his father did not smoke to great excess until after the capture of Fort Donelson. The story went through the nation that Grant had fought the battle with a cigar in his mouth. Friends congratulating him on this, the first great victory of his life, accompanied their messages with boxes of cigars. It is an extreme case of the damaging effect of the American treating habit.— *The Savings Journal, February, 1909.*

Don't Smoke, Boys

No man or boy is free who is tied to his cigar or cigarette. He is so much less a man as he is a slave to this indulgence. Anything that makes a man less a man, or a boy less a boy, must be nipped in the bud, though it be dear as a right hand or a right eye. God has given us our bodies

and our souls in trust; and we must return them to him in as good a condition as we received them, with the increase of talents which he requires of his faithful children. Character-building, next to service to God and man, is our chief business in this world; and we must steer clear of every taste, habit, or desire that stands in the way of making ourselves noble and true human beings.

Don't smoke, boys. Be pure, clean, sweet from all such habits. Have wholesome breaths, mouths undefiled. God by his laws has put up this notice in his universe, "No smoking here!" We ought to rejoice in all his laws, for they are for our good. Throw the cigar and the cigarette into the fire, and never light another. It will be a hard thing to do, but a victory over a bad habit is one of the noblest things we can achieve in this world. May our Heavenly Father help you in your efforts.— *Selected.*

The Effects of Tobacco Upon the System

The first effect of nicotine on the system is to excite glandular activity, and increase the fluid from the secreting and excretory glands. This result is brought about by its action upon the nerve-centers, and is but temporary; later results are depression and paralysis.

It has also a special action through the same channel of the nerve-centers upon the involuntary muscular fibers. These are located in the heart, walls of the blood-vessels, and beneath the mucous membrane of the alimentary canal. It is this contraction of the muscular fibers in the walls of the stomach that cause nausea, and possibly vomiting, in many individuals when they first attempt to use tobacco.

The contraction of the muscles of the walls of the arteries increases the blood pressure, which in some cases amounts to two or two and a half times the normal. The stimulating action through the inhibitory nerves upon the muscles of the heart first causes a slowing of the pulse, and later the inhibitory influence is paralyzed, and the pulse-rate is increased. This double action upon the heart and blood-vessels is a serious matter. It not only affects the circulation, but it interferes with the local blood supply to all the vital organs.

Perhaps with the heart itself this may be most felt; the arteries that supply blood to the wall of the heart being unable to carry the normal amount of blood, the nutrition in the heart muscle is diminished, and the action of the heart itself through its nerve relation is constantly increased or depressed through the effect of the drug. The sequel can only be, especially to the more susceptible individual, a constantly disturbed function which eventually develops into a chronic diseased state known as "tobacco heart."

Alder experimented with rabbits fed upon cabbage leaves which had been soaked with tobacco infusion, and found the function of the liver disturbed. Upon examination, the liver was enlarged, and a microscope revealed a great increase in the connective tissue, which had developed between the lobules of the liver, and which always means a serious interference with the function of the organ. It may be a factor in the development of sclerosis of the liver, which is supposed to be brought about mainly by alcohol.

The effect upon the blood has been studied by Vas on puppies. After feeding them for eight weeks with a substance containing nicotine, he noticed marked anemia; the hemoglobin and red corpuscles were diminished more than half.

The action of nicotine is very largely brought about by its direct influence upon nerve-centers. In giving a fatal dose of nicotine, death is brought about by paralysis of respiration, because the respiratory centers of the medulla are paralyzed. The nerve-centers mostly influenced are those of the sympathetic ganglia, which control the circulation and the function of all the vital organs. These centers, subjected to this slow and steady stimulating and paralyzing influence, can not but undergo functional or degenerative changes, which result in much harm to the system.

How many diseases owe their origin to this factor can not be determined, but Huchard and others have pointed out that they are positive factors in the production of various diseased conditions.— *A. J. Sanderson, M. D.*

Cigarette Poison

"You smoke thirty cigarettes a day?"

"Yes, on the average."

"You don't blame them for your run-down condition?"

"Not in the least. I blame my hard work."

The physician shook his head. He smiled in a vexed way. Then he took a leech out of a glass jar.

"Let me show you something," he said. "Bare your arm."

The cigarette fiend bared his pale arm, and the other laid the lean, black leach upon it. The leech fell to work busily, its body began to swell. Then, all of a sudden, a kind of shudder convulsed it, and it fell to the floor dead.

"That is what your blood did to that leech," said the physician. He took up the little corpse between his finger and thumb. "Look at it," he said. "Quite dead, you see. You poisoned it."

"I guess it wasn't a healthy leech in the first place," said the cigarette smoker, sullenly.

"Wasn't healthy, eh? Well, we'll try again."

And the physician clapped two leeches on the young man's thin arm.

"If they both die," said the patient, "I'll swear off — or at least, I'll cut down my daily allowance from thirty cigarettes to ten."

Even as he spoke, the smaller leech shriveled and dropped on his knee, dead, and a moment later the larger one fell beside it.

"This is ghastly," said the young man; "I'm worse than the pestilence to these leeches."

"It is the empyreumatic oil in your blood," said the medical man. "All cigarette fiends have it."

"Doc," said the young man, regarding the three dead leeches thoughtfully, "I half believe you're right."— *Evanston (Illinois) Index*.

Stubborn Things

"Have one?" and Fred Weston held toward his friend a package of cigarettes, having just placed one between his own lips.

"No, sir! thank you."

"Well, you needn't look so disgusted; aren't you ever going to smoke?"

"Not if I can help it; the game isn't worth the candle."

"What do you mean by that?"

"I mean that there isn't fun enough in it to pay me for taking the chance of ruining my health or making a drunkard of myself. Besides all that, too, money is worth more for some other things than for burning up, and men that smoke often burn up hundreds and thousands of dollars in that way during their lives."

"But they enjoy it, don't they?"

"Perhaps so; but if they never began to smoke they wouldn't miss it, and they'd be ever so much better off in every way. Only a day or two ago I saw in one of the papers something about a little Italian boy who was brought before a justice in New York City as a young tramp. The officer charged him with picking up cigar stumps from the streets and gutters, and showed the boy's basket half full of the stumps, water soaked and covered with mud.

"When the justice asked the boy what he intended doing with them, he said, 'O, I sell them to a man for ten cents a pound, to be used in making cigarettes.' And the article went on to state that in the large cities there are a great many cigar-butt grubbers, as they are called, boys and girls who scour the streets in search of half-burned cigars, which are dried, and then sold."

"H'm! but what has tobacco got to do with making a man a drunkard?"

"It creates a burning, or thirst, which water does not satisfy, and before a man realizes it, he is taking something stronger. Only the other day I heard a gentleman telling mother that out of his family, in which there were four brothers, the only one who had not drunk to excess was the one who never began to smoke. He himself had been nearly ruined by liquor, and said that from his own experience he was sure that the use of tobacco was one of Satan's opening wedges to drunkenness."

"Well, Bob, I don't see but what you make out a pretty

clear case; you would be a first-rate temperance lecturer."

"It isn't what I think, Fred, that makes the case a strong one; it's the facts that tell, and you know facts are stubborn things."— *Selected*.

The Cigarette Cure

No slave of the cigarette habit need consider his case hopeless. The same divine Person who spoke deliverance to the captives in the time of Christ, and who is ready to save the drunkard to-day, is just as efficient in rescuing the slave to cigarettes. Resolve to stop at once and forever. The sooner the nicotine can be eliminated from the system, the sooner the desire for it will pass away. As a large portion of the poison is eliminated through the skin, vigorous sweating will hasten the cure. Copious water drinking is also beneficial. In overcoming this habit, it is extremely important that all stimulating and irritating articles of food, as spices, condiments, flesh foods, tea, coffee, etc., should be excluded from the dietary. It is these irritating substances that create a demand for the after-dinner cigar of the ordinary smoker.

Properly prepared meals, consisting largely of luscious fruits, grains, and nuts, will hasten the deliverance of the slave of the cigarette, and reduce to a minimum the struggle necessary to win the battle. The distressing heart symptoms which sometimes appear can be relieved almost instantly by placing over the heart a towel wrung out of cold water, or a rubber bag filled with crushed ice. In order to strengthen the nervous system and improve the general tone of the body, it is a good plan to adopt the habit of taking a cold sponge-bath upon rising in the morning. Those who will take the trouble to adopt a few of these simple procedures, and at the same time earnestly seek God for his divine aid, will be saved from the insane asylum, the hospital, or an early grave.— *John Q. A. Henry, in "The Deadly Cigarette."*

POEMS

A Case for Charity

He was out at the elbows and out at the knees,
 But he had an old pipe in his mouth.
He was worse than a ragman by several degrees,
 But he had an old pipe in his mouth.
He was out of a job, and his plans had all failed,
He was "down in the mouth," and his luck he bewailed,
At the rich man he swore, at monopoly railed —
 But he kept that old pipe in his mouth.

He was woeful and shabby and hungry and lame,
 But he had his old pipe in his mouth.
He had saved little money — he was not to blame,
 For he must have a pipe in his mouth.
He would "go out to market,"— an every-day joke,—
And you knew what he'd say ere a sentence he spoke:
" A penny for bread and five cents for a smoke,"
 O, he must have that pipe in his mouth!

His wife sewed by lamplight, to drive the wolf hence
 (And to keep that old pipe in his mouth),
And he said, between puffs: "We must cut our expense,"
 But he kept that old pipe in his mouth.
Kind charity, come, without further delay,
This woman may die — what will happen, then, pray?
Here's a case you must help. Shall I tell you the way?
 Just take that old pipe from his mouth!

— Hattie H. Louthan.

The Cigarette

The cigarette! The cigarette!
Most subtle foe that youth has met!
 We boys should take alarm!
A dangerous thing it is, though small,
For in its tiny folds lie all
 The elements of harm.

An Ally of the Liquor Traffic

The cigarette! The cigarette!
O listen, boys, and don't forget!
 (The half has ne'er been told.)
There is a drug within it placed
To which directly may be traced
 Disorders manifold.

The cigarette! The cigarette!
To smoke it, boys, is to beget
 A thirst for liquors vile;
Within the victim's weakened will
Love for the products of the still
 Becomes intrenched the while.

The cigarette! The cigarette!
The smoker's pathway is beset
 With dangers not a few;
Physical vigor it impairs,
Mental and moral force ensnares,
 While death doth oft ensue.

The cigarette! The cigarette!
Worse than the old-time calumet!
 Boycott it, boys, I say!
Let every boy in every cot
Decide that he will use it not —
 Boycott it, boys, I say!
— *Rufus Clark Landon.*

A Fiend

I know a little impish fiend; he dresses all in white,
So innocent appearing he, you'd think him harmless quite.
So little space he occupies, he scarcely parts the lips,
He often rests, though quite unseen, between the finger-tips.
He has companions by the score; in bundles he's put up;
He often breathes his poison breath above the social cup.
The beer mug is his special chum, the wine glass is his fellow,
And often he seeks comradeship with punch so mild and mellow.

He's growing bigger year by year, and yet he looks so little
That any schoolboy, with a knife, might soon reduce to whittle.
He lies in wait for little boys, and tempts them for a penny,
And as for having one good point, he really hasn't any;
For he will win the boys' love, then poison hearts and brains;
And when they try to break away, he'll mock them for their pains;
Yes, he will chain them hard and fast, and make them helpless slaves,
And at the madhouse, in a cell, there many a victim raves.

You can see him in the drug-store; upon the grocer's shelf;
Wherever he can play a card so cunningly for pelf,
In candy stores he lies in wait, with ever-watchful eye,
To catch the pennies and the dimes of every passer-by.
And while his fiendish deeds are known, and blazoned far and wide,
Yet there are men with hearts so hard they're on the demon's side.
So strange it seems, and monstrous, too, you scarcely will believe it,
They sell the fiend for paltry gold, and gladly they receive it.

You ask, " Who is this fiend that lies in wait for boys,
And robs them of their birthright, of manhood's hopes and joys?
Where is the monster, great or small, who has victims by the score,
And yet is never satisfied, but is always wanting more?"
Ah, friends, it is the cigarette, that trifling little thing,
Which disease, insanity, and death to many youth doth bring.
If we could summon pictures up, and see the ruin wrought,
We never could be happy till we'd seen the monster caught.

His awful maw is never filled, as long as greed for gold
Shall rule the willing hearts of men, and make them hard and cold.
And mothers must give up the boys, to satisfy the greed
Of selfish men — no use to stand and plead.
We stand aghast with bated breath, and wonder how much longer

Our God will see and yet permit the sinning of the stronger;
For yet we know, though hard to see, that God is just and tender,
While love's the link from us to him, the cord is strong though slender.

O fathers, husbands, brothers here, come waken from your sleep!
Throw off your struggling apathy, your indifference so deep!
Let us join our hands and voices, plunge boldly in the strife,
Let us catch the sneaking demon, and crush out his worthless life!
It's your neighbor's boy, and yours, friend, who are sacrificed each day,
Who are smoking, yes, and drinking in the saloon across the way.
Put your heel upon the serpent, crush his ugly rising head,—
No more boys in our fair country to the monster shall be fed!

— *Lou E. Rall.*

The Tobacco User

Throw that filthy pipe away,
You can never make it pay;
Ever smoking as you go,
Where's the good? I'd like to know.

Now I say,— and 'tis no joke,—
Half your plans will turn to smoke;
All you earn from day to day,
You'll chew up, and spit away.

Is there aught that's noble, great,
You attain in such a state?
Are you living out the plan
God at first designed for man?

Break your pipe and be a man,
Cut the chain while yet you can;
Though you doubt it, soon, I think,
If you smoke, you'll want to drink.

If one sin breaks through the door,
It will soon make room for more;
Shut the door against the first,
Then you'll never meet the worst.

— C. M. Willis.

Be Careful What You Sow, Boys

Be careful what you sow, boys!
For seed will surely grow, boys!
The dew will fall, the rain will splash,
The clouds grow dark, the sunshine flash,
And he who sows good seed to-day
Will reap the crop to-morrow.

Be careful what you sow, boys!
For every seed will grow, boys!
Where it may fall you can not know;
In sun and shade 'twill surely grow;
And he who sows good seed to-day
Will reap the crop to-morrow.

Be careful what you sow, boys!
The weed you plant will grow, boys!
The scattered seed from thoughtful hand
Must gathered be by God's command;
And he who sows wild oats to-day
Must reap wild oats to-morrow.

Then let us sow good seed, boys!
And not the briers and weeds, boys!
The harvest-time its joys will bring,
And when we reap, our hearts will sing;
For he who sows good seed to-day
Will reap good seed to-morrow.

— Selected.

The Deadly Cigarette

The boy who smokes these filthy things,
  These cigarettes I mean,
With clothes and breath offensive, vile,
  Can never be called clean.

They stunt the growth of the physique,
  The brilliant eye bedim,
Befog the mental vision, too;
  For judgment, don't trust him!

If he's a servant anywhere,
  This slave of cigarettes,
His service can not be the best,
  His duties he forgets.

My boy, don't use these "coffin nails;"
  For surely if you do,
You undervalue manhood's worth,
  And crush your spirits too!

Say, "No!" when first you're tempted,
  Say, "No!" you surely can,
Say, "No!" to every evil;
  Be first and last a *man!*

                — *Selected.*

The Tobacco Aggression

Men of nations, rise to duty!
  Crush the vile, destructive foe;
Rise and fight for childhood's freedom,
  Lay this mighty tyrant low.
Up, ye men! be strong, courageous,
  Look with pity on the youth
Poisoned by the weed tobacco,
  Pitiable wreck, forsooth!

Stealthily it stalks among us,
  Poisoned arrows round it fly;

And our children, once so healthy,
   In its pathway droop and die;
For it saps the very life-blood
   Of our bright and winsome boys;
Sows its seeds, works fearful havoc,
   Devastates, and so destroys.

Rise and plant the tree of freedom
   In the ashes of the dead,
These our martyred little children,
   Blindfold by tobacco led.
Faith in God will be our watchword,
   Faith to crush the subtle foe,
Faith to trust him to deliver,
   Faith to lay the tyrant low.

—*Adapted.*

The Pledge That Makes Us Free

(Tune: "Marching Through Georgia.")

O, come on, boys, and join our ranks, and sing another song!
Sing it with a spirit that will start the world along,
Sing it as the victors sing who triumph over wrong —
   Down with the cigarette forever!

CHORUS:
Hurrah! hurrah! we bring the jubilee.
Hurrah! hurrah! the pledge that makes us free.
So we'll sing the chorus,— let us sing it out with glee,—
   Down with the cigarette forever!

As soldiers we will loyal be, and battle for the right;
To drive this demon from the land, we'll work with all our might;
Give us all a helping hand, and join us in the fight.
   Down with the cigarette forever!

—*Adapted.*

THE GREAT AMERICAN FRAUD

"It is far better to discard the use of drugs, and depend upon simple diet, exercise, fresh air, sunshine, cleanliness, cheerfulness, faith in God, and simple, rational home treatments, intelligently and faithfully applied. To be constantly resorting to drugs of any kind is a great mistake. Millions of dollars are annually expended on worthless and injurious nostrums. It would be far better for the people to spend a few dollars in the purchase of reliable works on the preservation of health and the rational treatment of disease, and to become intelligent in these important matters. In critical cases it is, of course, best to consult a reliable physician, or take treatment at a good sanitarium; but by following the instruction here given, vast sums of money might be saved, much suffering avoided, and the health of the people greatly improved."

PLEASE DO NOT ASK US

WHAT IS | ANY OLD PATENT MEDICINE | WORTH?

For you embarrass us, as our honest answer must be that

IT IS WORTHLESS

If you mean to ask us at what price we sell it, that is an entirely different proposition.

When sick, consult a good physician. It is the only proper course. And you will find it cheaper in the end than self-medication with worthless "patent" nostrums.

The Above Sign Was Displayed in a Chicago Drug-Store

PATENT MEDICINES AND DRUGS[1]

A Profitable Business

No apology is made for considering patent medicines in this book; for they constitute a formidable obstacle in the path of temperance reform. It seems that Satan has hit upon this modern device for leading on to intemperance those who shrink in horror from the glass; and the result of this effort is no discredit to his work as a deceiver. Disguised as friends of suffering humanity, these medicines not only take people off their guard, but receive a hearty welcome from the credulous multitude. They indiscriminately attack the innocent babe, the stalwart youth, and the aged sufferer. Rich and poor, ignorant and learned, are found among their victims. So prosperous has the patent-medicine business become, that it keeps thousands of persons employed in supplying the demands of the public. It is estimated that the sale of these medicines comprises two thirds of the business of the average small drug-store. Annually they cost the American people alone about seventy-five million dollars.

Splendid testimonials and the " sure-cure " advertisements beguile many to make the " tablespoonful before meals " a daily essential. After diagnosing their own cases, they choose some concoction which is little better or worse than so much alcohol and water, with perhaps some opium, cocaine, or morphine added. Could these victims of men's greed spend a day with the bureau which produces the testi-

---
[1] Those wishing to give further study to this subject can secure " The Great American Fraud," from the American Medical Association, 103 Dearborn Ave., Chicago, Ill. Price, post-paid, ten cents. The pamphlet contains one hundred sixty-eight pages, and is a compilation of two series of articles which appeared in *Collier's Weekly*.

monials for these compounds, or with the chemists who analyze them, the business of these patent-medicine concerns would very probably decrease. *Collier's Weekly* and the *Ladies' Home Journal* not long ago gave this matter considerable publicity. This agitation helped to secure the present United States pure-food laws.

The dealers in these nostrums evidently have "loved darkness rather than light," and have had no desire to acquaint the public with the contents of their medicines; for when the United States Legislature demanded that the labels of proprietary remedies should state the exact amount of opium, cocaine, alcohol, etc., they contained, these dealers cried out that such a law was destructive to business, and a crime against personal liberty.

In securing testimonials, they seem to follow the plan of letting the end justify the means. Some are honestly received from persons who write under the stimulating influence of the medicines; but many are forged. Of persons who thus suffer misrepresentation, few are as fortunate as was Miss Alice Wynne, who was awarded six thousand dollars damages for the unauthorized use of her photograph in an advertisement. Seldom do testimonials so completely defeat their purpose as did one which appeared in the Connecticut *Evening Citizen*. In one column Mrs. Mary Adams, of Adams Street, related her complete restoration to health, through the efficacy of a certain patent medicine; and in another column of the same issue was an account of her death.

Greed Is the Root

The patent-medicine business has for its foundation "the love of money." That greed for gain has induced many to identify themselves with a money-making concern which is morally a crime to the public; that same greed has silenced most of the voices which have been lifted to expose the fraudulent business, and has paralyzed most of the hands raised against it.

The Great American Fraud

The press, with few exceptions, is at the service of the patent-medicine dealers, who are leagued together to force their advertisements into the papers. Alliances to prevent the suppression of the business by legislatures have also been made with some papers. When Massachusetts tried to pass a bill regulating the patent-medicine trade, dealers telegraphed the newspapers in that State with which they had contracts, and the bill was killed. Later, however, Massachusetts passed such a law, as have also New Hampshire, Michigan, and North Dakota.

There must be money in it. The newspapers receive no small sum for helping quacks in their swindles. Samuel Hopkins Adams says, in his book, "The Great American Fraud," that Mr. Hearst's papers alone draw more than half a million dollars yearly from that source. A New York magistrate says that the patent-medicine business is robbing America of more money than is burglary. For instance, a bottle of Peruna which retails at one dollar, costs the manufacturers about eighteen cents — medicine, bottle, wrapper, and all. A conscientious druggist in Chicago put this notice in his window: "Please do not ask us what is any old patent medicine worth; for you embarrass us, as our honest answer must be, *It is worthless*. If you mean at what price we sell it, that is an entirely different proposition."

Intemperance in Disguise

These medicines, for the most part, fall into two classes —" the absolutely worthless and the absolutely dangerous." The evils resulting from their use are legion. They generally bring added pain, and often needless death. Perhaps there is no greater evil connected with them, however, than their tendency to lead to intemperance. That they should do this is not strange; for nearly all of them contain alcohol, and some contain opium, morphine, and cocaine.

Dr. Ashbel P. Grinnell, of New York City, says: " More

alcohol is consumed in this country in patent medicine than is dispensed in a legal way by licensed liquor venders, barring the sales of ale and beer."

Some patent medicines contain so much alcohol that they will burn with a light-blue flame.[1] Hood's Sarsaparilla contains 18.8 per cent; Ayer's Sarsaparilla, 26 per cent; Brown's Iron Bitters, 19.7 per cent; Paine's Celery Compound, 21 per cent; Peruna, 28.5 per cent; Jamaica ginger, 90 per cent; Hostetter's Stomach Bitters, 44.3 per cent; Lydia Pinkham's remedy, 20 per cent; while beer contains from 2.5 to 6 per cent, wine 10.12 per cent, and whisky 50 per cent. Some of the popular soothing sirups contain not only alcohol, but opium as well. Many catarrh remedies contain considerable cocaine. Mr. Adams's statement that the one thing Peruna "cures" is sobriety applies to most patent medicines, and by the use of them many men, women, and children are innocently quickening their pace to drunkards' graves.

Drug Medicines

Many of those who steer clear of such "cure-alls" as Peruna, become the prey of subtler poisons, like headache-powders and "drug-habit" cures. One wakes up with a throbbing head; "that tired feeling" overtakes another; sorrow or disappointment grips the soul of a third, and together they flock to this or that so-called remedy,— a remedy which, while it never cures disease, benumbs pain, and lures the user on to drug enslavement. Such is the story of thousands, especially in our great cities.

The only safety is, "Touch not!" The following incident, although probably among the extreme ones, was selected from a list of twenty-two similar cases. Coroner Dugan, of Philadelphia, gave the following verdict: "Mary

---

[1] The per cent of alcohol in different medicines has been somewhat changed by recent pure food laws. Peruna, for instance, has now only eighteen per cent.

A. Bispels, aged eighteen years, came to her death from kidney and heart disease, aggravated by poisoning by acetanilid taken in Orangeine Headache-powder." This headache-powder claims also to strengthen the heart and enrich the blood, but analysis proves its influence to be just the opposite. Another similar and equally dangerous headache-powder is Bromoseltzer.

Then there are the drug-habit cures. If there is any shading in the moral crime of the dealers in drug medicines, then those who prey upon drug fiends must wear the blackest badge. They come to persons, who, having tasted the bitter dregs of the drug habit, are struggling to liberate themselves, and, with medicines which promise to cure, they thrust the poor sufferers into greater slavery. Often the principal element of the drug-habit cure is the very drug against which the patient is battling.

Opium in China

It is not a new problem with which the nations are wrestling. Anciently the Arabs used opium. For some time Asia Minor remained the source of the supply, but gradually the plant became distributed over the globe.

No country has escaped the ravages of the opium curse; but perhaps none has suffered more than China. One of her proverbs says, "Eleven out of every ten use opium." It first came to China in the thirteenth century. In 1757 the East India Company monopolized the opium traffic, and made that fatal abuse of the Chinese a great money-making enterprise. Soon the trade increased five hundred per cent. China vainly legislated against its importation, and in 1839 she became so desperate that she destroyed ten million dollars' worth of opium. This plunged her into a war with England, who, at the point of the bayonet, forced her to permit the traffic. Mrs. H. Taylor says: "During the entire reign of Queen Victoria, opium was exported from India at the rate of one-half ton every hour, day and night. Almost all of this found its way to China." Doubtless opium is partly responsible for some of the so-called characteristics of our yellow brother. Certain it is that everywhere the opium habit spreads poverty, suffering, and woe. When the people of Shan-si were pleading with their foreign teachers to liberate them from the opium curse, they said: " Those who before protected their families are themselves reduced to the appearance of beggars. The beds have no coverlets; the household utensils contain no food; hungry, there is nothing to eat; cold, there are no clothes to wear. The fault is surely opium."

Recently China issued a decree that the use of opium must be discontinued within ten years. Literature telling of the deceptive nature of this drug is being circulated freely in the Celestial Empire. China's most intelligent people are trying to do with opium what America's temperance workers are trying to do with alcohol.

Drugs in Other Lands

While China is endeavoring to wipe out the opium evil, America is cultivating it. The use of morphine is also becoming quite common in America. There are at present brought into America over seven hundred fifty thousand pounds of opium every year, and over a ton of morphine. This is over five times the quantity that was consumed a few years ago. It is estimated that over one million persons in America are slaves to this habit. Among males, forty per cent of these are found in the medical profession, fifteen per cent are men of leisure, eight per cent are merchants; among females, forty-three per cent are women who rank high in society. There is consumed annually practically the equivalent of fifty grains of opium for every man, woman, and child in America; while in opium-cursed China there is consumed only twenty-eight grains per capita. Unfortunately, morphine is said to be supplanting opium in China to some extent. Heroine is made from morphine, and is

The Great American Fraud 107

widely used in America. It is by many considered a harmless substitute for morphine. This is not the case; heroine has all the dangers of morphine, and additional dangers of its own; it is one of the most toxic agents of the morphine group. Trade preparations containing heroine are widely advertised as cough sirup, asthma cures, headache cures, etc. Americans become addicted to these so-called remedies, not knowing that they are becoming slaves to this drug. When attempting to discontinue their use, they find an aggravation of their symptoms; this is instantly relieved by the supposed remedy. As a result, many are slaves to the opium or morphine habit, and are not aware of it.

Germany, France, and the United States are countries in which the use of opium and its derivatives is most uni-

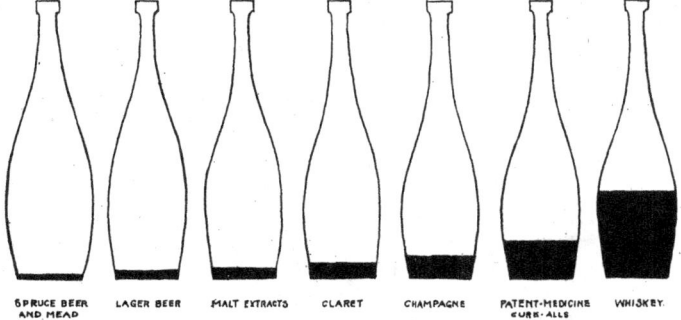

SPRUCE BEER AND MEAD LAGER BEER MALT EXTRACTS CLARET CHAMPAGNE PATENT-MEDICINE CURE-ALLS WHISKEY.

SHOWING RELATIVE AMOUNT OF ALCOHOL

versal. It has its victims, however, in all civilized lands.

In Germany it is said there are entire villages whose inhabitants are addicted to the use of the drug. The people of China and Germany know what they are taking, but in America and Great Britain drinks are sold in drug-stores and at soda-fountains which contain an appreciable quantity of this or other equally dangerous poisons, and the people do not know it. All the drinks advertised to relieve fatigue should be regarded with suspicion. Coco-cola, one of the most widely advertised drinks in America, contains about three grains of caffeine to the glass, and many other drinks now contain both cocaine and caffeine. Yet a great many, when fatigued, take these drinks as "pick-me-ups," never suspecting their contents. Unconsciously, men and women who depend upon these drinks for vim and strength when tired and fatigued, and in need of rest, finally become nervous wrecks. The rapid increase of insane and mentally unbalanced persons during the past few years is doubtless largely due to the use of these soft drinks containing drugs. The sale of these poisons should be prohibited by law in America, just as truly as in China. But until this is done, the only wise course to follow is to refuse any drink that is supposed to impart energy and new life, or that claims to relieve fatigue.

The Doctor's Story

Deacon Rogers, he came to me;
"Wife is a-goin' to die," said he.
"Doctors great and doctors small
Haven't improved her any at all.
Physic and blisters, powder and pills,
An' nothin' sure but the doctors' bills!
Twenty women, with remedies new,
Bother my wife the whole day through.
Sweet as honey, or bitter as gall—
Poor old woman, she takes 'em all.
Sour or sweet, whatever they choose,
Poor old woman, she daren't refuse.
So she pleases whoe'er may call,
An' Death is suited the best of all.
Physic and blister, powder an' pill—
Bound to conquer, an' sure to kill!"

Mrs. Rogers lay in her bed,
Bandaged and blistered from foot to head.
Blistered and bandaged from head to toe,
Mrs. Rogers was very low.

Bottle and saucer, spoon and cup,
On the table stood bravely up.
Physics of high and low degree;
Calomel, catnip, boneset tea;
Everything a body could bear,
Excepting light and water and air.
I opened the blinds; the day was bright,
And God gave Mrs. Rogers some light.
I opened the window; the day was fair,
And God gave Mrs. Rogers some air.
Bottles and blisters, powders and pills,
Catnip, boneset, sirups, and squills,
Drugs and medicines, high and low,
I threw them as far as I could throw.

"What are you doing?" my patient cried;
"Frightening Death," I coolly replied.

Deacon Rogers, he came to me;
"Wife is a-gettin' her health," said he.
"I really think she will worry through;
She scolds me just as she used to do.
All the people have poohed an' slurred —
All the neighbors have had their word;
''Twere better to perish,' some of 'em say,
'Than be cured in such an irregular way.'"

"Your wife," said I, "had God's good care,
And his remedies — light and water and air.
All of the doctors, beyond a doubt,
Couldn't have cured Mrs. Rogers without."

The deacon smiled and bowed his head;
"Then your bill is nothin'," he said.
"God's be the glory, as you say!
God bless you, doctor! good-day! good-day!"
— *Will Carleton.*

SPARKS FROM THE ANVIL

One patent-medicine firm uses each week five hundred barrels of cheap whisky in the manufacture of its products.

The baby cries, and the mother quiets it with a dose of soothing sirup, thus starting it down the path that leads to the slavery of intemperance.

Despite the enactment of drastic laws looking to the suppression of illicit traffic in opium, it is estimated that between one hundred twenty-five thousand and one hundred seventy-five thousand ounces are annually consumed in the United States, the greater part being in New York City, by its five thousand opium smokers.

Japan, New Zealand, and Australia have forbidden the importation of opium, except as a medicine. The United States government has made it illegal to import opium into the Philippine Islands except by government order.

All Mohammedan lands are said to proscribe opium and liquor, and some of them proscribe tobacco.

When the Dutch flag was raised in a certain island in the East Indies, the first building was not a church, nor a school, but an opium den.

Patent-medicine dealers are said to do a big business in prohibition territory. There this servant of the liquor traffic helps to keep alive the insane craze for alcoholic beverages.

The United States government has prohibited the sale of Peruna among the Indians.

Japan is trying to rid Formosa of the opium curse.

The use of opium is increasing in London. Several opium "joints" have been opened in the West End. They are run on the lines of social clubs. Introductions are necessary for admission, and a fee of ten dollars is charged

The Great American Fraud

for each visit. They are said to be the most luxuriously fitted-up opium dens in the world.

In some of the schools in New Jersey cocaine was introduced by some depraved older students, who conducted a thriving business selling the drug to children for the pennies given them for candy and lunch. Some children under ten years of age thus became addicted to the use of the drug.

Dr. T. D. Crothers, whom the American Pharmacy Association appointed to study into the drug habit, reports that within six years (1902-08), the demand for cocaine has increased four hundred per cent, for morphine and opium five hundred per cent. This is especially alarming when he adds that the increase for legitimate purposes has been less than twenty per cent.

Liquozone is chiefly a weak solution of sulphuric and sulphurous acids. It claims to cure thirty-seven different diseases.

An opium smoker wrote on the walls of his den: "While smoking opium, we are transported to paradise; while breaking the habit, we are tortured in hell."

It has been observed that one of the readiest ways of using cocaine is by means of taking snuff. Most of the so-called catarrh cures are compounded with cocaine, and lead up to the use of that drug.

The chief of police of Tampa, Florida, says that cocaine fiends, more than any other class of individuals, are responsible for an increase of crime, and they are more difficult to handle. According to this official, there is as much need of a national campaign against the sale of snuff and other compounds containing cocaine, as against the sale of alcoholic liquors.

"Should the newspapers, the magazines, and medical journals," declares Samuel Hopkins Adams, "refuse their pages to patent-medicine advertisements, the nation would be the richer not only in lives and money, but in drunkards and drug fiends saved."

Jamaica Ginger

"I am tired and cold, aren't you?" said one lady to another, as they were shopping one winter day.

"Yes," replied her friend. "Come in here and get a hot ginger," invited the first; and the two quiet, cultured women took their places with others at the counter of a fashionable drug-store, and ordered each a "hot Jamaica ginger."

They, and others, sipped and talked, and after a time passed out, but the proprietor said to a bystander, "Those women would scorn to go to a bar and get a hot whisky sling, but they've taken their ginger for just the same reason the toper takes his dram, because it braces them up; and they have taken it for the alcohol in it, too, though perhaps they do not know that part of it."

"Does it contain so much liquor as that?" questioned the hearer. "Certainly," replied the druggist, "it contains about twice as much alcohol as there is in whisky, and a 'ginger tipple' is getting to be a common thing with women." After a moment he added, thoughtfully, "I am not at all sure that the drink habit of many young men and women of to-day may not have been cultivated by the ease with which the Jamaica ginger bottle is opened and used in the home."

This may seem a harsh statement, but any one who will pour a little Jamaica ginger into a small dish and touch a match to it, will see that it is almost pure alcohol.

In these days when so much is being said of the danger and harmfulness of patent medicines, let us not forget that one of the most insidious is found in the bottle of Jamaica ginger which has its place on so many pantry shelves.—*Emma Graves Dietrick.*

THE TEMPERANCE MOVEMENT

In 1878 Rev. Robert Cuyler said of the temperance cause: "The good cause is yet under the mid-vollies of hot encounter, but as surely as God is at the helm of the universe, our cause shall have a final and substantial victory. In my humble judgment the three Thermopylæs of our conflict are the legal veto of the rum traffic, the medical argument against alcohol, and the individual effort to save the tempted by God's grace and the abstinence pledge."

FOUNDERS AND HOME OF FIRST TEMPERANCE SOCIETY

Dr. Clark, who is mentioned on page 116, stands in the rear of the group in this cut.

TEMPERANCE IN AMERICA

Beginning of the Temperance Work

Crusades against intemperance are not modern movements. The prophets were possessed with the terror of strong drink. Solomon preached against it, Daniel held aloft the banner of total abstinence, and Paul advocated it. But since the New Testament writers laid down the pen, a deep silence seems to have settled over the civilized world; and for eighteen hundred years the advocates of temperance have been almost entirely mute, while in the luxury of the ages, social life drifts on in the course of intemperance and self-indulgence.

Then turn to America. The hearts of its early settlers had been impregnated with the noble influence of the Reformation; and it was in the soil of those hearts that the seeds of modern temperance sprang up and grew. Many a time has the Master Gardener had to prune the plant, and now and then a twig has been grafted in; but under his careful hand it has continued to flourish.

Away back in 1650 some of the colonies tried to regulate the liquor traffic. But more than a century rolled by before any organized efforts were made. The revival then started among some Connecticut farmers. Two hundred of these men leagued themselves together, and resolved "not to drink more than was good for them." That does not sound much like a twentieth-century temperance pledge, yet these farmers stand forth as heroes; for in those days many of the worthy pioneers would hold one license from the state to sell whisky, and another from the church to preach. Alcoholic beverages were considered a necessity. Few men would work for those temperance farmers. They served no liquors on their tables, and that was looked upon as an infringement of the inalienable rights of hired help. The farmers were called stingy, gossipers ridiculed them, their fences were torn down, and sometimes the reformers themselves seemed in danger of becoming martyrs to the cause. But God blessed, and the temperance " tide heaved onward." Some years later the members of the Methodist Conference in Virginia enjoined their ministers to preach against the sin of intemperance.

During the Revolutionary War the foreign trade of the colonies was almost entirely cut off. This stopped the importation of rum and wine, and resulted in the establishment of distilleries all over the land. This waste of grain threatened at one time to cause a famine; and in view of this, Congress in 1777 passed the following resolution: —

"That it be recommended to the several legislatures of the United States immediately to pass laws the most effective for putting an immediate stop to the pernicious practise of distilling grain."

Crossing the threshold of the nineteenth century, we find other important events. In 1808 what is often called the first temperance society in America was formed near Saratoga Springs, New York. Dr. Billy Clark was the founder of it. For nine years, it is said, the burden of the drink evil pressed more and more heavily upon his heart. His attempt to get the local court to help him to organize a temperance society had failed, for " all the members of both bench and bar pronounced the project visionary and impracticable." But this did not discourage the invincible doctor. One cold, dark night in March, 1808, he rode to the home of his pastor. " Sir," said he, " we shall become a community of drunkards unless something is speedily done to arrest the progress of intemperance." The pastor was ready to listen, and ready to unite his efforts with those of Dr. Clark. They planned a meeting for organizing a temperance society. It was held April 13. Little did Dr. Clark and his associates know that the acorn they planted was destined to become a stately oak.

Rapid Development

Within four years, largely through the efforts of Lyman Beecher, the work developed into a national movement. In 1827 the Fairhaven Temperance Society was formed by Capt. Joseph Bates. He had seen the debasing influence of liquor among the sailors; and for several years he had not only abstained from all intoxicating liquors, but had also refrained from the use of tobacco. Perhaps one of the most interesting outgrowths of this early effort was the "Cold Water Army" of children, which in Fairhaven, Massachusetts, had three hundred members. Temperance papers, tracts, lecturers, and societies multiplied throughout the field. Already the temperance revival was bringing good results. It is claimed that during the third and fourth decades of that century, from one half to two thirds of New York's distilleries were closed, and it was estimated that during twelve months the commonwealth had saved six million two hundred fifty thousand dollars by the lessened use of ardent liquors. Together with a greater prosperity, the temperance revival also brought higher morals, and led to a religious awakening.

In 1833 Congress had a temperance society of its own members. But more important than this was the position taken in 1836 by the American Temperance Union. Its leaders had learned that efforts to reform which reserved the privilege of indulging now and then, meant absolute failure, and accordingly they hoisted the flag of total abstinence. That was a splendid platform, but it had one weak plank. Its pledge said nothing of stimulants, and because of this, some of the reformers relapsed into drunkenness through the use of milder intoxicants. On the other hand, the public, holding that it was the "*abuse, and not the use,*" of liquor that was wrong, refused to indorse total abstinence. This brought the temperance movement to a standstill for a time. But the spell soon broke; and in 1846 the Total Abstinence Society showed a membership of seven million in the United States, three million in England and Scotland, one million in Ireland, and three million in other countries. That was the high-water mark of early temperance efforts. One cause for such a great temperance victory was the labor of "Father" Matthew in Ireland, and of John B. Gough, a reformed drunkard, in England and America.

Recruits From the Enemy's Ranks

New blood coursed through the arteries of the temperance movement when some reformed drunkards stepped into line. They themselves were evidences of the saving grace, and could speak with persuasive power of the terrible slavery of intemperance. Several societies were formed by these rebels of King Alcohol. Among the most important were the Washingtonian Total Abstinence Society, and the Red Ribbon and Blue Ribbon reform movements.

The first of those mentioned was formed in Baltimore, Maryland, in 1840. Its charter-members were six tipplers, who pledged themselves to total abstinence. Their first meeting was called in a carpenter shop. To this gathering each of the six agreed to bring one other. The movement spread rapidly. In a month one thousand reformed drunkards joined its ranks; and in two years its membership reached six hundred thousand.

Reaction

The Civil War brought a reaction. While temperance workers were on the battle-field helping to settle the slavery question, many of the liquor dealers, busying themselves at home, began a work which finally secured the repeal of all prohibition laws, save those in Maine. That State remained true to the principles which Neal Dow had taught it several years before. There were some who felt this relapse very keenly. Lincoln, on the very day of his tragic death, said, "The next snare we have got to straighten out is the liquor question." Yet for about ten years temperance remained practically a dead issue. People were busy regaining lost fortunes, and protected the business which promised to help fill the treasuries and lessen the taxes. The liquor traffic boomed. But finally the temperance workers arose, and slowly but steadily their ranks advanced in the power of Him who fights the battles of justice and liberty.

The Woman's Christian Temperance Union

One of the leading temperance associations formed since the Civil·War is the Woman's Christian Temperance Union. It was in 1873 that a band of earnest women, led by the governor's daughter, entered the saloons of Hillsboro, Ohio, to pray and sing. The event seems an insignificant one; but God's clock had struck the hour for a temperance pentecost. From that village a wave of influence went out which touched nearly every hamlet and town in the country. As these women went forth in their noble crusade, they made the forty-sixth psalm their "Magna Charta," and here are the words of their crusade hymn:—

"Give to the winds thy fears,
  Hope and be undismayed.
God hears thy sighs, and counts thy tears,
  He will lift up thy head.

"Through waves and clouds and storms,
  He gently clears thy way.
Wait thou his time, so shall this night
  Soon end in joyous day.

"Far, far above thy thought,
  His counsel shall appear,
When fully he the work hath wrought
  Which caused thy needless fear."

About a year after the first meeting at Hillsboro, the movement was permanently organized, and became known as the W. C. T. U. To-day it belts the globe, and has its pledges printed in nearly every spoken tongue. Forty departments plan, pray, and work for the advancement of the different phases of this movement. Through its efforts, scientific temperance is in the public-school curriculum, and temperance is one of the subjects taught in Sunday-schools. It has worked in behalf of men in every zone of human activity, and it has helped to establish homes for the drunkard and his suffering children. Of it Miss Willard said: "The mission of the White Ribbon women is to organize the motherhood of the world for peace and purity, the protection and exaltation of the home."

Red and Blue Ribbon Movements

The Red Ribbon reform, with its motto, "Dare to do right," and its red ribbon badge, was founded by Dr. Reynolds in 1874, a few months after he reformed. It has been especially successful in Massachusetts, Michigan, and Illinois. The Blue Ribbon reform, of which Francis Murphy is the hero, has a similar record, and was formed about the same time. The Murphy temperance pledge bore these words: "With malice toward none and charity for all."

Yesterday — To-day — To-morrow

Many battles have been fought and won in the past, but a strenuous conflict is still impending. It is a warfare against avarice and appetite; against an enemy which almost universally has had the law for its shield, and politics for its sword. But there is cause for courage. The eyes of the public are turning wistfully to the trail of blessings which temperance brings; and science is acquainting the people with the deceptive nature of alcohol. In the nineties of the last century, American industries began to realize the value of temperance labor. To-day, according to the report of the national Department of Labor, ninety-six per cent of the railroads, seventy-two per cent of agriculturists, seventy-nine per cent of manufacturers, and eighty-eight per cent of trades in the United States are discriminating against the man who drinks. Two strong organizations not yet mentioned, the Prohibition Party and the Anti-Saloon League, are determined that we shall have " a saloonless country and a stainless flag," and their well-organized efforts are giving the liquor dealers considerable uneasiness.

These conditions are helping to prepare " in the desert a highway " for the temperance army. The mistakes made in the past serve only to help light the torch of the future. Methods have been tested, and more rapid progress is possible. It has begun. Within the last few years there has swept over both sides of the globe such a wave of temperance sentiment as the modern movement has never before known. It still rolls on. Charles Stelzle, in the *Sunday School Times* of Nov. 29, 1908, speaking of the movement in the United States, says: " The saloon is going at the rate of thirty a day." To-day is reaping the harvest of past sowing. Every civilized nation in the world is represented in the crusade against King Alcohol's forces. Our temperance warriors are moving on. Their drums beat no retreat.

> " It has been weary watching wave on wave,
> And yet the tide heaves onward.
> We build, like corals, grave on grave,
> And pave a pathway sunward.
> We're beaten back in many a fray,
> But newer strength we borrow;
> For where the vanguard rests to-day,
> The rear shall camp to-morrow."

But whether the ground already gained shall be held, and a glorious and triumphant victory finally be achieved, will depend upon the thoroughness with which the work in all its phases is prosecuted now, and the faithfulness of men to principles of right and duty. Unless the work is genuine, thorough, broad, and deep, the forces of wrong will recover the ground they have lost, and yet triumph.

The March of Progress

1789 — Connecticut Farmers' Temperance Association organized.

1808 — First temperance society in the United States was formed near Saratoga Springs, New York.

1827 — Fairhaven Temperance Society, organized by Capt. Joseph Bates.

1828 — First temperance paper, the *National Philanthropist,* started.

1836 — Temperance societies adopted total abstinence.

1846 — High-water mark in early temperance movement.

1851 — Maine adopted prohibition.

1872 — Prohibition Party began its national existence.

1873 — Woman's Christian Temperance Union organized.

1874 — Red Ribbon movement founded by Dr. Reynolds.

1874 — Blue Ribbon movement started by Francis Murphy.

1880 — Kansas made prohibition constitutional.

1882 — Vermont passed the first law to teach temperance in public schools.

1883 — Frances E. Willard organized the World's Woman's Christian Temperance Union.

1889 — North Dakota went under constitutional prohibition.

1893 — Anti-Saloon League was formed.

1902 — Georgia passed law for temperance education, all the other States having taken this step before.

1907 — Oklahoma adopted prohibition.

1908 — World's Temperance Congress at Saratoga Springs, New York.

1908 — North Carolina and Georgia adopted prohibition.

1909 — Alaska-Yukon-Pacific Exposition, the first Prohibition World's Fair.

1909 — Alabama, Mississippi, and Tennessee adopted prohibition.

TEMPERANCE IN OTHER LANDS

Alaska

The prohibition of the traffic in Alaska, which was adopted by the United States when it purchased the territory from Russia in 1868, continued until 1899, when Congress granted a license law permitting the sale of liquor to whites. The law still prohibits the sale of intoxicants among the Indians.

Hawaii

The act of the United States government which annexed Hawaii, contained a clause prohibiting the sale of intoxicating liquors there, but an amendment was added, granting the territorial legislature the privilege of substituting a license law.

Germany

A temperance movement began seventy years ago, but made little headway until the beginning of the twentieth century, when the great increase in the consumption of liquor began to alarm those in authority.

Great Britain

In 1494 the evils of the liquor business became too apparent to be borne longer passively. Justices of the peace were empowered to stop the sale of ale. Later inns were forbidden to deal in liquor. In 1736 a very strict gin law was made, but public sentiment made it impossible for those in authority to enforce it. Great Britain is still battling against the destructive traffic.

France

Alcoholism is held as one of the most terrible scourges of the day, and one of the chief causes of death. France is battling against the popular drink, absinthe, which about the middle of the nineteenth century was introduced by the soldiers returning from Algiers. Some of the newspapers which have conducted an energetic campaign against absinthe have been intimidated by the storm of protest from the dealers.

Belgium

Having faced the peril of the absinthe habit, Belgium has passed a law prohibiting the manufacture, importation, transportation, storage, or sale of the liquor or any substitute for it. For a number of years she has made an appropriation for the teaching of temperance in the public schools.

Russia

The sale of spirits has been a government monopoly since 1896. There seems to be a loud call for local option. The sale of spirituous liquors is prohibited on steamers and in railway stations.

Hungary

Reports indicate that Hungary consumes less intoxicating liquor per capita than any other country in Central or Southern Europe.

Sweden

In 1855 Sweden adopted local option. This resulted in two thirds of the territory going dry. Ten years later the Gothenburg system, a system by which the government controls the trade in spirits, was adopted. However, Sweden still spends more than twice as much for alcoholic liquor each year as for her military defenses. In 1907 her army of total abstainers passed the ten-thousand mark; she is still fighting for direct local veto.

Norway

The experience of Norway is much the same as that of Sweden. Her people, according to a statement made in the International Congress on Alcoholism (June, 1909), are the smallest consumers of alcohol in the world. Every fifth person is an abstainer.

Switzerland

In 1887 Switzerland introduced state control of the liquor traffic; but while this has reduced the sale of distilled spirits slightly, the manufacture and sale of fermented liquors, have increased. The sale of absinthe on the boats on Lake Geneva and adjacent lakes is forbidden. Much is being done throughout Switzerland for the cause of temperance.

Holland

Holland adopted a law in 1880 which has helped to check the growth of the liquor traffic. She spends about four thousand dollars yearly for temperance instruction in her public schools.

Denmark

Denmark teaches scientific temperance in her schools. Her liquor bill costs her about four times as much as her army and navy.

Spain

Spain consumes a great deal of light wines and liquors.

Austria

Austria forbids all temperance teaching for children under fourteen and for secondary schools under eighteen.

Bohemia

In Bohemia exists the same difficulty as in Austria.

Abyssinia

Abyssinia will not suffer the liquor traffic to enter her borders.

Japan

Temperance is retreating. Some years ago Japan had no saloons; but in recent years American and European breweries have been opened there.

China

As far as the liquor traffic is concerned, China is under prohibition. The prohibition law dates back to 459 A. D. One writer says that whatever nullification there is of this decree is largely due to European influence.

India

Her religions — Buddhism, Hinduism, and Mohammedanism — prohibit intoxicating liquors. However, she now manufactures some wine and spirits; but the great foe to temperance in India is English liquor.

Turkey

Her religion forbids the use of intoxicating liquors. Moslems say, when they see one of their number drunk, "He has left Mohammed and gone to Jesus." The liquor consumed in Turkey comes mostly from England and the United States.

Canada

Canada has local option in most of her provinces. All sale of liquors is prohibited in the army and military camps. The consumption of liquor in Canada is much less per capita than in England and America.

Australia

Australia makes temperance education compulsory in its schools in many of its provinces.

Mexico

Scientific temperance is now being taught in the schools of old Mexico.

BEACON LIGHTS IN THE TEMPERANCE MOVEMENT

All reform movements are more or less the "lengthening shadows" of persons who are great enough to turn away from themselves, and to live for the betterment of the world. Being at leisure from selfish pursuits, they become occupied with the needs about them, and give expression to the discontent and suffering of the silent millions. More than that, they help the people to place their feet upon the circumstances that tend to crush them. This is true of the temperance workers, and the records of their noble lives are a call to us for service. Study those lives to gain inspiration from their courage, faith, and untiring zeal; and study them to obtain a glimpse of the temperance cause from a new view-point.

THE LORD OF HOSTS IS WITH US.

T. C. Harper. Ira Long.

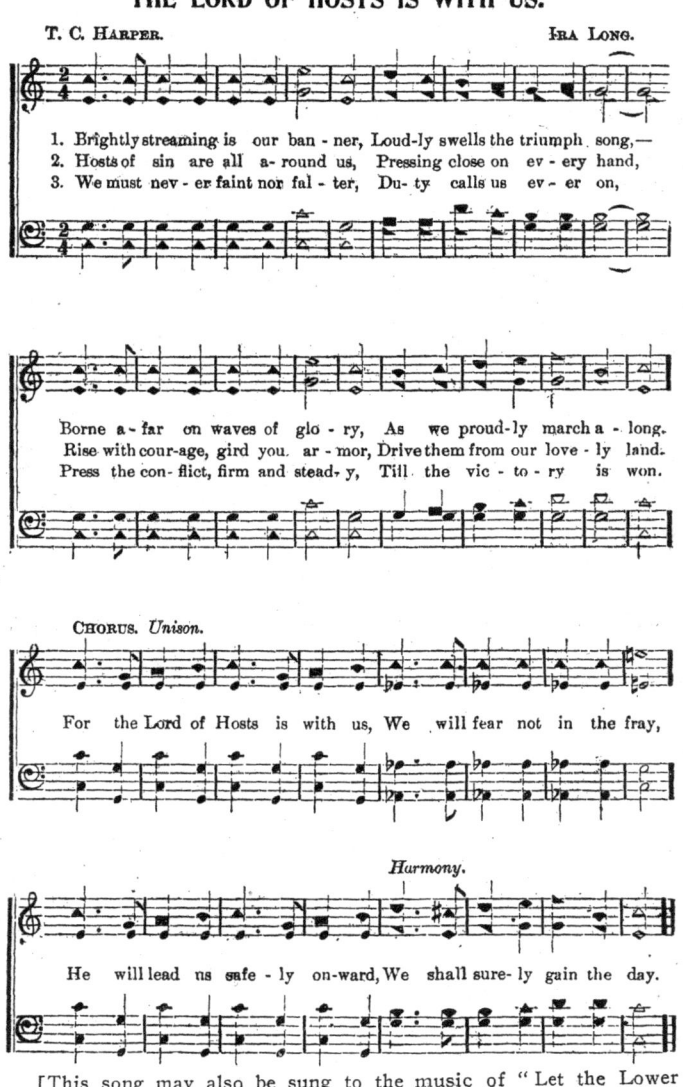

1. Brightly streaming is our ban-ner, Loud-ly swells the triumph song,—
2. Hosts of sin are all a-round us, Pressing close on ev-ery hand,
3. We must nev-er faint nor fal-ter, Du-ty calls us ev-er on,

Borne a-far on waves of glo-ry, As we proud-ly march a-long.
Rise with cour-age, gird you ar-mor, Drive them from our love-ly land.
Press the con-flict, firm and stead-y, Till the vic-to-ry is won.

CHORUS. *Unison.*

For the Lord of Hosts is with us, We will fear not in the fray,

Harmony.

He will lead us safe-ly onward, We shall sure-ly gain the day.

[This song may also be sung to the music of "Let the Lower Lights Be Burning."]

SHORT BIOGRAPHIES

Dr. Benjamin Rush

Benjamin Rush (1745-1813) was a blessing to the world. When he was six years old, his father died; his mother had only limited resources, yet her boy was sent to school. He was a diligent student, and while still a young man, was graduated from both Princeton and Edinburgh. While in school, he was exposed to the temptations of the great cities; but in him the college sent forth not only an intellectual giant, but a young man with a clean record and a strong Christian character. He had now completed his medical course, and went abroad for two years, returning to Philadelphia in 1769 to practise medicine. Business flourished. He gave his life to his work. In 1793 an epidemic visited Philadelphia; traffic was closed down, and the terrible solitude of the city was rarely broken save by the sound of the hearse or the thud of the doctor's foot. Nearly all the physicians had fled from the city, or fallen by the indiscriminating hand of death; yet in all that crisis Dr. Rush remained at his post. Day and night he served. One week he visited and prescribed for about one hundred twenty patients daily.

That busy doctor was more than a physician. In him every noble cause found a friend. He was a noted teacher in the medical department of the Pennsylvania University; he signed the Declaration of Independence; he was vice-president of the Philadelphia Bible Society; when slavery began to be agitated, he was made president of the American Society for its abolition. With tongue and pen he advocated the establishment of free schools throughout the country. In the temperance war for independence, he " fired the opening shot heard round the world." He wrote essays and pamphlets on the evil effects of ardent spirits and tobacco. This literature was distributed gratuitously. It contributed much to dim the vice of intemperance, and won for Dr. Rush the honor of being "the father of the modern temperance reform."

Mrs. Annie Wittenmyer

Mrs. Annie Wittenmyer became the first president of the Woman's Christian Temperance Union. During the Civil War, she superintended the special diet kitchens, to the great advantage of the health of the soldiers. After the war, she became the founder of the first home for soldiers' orphans in Iowa. As a W. C. T. U. worker, she did extensive lecture work, and edited two papers. In 1875 she presented a petition to Congress asking for the prohibition of the liquor traffic. First and last, she was a woman's woman, devoted to the advancement of her sex in usefulness and opportunity. One day a gentleman said to her, "Madam, if you go on and have success, you'll break up my business." "I hope I shall," she replied, "if you are a liquor dealer." "No, I am not a liquor dealer; but I keep the jail, and that's about the same thing."

Neal Dow

Neal Dow (1804-1897) was one of the first temperance lights to shine in America. First we find him in his father's

tannery, next as mayor of Portland, Maine, and then a worker in the great temperance cause. In Maine, his native State, in America, and in Great Britain he labored without compensation. It was one of the thousands of sad cases caused by the liquor traffic that turned his attention to temperance. The unhappy wife of a drunkard asked him to urge the saloon-keeper to sell her husband no more liquor. Mr. Dow gladly acquiesced, but the saloon-keeper invited him to cease "whining around" his place of business. Of this occurrence Mr. Dow says:

"Surprised, disappointed, indignant, I replied to the effect that sooner or later I would see that he and all like him were driven from the community unless they abandoned their infamous business." And he did see to it. In 1851 his State passed a prohibitory law. He was beaten back a dozen times; but never acknowledging defeat, he pushed on to success. As a youth, his temperance principles were a strength to his associates; as a worker, he became a blessing to his country.

Lady Henry Somerset

Lady Henry Somerset, the wife of one of Queen Victoria's officials, was by virtue of her position brought into the gaiety of court circles. But that life could not satisfy her cravings for better things; yet it was not until a keen personal sorrow gripped her heart, that she proved the utter emptiness of worldly pleasures, and sought for comfort in the path of Christian service. She found it.

Long she worked for her tenants, and would go over the hills in stormy days to attend their cottage gatherings. Then she conducted a mission in the poorer districts of the city, where she came to realize the curse of the liquor traffic. For years she held gospel-temperance meetings among the Welsh miners. Later she secured a two-hundred-acre farm, where she made homes for women and children whom she could rescue from drunkenness. In 1898 she was made president of the World's W. C. T. U., which office she held until succeeded by the Countess of Carlisle in 1906. "Her logical reasoning, keen analysis, vast fund of information, and full understanding of political conditions, made her of all speakers the best equipped to present the great theme of total abstinence."

John B. Gough

John B. Gough (1817-1886) was not sober when he signed the temperance pledge, but he was in earnest. The day after signing the pledge, the terrible gnawing within was about to conquer him when he felt a hand on his shoulder, and heard a voice saying: "I am glad you signed the pledge; other young men will follow your example." Some one did care what became of him. Again he asserted his manhood. The struggle was desperate, but he came out victorious.

John Gough's career had been a checkered one. His parents were poor; and when he was only twelve years old, he left England to come to America. After working awhile on a farm, he went to the city, and apprenticed himself to a bookbinder; but because of dissipation he soon lost his position. Then followed seven years of reckless living. He sang and recited in grog-shops. Drinking brought on delirium tremens. His young wife and little child sank into the grave. Still he continued carousing.

But after a temperance meeting in 1842, he was a changed man. He rapidly developed into a great lecturer, and became one of the most noted temperance workers in Europe and America. Of him one biographer says: "No other man has ever done so much to silence opposition." For thirty-four years he worked to save his fellow men from the terrible demon, drink. Often he told others of his hatred for it, and how he never hated it worse than when he was its abject slave. He also said that he never felt so strong to resist the demon of drink as when he was battling against it. It seemed impossible to break the chains, but by God's grace he did it. "There is not so pitiful a slave on this earth," he said, "as the man that is the slave of evil habits and passions." His last words were, "Young man, keep your record clean."

Jennie Casseday

It seemed that she had no life to give the world; yet she made a princely investment of her days. When at the age of twenty she learned that her life must be one of pain, she lifted her heart to God for his indwelling. For thirty years the bed was her world, but by God's grace she defeated seeming impossibilities, and became a blessing to others.

Through her influence, a home was founded for working girls. She was a White Ribboner, and for ten years served as superintendent of one of its departments. The special work of her department was gospel and temperance work among prisoners. To bouquets tied up with ribbon were fastened Scripture texts and quotations on temperance. These gifts were sent to cheer lonely prisoners. Then would follow select literature and the total abstinence pledge. She was a Christian friend of all poor criminals, and for this reason her anniversary has been celebrated as "prisoner's day."

Her greatest peculiarity, says Miss Willard, was that she always had "a heart at leisure from itself, to soothe and sympathize." In darkest gloom she saw some faint ray of light and cheer, and made the best of "now and here." Her self-forgetful life built, in the hearts of those who knew her, a monument which death alone can destroy.

Anna A. Gordon

Anna A. Gordon heard the moan of sinning, suffering humanity. It was to her a call to service. Her beautiful,

self-forgetful career began in 1877. It was a little thing that broke the shell of self-service. Miss Willard was holding meetings. There was no one to play the organ. After a painful pause, Miss Gordon came shyly up the aisle, and whispered, "As no one else volunteers, I'll do the best I can."

That was her first acquaintance with Miss Willard; but from that day those two lives were indissolubly knit together until death broke the strands. Miss Gordon has filled various offices in the W. C. T. U., and has done extensive traveling in behalf of that movement. Her musical compositions have done much to popularize the work

Frances E. Willard

Frances E. Willard (1839-1898), the uncrowned queen, was one of the brightest lights in the temperance world.

New York was her birthplace, but most of her childhood days were spent in Wisconsin. She loved nature; and often with her brother and sister she would roam over the prairies that stretched away mile after mile about her forest home. But not always was she thus to roam. Humanity needed her. Her parents moved to a Chicago suburb, where she lived for nearly forty years.

Miss Willard was a hard worker, and served humanity in many spheres of usefulness. For some time she was in the public schools, then dean of the woman's department of the University of Evanston, and professor of rhetoric in the same school. Her fertile pen has produced much good literature on social purity, labor reform, and temperance subjects.

In 1874 she handed her resignation to the university. Many attractive and remunerative positions were offered her. She had no income, and her mother, who was advancing in years, leaned on her for support; yet she turned from all else to take up the work to which she felt God had called her. Like Moses, she turned from the wealth of Egypt to face the desert with God.

That decision has brought great blessing to the world. Few have done more to lift humanity heavenward than Frances Willard. For several years she was president of the W. C. T. U. She originated the Polyglot Petition for the prohibition of the liquor traffic and the opium trade.

This petition was presented in both England and America.

Miss Willard has been called "the best-loved woman in America;" and consistent with that phrase, hers is the first woman's statue to be placed in the great statuary hall of the national capitol. Her death seemed an irreparable loss to the temperance cause, but to be robbed of the influence which she wields in the world would be a still greater calamity. "She threw her lance into the thickest of the fight, and when she fell, it was with face to the foe and harness hacked in front."

Francis Murphy

Francis Murphy (1836-1907) in the summer of 1870 sat in a prison cell. When under the influence of liquor, he  had pushed a man down-stairs, and the verdict was, "Guilty of manslaughter." As he looked at the iron bars before him, he cried out, in terrible despair, "I am lost." God heard that cry. A Christian worker visited the prison, and laying his hand on the shoulder of the distressed man, whispered words of courage. Then came the little prayer-meetings in Mr. Murphy's cell, his conversion, and his wonderful work. That warm-hearted Irishman, through love and sympathy, induced many to reform.

Often he told others his story. It was a guest in his mother's home who first put the glass to his childish lips, and he never forgot the tingling sensation. Poverty soon drove him away from his mother's care. He came to America, and for some years lived the life of a sober farmer. While on the farm, he married a worthy young woman. Later, his brother induced him to go to the city; and against his wife's pleadings, he opened a hotel in Portland, Maine. Here began his fall — first a popular landlord; next the drunken keeper of a grog-shop; and then a criminal behind prison-bars, with a starving, heart-broken family in a stricken home.

But the loving Father took the smutched, torn fragments of his life and made him a new man. Three months after his conversion he buried his wife. The terrible sorrow that intemperance had thrust upon the home had wounded her unto death. This was a severe blow to the new convert, but by the grace of God, Mr. Murphy labored unceasingly. His work was extensive, his success marvelous. He had tasted the bitter dregs of the cup, and knew from experience that God could save the drunkard. The following story is characteristic of him. Going into a saloon in a Western State, with a friend, on one occasion, and finding a number of men about to drink, he said, "Hold on, boys, hold on! Drink with me!" Upon being asked by the saloon-keeper what he would have, whether wine, whisky, gin, or rum, Mr. Murphy replied, "No, give us lemonade all around," and the treat was prepared as ordered.

It is said that during his nearly forty years' labor in the temperance cause he succeeded in inducing more than three million to sign the pledge.

Mrs. Mary Hunt

Mrs. Mary Hunt, who prevailed on the American government to educate its children in scientific temperance, spent her childhood in the open air of Connecticut. Her fun-loving nature often brought her teachers to despair, while her scholarly instincts wrung from them merited admiration. She showed a fondness for chemistry and physiology, and of these branches she later became professor.

In 1879 she was made chairman of a committee which planned and worked to make scientific temperance education compulsory in the schools. Untiring efforts brought success. Congress passed the statute she had drafted. Then came the work of preparing manuals for giving such instruction. To this she lent valuable assistance. "We must save the children to-day," she said, "if we would save the nation to-morrow."

In 1897 she attended the International Anti-Alcoholic Congress in Brussels. Six years later she visited Germany, and also gave several addresses in England. For twenty-five years she has worked without a salary, and has given the proceeds of her literary work to the cause she loves. Her biographer says: "She has stood unfaltering for that truth which alone can bring liberty from the bondage of alcohol."

Mrs. Lillian M. N. Stevens

All whose eyes are upon the temperance forces to-day, recognize Mrs. Lillian M. N. Stevens as one of the captains  in that noble army. She is the dauntless, unfaltering leader of the National Woman's Christian Temperance Union, and with her loyal co-laborers in that organization, she unflinchingly meets the attacks of the enemy. With wisdom she adjusts the grave problems before her; and to her remarkable executive ability she adds rare gifts as a speaker.

This gifted daughter of New England is a born leader, one who is well trained for service in the great work of uplifting humanity. She received a thorough education under New England's best instructors, and, like many others, her first public work was in a schoolroom as teacher. When she was twenty-one years old, she left that vocation and married, and it is a pleasure to mention that Mr. Stevens has ever been in full accord with his wife's principles and her chosen work. Her home has always been in Maine, so from childhood she has been inhaling the good, vigorous air of the Pine Tree State, where the temperance principles of Neal Dow have so long been honored.

In 1875 Mrs. Stevens first met Frances E. Willard. That was the beginning of a lifelong friendship. Together they labored in the cause they loved, and when in 1898 the angel of death called Miss Willard to rest, it was Mrs. Stevens who was called upon to grasp the reins of national leadership. The death of Miss Willard was a tremendous blow to the W. C. T. U., but perhaps none felt the loss more keenly than did Mrs. Stevens, who had been Miss Willard's first assistant; yet, burying her own grief, she led her co-workers on through the lowlands of sorrow in the great struggle of reform.

"For many years Mrs. Stevens was reckoned as Neal Dow's chief coadjutor, and since his death she is recognized throughout the State as the leader of the prohibition forces. Indeed, in the well-fought battle of 1884, which placed prohibition in the State constitution, Mrs. Stevens won for herself a fame as organizer and agitator hardly second to Neal Dow himself." Besides her distinctive temperance work, she is prominently identified with other reform and philanthropic movements. Wherever she goes in public work, she takes with her the sweet, pure atmosphere that always surrounds a noble woman, and in her work she "holds the sincere esteem even of those who oppose the principles for which she so untiringly strives."

Biographies of Daniel, John the Baptist, Paul, and other Bible characters, would be in place in this series. Aside from those given here, mention might be made of Billy J. Clark, M. D., Judge L. M. Sargent, Hon. Samuel Dexter, Justin Edwards, Anthony Benezet, Joshua Leavitt, Lenard Woods, Nathaniel Hewitt, Eliphalet Nott, Lebbeaus Armstrong, Mason L. Weens, and Lyman Beecher; Countess of Carlisle, president of the World's W. C. T. U. (1909); etc.

THE LAW AND THE LIQUOR TRAFFIC

"The state may not make men good by law, but it certainly should not permit men to be made bad in accordance with law."

"If there were a railroad in any State which every year killed one tenth of all the passengers, dropped one tenth at way stations so badly injured that they must go to the hospital or asylum, robbed three tenths of the money needed for the support of their families, carried three tenths where they did not wish to go, and left the remaining two tenths at least no better off for their ride, is there any doubt that the first legislature that convened would deprive that road of its charter and compel it to take up its tracks?"

"The only way to regulate the liquor traffic is to annihilate it."

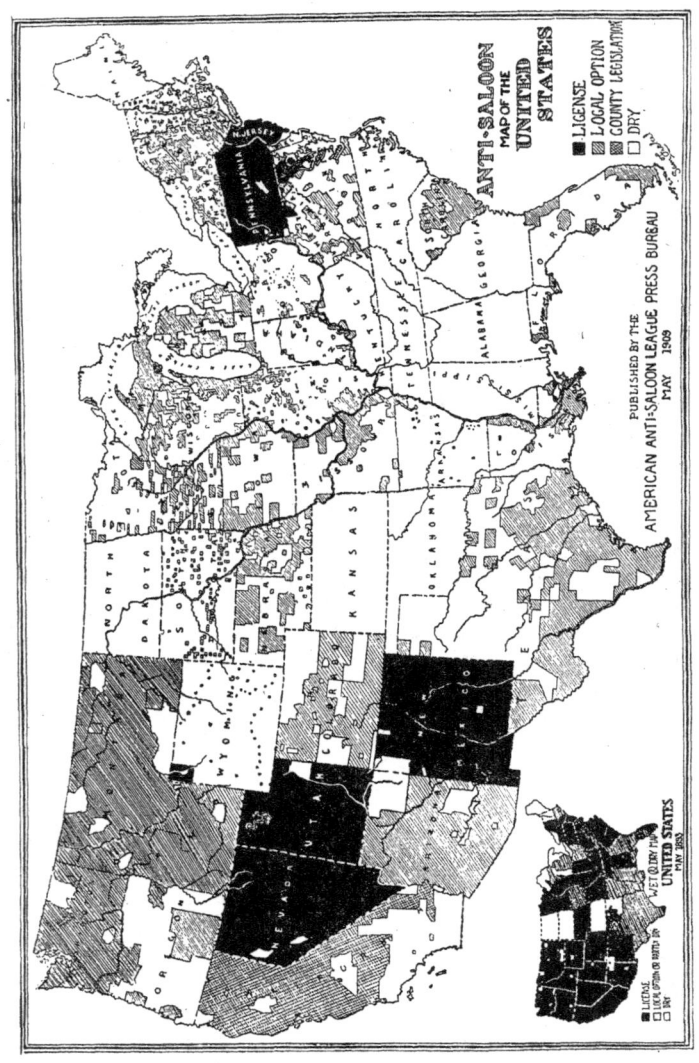

PROHIBITION

By Its Fruits

The saloon in your town is as truly a legal institution as the school in your district or the church in your community. It is protected by the nation, and in turn it renders "to Cæsar the things that are Cæsar's." But nations sometimes err. For more than three hundred years slavery was a legal institution in the United States. Family ties were disregarded; men, women, and children were sold at auction, to bring gain to the dealer's purse. Finally, however, when the mist of false reasoning cleared away, men saw that legislation could not make wrong right, and at the cost of four billion dollars and the sacrifice of a million lives, that evil was wiped from the land. It left many slaveholders bankrupt, yet to-day we honor the nation which loosened the shackles from the feet of four million people.

But what about the saloon? Before us lies a pamphlet published by the United States Brewers' Association. In it the secretary of that corporation says, "I wonder sometimes if any of us really know enough about the saloon to pass judgment upon it." In respect for the opinion of one who must be thoroughly acquainted with it, we naturally defer judgment. However, as the farmer does not go into a detailed study of botany to determine the worth of a tree in his orchard, but values it according to what it *produces,* so we must judge the saloon by its fruits.

Found Wanting

This age of commercialism asks, "Does it pay? Does it pay to support the liquor traffic?" Each year the traffic turns into the national treasury about two hundred million dollars. That is nearly one half of all the revenue received. But does the government get sufficient returns to license a business that increases the cost of the necessities of life; that makes the taxes heavier, in order to provide the courts, the reformatories, the asylums, the orphanages, the prisons, and the jails which are needed to care for the products of the business? In 1907 saloons in the District of Columbia paid half a million dollars in revenue, but "on the institutions in the District that look after the saloon's finished articles, was expended more than five millions." Did that pay?

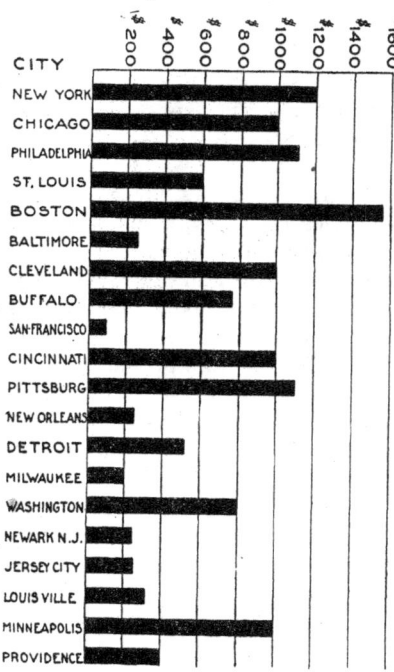

LICENSES IN VARIOUS CITIES

The nation pays too much for the revenue it gets from the liquor traffic. During 1908 the traffic received more than two billion one hundred million dollars from America. In return it gave her nothing with which to clothe, to feed, to develop, or to comfort her people. For value received it gave about "two thousand five hundred smothered babies, five thousand suicides, ten thousand murders, sixty thousand fallen girls, three thousand murdered wives, forty thousand widowed mothers, one hundred thousand paupers, one hundred thousand orphaned children, one hundred thousand criminals, one hundred thousand drunkards' graves, and one hundred thousand fallen boys."

The Law and the Liquor Traffic 143

If statistics prove anything, they show that the liquor traffic is a loss to the nation. If the traffic has been given a fair trial, the verdict must be, " Weighed in the balance, and found wanting." It is more than an economic loss. It is a terrible barter of public health and public morals; and so long as the saloon shall continue to yield crime, poverty, disease, and woe, the licensed liquor traffic must stand forth as legalized crime.

Does Prohibition Prohibit?

" Prohibition doesn't prohibit!" That phrase has been worn threadbare by friends of the liquor traffic. They claim that as much liquor is sold in " dry " districts as in " wet." Yet they do not look with indifference upon the strides made by prohibition; they are working as if the very life of their business depended upon the defeat of the temperance forces. And it probably does; for every distillery, brewery, and saloon must have a license before its doors can swing open for business. In France the liquor dealers found it most profitable to have no prohibition law; for when the government granted liberty to the liquor trade, the consumption of alcohol increased nearly one hundred per cent.

Yet "prohibition doesn't prohibit"! The daily newspapers give abundant evidence to the contrary. Lawbreakers will probably always be with us, for the wheat and the tares grow together until the harvest. The laws of the land forbid theft, but some persons still steal; the laws forbid the taking of life, but on an average twenty-five persons are murdered every day in the United States. Still we would shudder if the laws prohibiting theft and murder were to be blotted from the criminal code. We would take no pleasure in contemplating that our lawmakers would fold their arms while some one was appropriating our property or dealing a death-blow to a friend. And yet the prohibition of theft and murder does not fully prohibit. So some men will probably get whisky even if the liquor traffic is outlawed, but experiments prove that prohibition in regard to it is as effectual as any other law against crime.

What Prohibition Does

Liquor dealers warned people that prohibition would destroy business, lessen bank deposits, increase taxes, etc. But thus far no such results have been reported by Maine, Kansas, Tennessee, or any other State which has outlawed the liquor traffic. On the other hand, every State that has enforced prohibition has realized a shrinkage in crimes, an increase in prosperity, and a higher intellectual and moral standard.

The following telegram came from Atlanta after Georgia had abolished the saloons in January, 1908: " Such a scene as that in the police court this morning is undoubtedly without a parallel in the history of a city the size of Atlanta. But one lonely case appeared on the docket for trial." An Oklahoma sheriff says that prohibition has reduced crime in his county seventy-five per cent. Out of nine thousand three hundred fifty murders and homicides in the United States in 1906, Maine furnished but three.

Prohibition is not hard on bank accounts. The State of New York receives annually about twenty million dollars in revenue from her saloons. Maine receives nothing. Yet while New York has only ten and one-half times more people than Maine, she has forty-two times more homeless families. After one year of prohibition in one large community, building operations increased two hundred per cent; and in Kansas City, Kansas, bank deposits advanced one million seven hundred thousand dollars. " The traveler in Missouri," says the *Drover's Telegram,* " looks out of the car window at the saloons along the track, and notices the usual lot of barroom soaks sitting on beer kegs in front of one-story shacks. Crossing the line into Kansas, there are no such evidences of blasted lives and depleted pocketbooks. There are no beer-keg touts." A Japanese statesman was asked why Japan had

The Law and the Liquor Traffic 145

so few paupers and Great Britain so many. He replied, "The Japanese drink water, and the British people drink alcohol."

After prohibition was adopted by a certain State, six hundred children from twelve to sixteen years old entered school for the first time. Formerly they had assisted drinking fathers to support the family. Maine has a larger per cent of her population in schools than has any other State in New England.

These are some of the facts which demonstrate the value of prohibition so fully that "to doubt the wisdom of the prohibitory law is to take issue with common sense."

Making Progress

"The truth is, the enemy is gaining ground rapidly upon us, and we are being overpowered by the tremendous forces battling against us." Such were the words of the president of the National Liquor Dealers' Association in 1907, in their meeting at Pittsburg. There are other evidences that the temperance sentiment is gaining ground. An increasing number of temperance societies are at work; various industries are refusing to employ men who drink, and some labor organizations are opposing the traffic.

During 1908 the temperance forces seemed to advance at breathless pace. Here are some of the mile-posts of progress in the United States. Eight thousand men left the Bartenders' Union, mostly because the bars over which they had served were closed. In Pittsburg, Pennsylvania, three hundred fifty thousand fewer barrels of beer were consumed than the year before. "Seventy-five car-loads of fixtures were returned to one Western brewery from closed saloons. A million railroad men have sworn to total abstinence through rules of their own brotherhoods." In ten months five entire States banished their saloons. Three others had already done so. While ten years ago only about six million persons lived in prohibition territory, to-day about forty million do. More than forty leading magazines took the position of total abstinence, and have refused to publish any liquor advertisements.

Victories are being scored in other countries also. The British war department forbids the use of stimulants in camp. Switzerland has recently put scientific temperance in the public-school schedule. Lack of space forbids other evidences. Almost everywhere the temperance forces are enlarging the place of their tent so rapidly that he who surveys the territory to-day, finds new acquisitions awaiting him to-morrow. "The great wave of total abstinence which has swept, and is still sweeping, over the English-speaking world, is something that will stand out in history as phenomenal."

Another View-Point

With such glowing accounts of prohibition, it would almost seem safe to lay aside the weapons of warfare, and retire from the field. But the Philistines have not yet fled; David has only stunned the modern Goliath. The conflict is but well begun. "This war," says one, "is destined to be the greatest struggle the United States has ever seen."

The liquor traffic has both men and money. It has more men enlisted than were put under arms by Japan during her war with Russia. According to the August, 1908, number of the *Broadway Magazine,* there are engaged in the struggle against temperance one million two hundred thousand men, who are backed by six and one-half billion dollars. That amount is almost equal to the total capital stock of all railroads in the United States, and it is one thirtieth of the aggregate wealth of the nation.

The traffic has also powerful allies. Among them are certain trades which are somewhat dependent on it, such as the coopers' and bottlers' trades, farmers who supply raw material, and icemen. There are also the sots and tipplers, who each day turn over to the traffic nearly six million dollars.

The methods used by the liquor dealers are as varied as the perplexing situation demands. Huge bulks of literature are being distributed. One liquor company is said to be spending a million dollars for a twelve-months' advertisement in a certain paper. The dealers are putting the newspapers under tremendous pressure. "All these different papers that fail to suppress prohibition news hereafter will not only lose our patronage, but that of almost every brewery in the United States." So reads an extract from a letter written by a Milwaukee brewing company to the New Orleans *Times*.

The liquor dealers realize that appetite is one of their strongholds, and through various means they are cultivating a thirst for liquor. The same glass that contains the sting of the serpent contains his subtlety also.

Aside from these methods, deceptive arguments are put forth. The liquor people point to great men who drank wine. They argue that social life needs the saloon, and the nation needs the revenue. But perhaps no arguments are more subtle than those that reach the public through so-called religious publications which are either owned or "influenced" by the liquor traffic. In one of these papers, Rev. William A. Wasson says: "The church can not longer afford to have its name exploited by prohibitionists. The church and the liquor trade should stand shoulder to shoulder in this great fight. We need each other." These are some of the campaign plans of the liquor army, whose vast wealth is being freely used in the desperate struggle against extermination. How will the battle end? Will the forces of evil be defeated, or will they be suffered again to cast their hellish shadows over the territories now brightened with the beneficent rays of prohibition?

What Shall Be Done?

Experience has taught no lesson more clearly than that regulation of the liquor traffic is a stupendous failure. Recently the liquor dealers did some "house-cleaning." Numerous dives and grog-shops were closed. This served to pacify many, but the past proves that the liquor business is not susceptible of reformation. You can no more reform the liquor traffic than you can change gunpowder to gold. Some years ago a "reformed" saloon was opened in New York City. "It was inaugurated with religious services, and was blessed by Bishop Potter. It was to be a good moral saloon, where men could get what they wanted to drink without coming in contact with the obnoxious and demoralizing features of the ordinary saloon." But that place can not be found to-day. In the words of the new owner of the place, "You can't follow the Lord and chase the devil at the same time." Men who wanted drink usually hankered for the ordinary accompaniments, so the "reformed" saloon soon sickened and died. But the liquor traffic did not go down. It has survived all panics, pestilences, and famines. Some decades ago a fearful famine visited Ireland. Yet within that year Ireland distilled nine million bushels of grain into whisky, while hundreds of her people died of hunger. The modern Moloch still continues to feed on human souls. What shall be done?

Abolish the Saloon

Should prohibition be secured, the government would be minus nearly one half its revenue. But each year America would save about ten times the national revenue; Germany would save about three billion marks; Sweden eighty million kroner; and Denmark about sixty-three million kroner. This being true, can not all join in Gladstone's sentiment: "Give me a sober England, and I will take care of the revenue"?

But as life is more than raiment, so is there a greater reason for prohibition than mere economy. William McKinley once said: "By legalizing this traffic we agree to share with the liquor sellers the responsibilities and evils of his business. Every man who votes for license becomes of necessity a partner to the liquor traffic and all its consequences." It hardly seems consistent to pray, "Lead us not into temptation," and then vote to place temptation in the path of everybody; to pray, "Deliver us from evil," and then vote to retain among us the greatest evil known to society. It hardly seems in keeping with the principles that have produced the greatness of the American nation, to license a business which antagonizes and largely neutralizes every good influence of the home, the school, and the church.

So long as the government holds its protecting hand over the saloon, the liquor traffic seems to be immortal; prohibition may not usher in a Utopia, but where it has been given a fair trial, it has proved to be effectual and productive of much good. It gives drink-maddened men an opportunity to escape from their thraldom. It erects a barrier between the unpolluted lips and the intoxicating cup. And although cherishing no malice toward the men engaged in the liquor traffic, every one who has the welfare of humanity at heart can ask for nothing less than the abolition of the traffic. May God hasten the day when the nations in both hemispheres shall be divorced from the "infamous business of making drunkards."

SOME RESULTS OF PROHIBITION

Prohibition has worked well in those sections of the State where popular sentiment is behind the law, and some of the most prosperous towns and parishes are those where prohibition has prevailed for a period long enough to afford fair tests of its merits.— *Governor Sanders of Pennsylvania.*

The moral advantage of prohibition is of incalculable benefit to any people.— *Chancellor of Kansas University.*

I consider the prohibition law in Kansas as worth more to the railroad men than any other one thing.— *Superintendent of Santa Fe Railroad.*

The five "wettest" counties of West Virginia have four hundred fifteen convicts; the other fifty counties have four hundred thirteen. One eleventh of the counties furnish one half of the convicts.— *Statistics of 1909.*

There is more hypocritical, illegal selling in license States than in Maine; for every joint or blind tiger under prohibition in Maine, there are sixteen blind tigers in licensed New York, plus twenty-seven thousand State licensed saloons.— *Mrs. Lillian M. N. Stevens.*

Atlanta, at the end of 1908, showed 3,903 fewer arrests for drunkenness, and 8,102 fewer arrests for all disorderly conduct — 200 fewer juvenile arrests.— *Mrs. Mary Harris Armor.*

One third of our counties are without prisoners in their jails or paupers in their almshouses; one half of our counties sent *no convicts* to our prisons this year, and one half of our prison inmates never lived in Kansas long enough to acquire a residence here. Churches and schools flourish, the spiritual outlook is hopeful, and the saloon is practically banished. — *Governor Hoch, of Kansas, in his Thanksgiving Message.*

The years of experience which have been mine to enjoy, together with the words which are constantly coming from all over the State, lead me to conclude that our people are more strongly in favor of the law now than ever before, and that there will be no steps backward upon the question in the future.— *Charles A. Pollock, district judge in North Dakota.*

A certain county in North Carolina, which endorsed prohibition in 1899, is now the richest county south of the Mason and Dixon line.

Abyssinia has prohibition, and the penalty for taking liquors into that country is death. In the capital of the country only two murders have been committed in the last forty years. Smoking is also prohibited.

It is stated by Lady Henry Somerset that in one district in Liverpool, England, in which there is no saloon, there is but one pauper to every one thousand inhabitants. In another district, in which there are two hundred saloons, there is one pauper to every twenty-eight inhabitants.

Without one dollar of revenue from the saloon, Maine has a larger percentage of the total population in the public schools than any other of the New England States, or New York, with its twenty million dollars of revenue from the saloon. It has more teachers employed in proportion to the school population than any other State.

ATLANTA, GEORGIA.— For the first time in its fifteen years of existence, every cell at the police jail yesterday afternoon was empty. Not a prisoner was incarcerated, and the turnkeys and matrons were having a very dull afternoon. The police attribute this remarkable condition to the prohibition law which went into effect the first day of the year.—*Washington Times, Jan. 25, 1908.*

Do you know of even one good reason why the sale of liquor for beverage purposes should not be prohibited?

"THE TIDE HEAVES ONWARD"

The first American prohibition law was passed in 1735. "The importation of rum or brandies" into Georgia was forbidden. James Oglethorpe enforced the law strictly in Savannah.

On the first of November, 1908, the parliament of Finland, by unanimous vote, passed a State-wide prohibition law — the first on European soil.

The managers of twenty-five different railway lines in the United States, employing one hundred eighty thousand men, will not tolerate a drinking man in their employ.

A law recently passed in Denmark provides that all drunken persons shall be taken home in carriages at the expense of the landlord who sold them the last glass.

Sweden has seventy-seven daily newspapers representing total abstinence, and thirteen more whose management refuses to insert advertisements recommending alcoholic liquors. Norway, with its smaller population, has forty daily papers that stand for total abstinence. In both these countries no support outside of the large cities can be found for a paper that does not stand for total abstinence.

There are to-day (1909) three hundred prohibition cities in the United States, with a total population of more than three million and a half.

The Law and the Liquor Traffic

Nine States — Maine, Kansas, North Dakota, Georgia, Oklahoma, Alabama, Mississippi, North Carolina, and Tennessee — have already by statute dethroned King Alcohol. Alabama has passed the most rigorous prohibition laws the country has ever known.

General Von Moltke said: " Beer is a far more dangerous enemy to Germany than all the armies of France." The kaiser has awakened to this fact through the report of his commissioners, who found that Germany's liquor bill had been increased during the last five years by six hundred million dollars. The kaiser says the " drinking must be stopped," and he is taking active measures to this end. It is expected that brandy and beer as a part of the army ration will be wholly eliminated.

The national revenue from the liquor traffic in the United States in 1908 was nearly sixteen million dollars less than in 1907.

Statistics show that the quantity of wine used in Great Britain has decreased from 16,600,000 gallons in 1899 to 11,350,000 gallons in 1908, and that the decrease in the consumption of spirits has been from 45,429,000 gallons in 1901 to 39,150,000 gallons in 1908.

Magazines Which Insert No Liquor Advertisements

All-Story	Designer
American Boy	Education
American Magazine	Everybody's Magazine
Arena	Good Health
Argosy	Good Housekeeping
Century	Housekeeper
Christian Education	Housewife
Circle	Ladies' Home Journal
Collier's	Ladies' World
Country Life in America	Liberty
Current Literature	Life Boat
Delineator	Life and Health

Literary Digest	Scrap-Book
Living Age	Signs of the Times Monthly
London Daily News	St. Nicholas
McClure's Magazine	Suburban Life
Munsey's Magazine	Success Magazine
New Idea Woman's Magazine	Uncle Remus's Magazine
New England Magazine	Watchman
Ocean	Woman's Home Companion
Outlook	Woman's Magazine
Protestant Magazine	Woman's National Daily
Railroad Men's Magazine	World To-day
Review of Reviews	Youth's Companion
Saturday Evening Post	Youth's Instructor

Taken a Determined Stand

The United States Steel Corporation has taken a determined stand against its workmen drinking liquor.

The corporation has found that much time has been lost daily by the workmen leaving for a few minutes to go out after a drink, perhaps several times a day. In addition to this, those in direct charge of the men say they do not do good work when they are allowed to fill themselves with drink, and so the order is imperative.

Many men have been discharged in the past week on being found carrying liquor into the mills in bottles.—*Washington Post, June 9, 1909.*

World's Largest Dry-Goods Firm Favors Prohibition

Marshall Field & Co., of Chicago, is perhaps the largest dry-goods firm in the world. The following letter to Bishop Berry, while editor of the *Epworth Herald,* indicates the position of the firm with reference to the employment of those who drink intoxicants: —

"DEAR MR. BERRY: Answering your letter of January 3, we will say that we will not, to our knowledge, place a young man who drinks, in our business, and even though a man should apply for a position whose ability and other all-round qualifications would seem to fit him for the position, if we knew or discovered that he was a drinking man, we should decline to consider his application. Any man in our employ who acquires the habit of drink, even though moderately, is to a certain extent marked down in our estimation, and unless we can remove from him this serious fault and show his error, we feel compelled to do without his service. Yours respectfully,

"MARSHALL FIELD & Co."

A Strong Resolution

The following resolution was passed May 23, 1909, by the World's Conference of Seventh-day Adventists, held at Washington, D. C.: —

"*Whereas,* The liquor traffic is a gigantic evil, condemned by the Word of God, by medical and scientific investigation, and by the experience of all time; and,—

"*Whereas,* It is destructive of law, order, and the civil rights of humanity; therefore,—

"*We recommend,* That our ministers, teachers, physicians, nurses, and people generally, engage in a vigorous campaign in behalf of total abstinence, by means of lectures, demonstrations, and the distribution of health and temperance literature; and that, whenever consistent, our people by voice, pen, and vote, place themselves on record as favorable to restriction and entire prohibition."

No Drunken Barkeepers!

The liquor dealers have made a resolution that they will have no drunken barkeepers, because they would ruin their business.— *Robert E. Glen, Ex-Governor of North Carolina.*

WHY WE FAVOR PROHIBITION

Liquor Is Not a Proper Source of Revenue

I can not consent, as your queen, to take revenue from the sale of liquor, which destroys the souls and bodies of my subjects.— *Queen of Madagascar.*

It is true that I can not prevent the introduction of the glowing poison. Gain-seeking and corrupt men will, for profit and sensuality, defeat my wishes; but nothing will induce me to derive a revenue from the misery and vice of my people. — *Emperor of China.*

TAINTED MONEY

The encouragement of drunkenness for the sake of the profit on the sale of drink is certainly one of the most criminal methods of assassination for money hitherto adopted by the bravos of any age or country.—*John Ruskin.*

The deriving of vast sums for revenue from the bitter sufferings and grinding pauperism of the people is a terrible offense. If Judas had received one thousand instead of thirty pieces of silver, would that have justified his conduct? — *Canon Wilberforce.*

Luxury, my lords, is to be taxed, but vice prohibited.— *Lord Chesterfield.*

Nine Reasons for Prohibition

Intemperance is one of the greatest foes to national life and prosperity.

The Law and the Liquor Traffic

Intemperance undermines the very foundations of civil society.

Intemperance unfits the citizen for the proper discharge of his duties in either private or public life.

Intemperance leads to the disregard of the natural rights of man, and, consequently, to the increase of crime.

Intemperance is the most effective agent in filling the courts with criminal cases and the jails and prisons with convicts.

Intemperance imposes a burden upon society by subtracting from the producing power and adding to the consuming power.

Intemperance changes homes into hells; and hells do not constitute a safe foundation for civil government and national existence.

Intemperance tends to produce an indigent class, an unemployed class, an ignorant class, and an unprincipled class, — the greatest foes of society and free institutions.

History furnishes no example where a nation or an individual has been injured by the restriction of the traffic in intoxicating liquors, while hundreds of volumes would be insufficient to contain the record of disaster, crime, and decay directly traceable to intemperance.— *W. W. Prescott.*

Seven Good Reasons for Prohibition

During a temperance campaign, a lawyer was discussing, with no little show of learning, the clauses of the proposed temperance law. An old farmer, who had been listening attentively, shut his knife with a snap, and said: "I don't know nuthin' about the law, but I've got seven good reasons for votin' for it." "What are they?" asked the lawyer. And the grim old farmer responded, "Four sons and three daughters."— *Youth's Instructor.*

"One out of every three persons who drink dies of tuberculosis."

READING WORTH WHILE

Vote for Prohibition

There is a cause for the moral paralysis upon society. Our laws sustain an evil which is sapping their very foundations. Many deplore the wrongs which they know exist, but consider themselves free from all responsibility in the matter. This can not be. Every individual exerts an influence in society. In our favored land, every voter has some voice in determining what laws shall control the nation. Should not that influence and vote be on the side of temperance and virtue? The advocates of temperance fail to do their whole duty unless they exert their influence, by precept and example, by voice and pen and vote, in behalf of prohibition and total abstinence. We need not expect that God will work a miracle to bring about this reform, and thus remove the necessity for our exertion. We ourselves must grapple this giant foe, our motto, "No compromise," and no cessation of our efforts till victory is gained. — *Mrs. E. G. White.*

"Show Consideration? — Emphatically, No!"

Not one syllable can be spoken in favor of the liquor traffic that is not dictated by self-interest. It poisons the political life in every town and city in which it exists, disgraces public offices and betrays public trusts, defiles public service and degrades public servants.

It has no legitimate place, because wherever it touches it blights like fire, and leaves only the ashes of former prosperity and former happiness in its wake. It gives nothing, but takes everything. It builds nothing, but is ever destroying. It panders to the weakest and worst traits of man, and strangles every impulse for good and decency. It is the father of murder and the mother of theft, the sister of harlotry and the blood-brother of degeneracy.

It knows that it is wrecking manhood, debauching politics, and binding people to a hellish slavery. It knows that it is stealing the honor of the man, the virtue of the woman, and the future of the child — and it continues stealing them. What thief in all criminal history can approximate this record?

"Show this traffic consideration? — Emphatically, No!"

We hang the murderer it has manufactured, we ostracize the harlot whose livelihood it furnishes, and incarcerate the thief whose honesty it has destroyed. "Show it consideration?" What a travesty upon justice! — *Nashville Tennessean.*

A Court-Room Scene

SATIRE WHICH ILLUSTRATES THE UNREASONABLENESS OF THE LICENSE SYSTEM

Did you ever hear of a scene in a court room like the following? —

A young man is brought into the court and charged with stealing a horse.

"Do you plead guilty or not guilty?"

He answers: "If I had not stolen the horse, some other man would."

The court replies: "That has nothing to do with the question. It is a simple question of fact; are you guilty or not guilty?"

The prisoner replies: "People have always stolen horses, and always will, and it is not fair to pitch onto me."

The court indignantly puts the question the third time: "Are you guilty or not guilty?"

The prisoner answers: "Suppose I am, what are you going to do about it? All prohibitory laws have failed. Persons steal everywhere. You can not stop it. Prohibition is a failure. Let me tell you what I will do. If you will let me go, and give me permission to steal, I will give you half the money I receive for the horse."—*American Issue.*

Well Answered

A liquor organ says: "The liquor traffic in this country employs three hundred sixty-four thousand persons, and one million eight hundred thousand people derive their support as families of the former directly from the manufacture of liquor," and then asks, "Will the 'Prohibs' please tells us what they would do with this army of people if they should succeed in abolishing the traffic?"

A prohibition paper makes this reply: "We would set them to raising grain and meat to fill the hungry mouths of the wives and children of the patrons of the saloon. We would employ them in the production of cotton, wool, and hides, and in making them into clothing, hats and caps, boots and shoes, for those who, on account of the saloon, are never comfortably clad. We would set them to felling trees and sawing them into lumber, and making them into homes for those who live in hovels because the husband and father spends his wages for drink, if indeed the patronage of the saloon has not put him 'out of a job.' We would keep them busy making carpets, furniture, pictures, pianos and organs, books and newspapers, for the millions, by whom, on account of drink, most of these things are considered as luxuries intended only for saloon-keepers and other fortunate people."

Sunday Closing

"It is simply impossible to create a one-day morality. What is right on Saturday is right on Sunday. When religious people give up this whole impossibility, and insist that a wicked thing shall not be done on any day, and a right thing shall be done every day, they have a basis for law and order that can be enforced. If whisky peddling is a crime on Sunday, it is on Monday."

"The enactment of Sunday laws," this same logical writer says, amounts merely to "putting the handcuffs on

The Law and the Liquor Traffic

for one day, and then taking them off for six." So far as these laws affect the liquor traffic, they are, he avers, "simply a determination to let saloons drive their unwholesome trade six days, but the seventh is a sop to the Lord."
—*Literary Digest, quoting Rev. E. P. Rowell.*

" The only States which enforce Sunday closing are those which prohibit liquor selling on all days."— *Dr. W. F. Crafts, Superintendent of International Reform Bureau, in his work entitled " The Sabbath for Man," edition of 1885, page 86.*

The License System

[Extract from an address given by Hon. Seaborn Wright, of Georgia, before the National W. C. T. U. Convention held 1908 in Denver, Colorado.]

The trouble in this big republic of ours is this,— we are money mad. We have the idea in our heads that money will make anything right. But it will not do it. The license system breeds vice; the system breeds crime; bad government comes from it, as straight as a ball from the barrel of a rifle; and so long as you tolerate the system, these things will live and flourish.

We stand for the total abolition of a system inherently wrong, not for its reformation. You, as citizens, deliberately, for a hundred or two hundred thousand dollars, plant upon your street corners saloons, reaching out invitations, — saloons with open arms, appealing to the passion for strong drink in your men and women,— saloons whose inevitable end is to destroy the great virtues of manhood! You capitalize the passion for strong drink in your people. You deliberately set a price upon it. You turn over your men who are living to-day, you turn over the coming generation, to an institution and a system whose basic principle is the destruction of the great virtues of manhood. You do it for money.

The man who votes to keep a saloon in any city, or any State, or any nation; who votes to keep it there because of his part of the profit in the saloon, stands upon a dead equal with the man who robes himself in his white apron, and boldly stands behind the counter, and serves the drink. If I bring no other message to you from the South from my long experience of years in the struggle against the saloon, I bring you this one at least,— that the thing that is holding the saloon in this republic is avarice, avarice, avarice.

Capitalizing vice! Deliberately selling out the virtues of your people for money! Stop capitalizing vice. Put a premium on manhood, and not on dollars.

Why I Do Not Believe in the License System

License is a *permit*. Government is organized for the preservation of the public welfare; therefore, it can not grant permission to conduct a traffic subversive of the public welfare.

License does not lessen the amount of liquor consumed; and does not, therefore, decrease the number of criminals, paupers, and insane persons produced by the liquor traffic. The curse is in the concoction sold, and the fact that the seller pays a high price for the privilege of selling does not lessen the evil. The consumer pays even the license fee.

License does not meet the cost to the government of the liquor business. The liquor business of Chicago pays to the city seven million dollars in license fees; but it costs the city nearly seventy million dollars to maintain the traffic with all that it entails. And Massachusetts spends nearly two and one-half million dollars a year for expenses incurred from the liquor traffic, and receives only $866,744 from the saloon.

License does not meet the cost to the government of the saloons. Doubling the license fee of Chicago, making. it one thousand dollars, decreased the saloons only from 7,353 to 7,231; and these disposed of as much liquor as was sold before.

One thousand two hundred dollars a year is the license fee of Salt Lake City; yet in less than twenty years the number of saloons has increased in that city from 39 to 184 — a gain of 450 per cent.

The number of commitments to houses of correction for drunkenness in the State of New Hampshire increased from 473 in 1902, when the State was under prohibition, to 2,182 in 1906, when it was under license law. Commitments for all causes increased from 592 to 2,470. The number of delinquent children increased twenty-four per cent.

Those who vote for license make themselves responsible with the saloon-keeper for the evils resulting from the business.— *The Youth's Instructor, March 16, 1909.*

Inconsistency of Licensing the Liquor Traffic.

The licensing of the liquor traffic is advocated by many as tending to restrict the drink evil. But the licensing of the traffic places it under the protection of law. The government sanctions its existence, and thus fosters the evil which it professes to restrict. Under the protection of license laws, breweries, distilleries, and wineries are planted all over the land, and the liquor seller works beside our very doors.

Often he is forbidden to sell intoxicants to one who is drunk, or who is known to be a confirmed drunkard; but the work of making drunkards of the youth goes steadily forward. Upon the creating of the liquor appetite in the youth the very life of the traffic depends. The youth are led on, step by step, until the liquor habit is established, and the thirst is created that at any cost demands satisfaction. Less harmful would it be to grant liquor to the confirmed drunkard, whose ruin, in most cases, is already determined, than to permit the flower of our youth to be lured to destruction through this terrible habit.

By the licensing of the liquor traffic, temptation is kept constantly before those who are trying to reform. Institutions have been established where the victims of intemperance may be helped to overcome their appetite. This is a noble work; but so long as the sale of liquor is sanctioned by law, the intemperate receive little benefit from inebriate asylums. They can not remain there always. They must again take their place in society. The appetite for intoxicating drink, though subdued, is not wholly destroyed; and when temptation assails them, as it does on every hand, they too often fall an easy prey.

The man who has a vicious beast, and who, knowing its disposition, allows it liberty, is by the laws of the land held accountable for the evil the beast may do. In the laws given to Israel the Lord directed that when a beast known to be vicious caused the death of a human being, the life of the owner should pay the price of his carelessness or malignity. On the same principle the government that licenses the liquor seller, should be held responsible for the results of his traffic. And if it is a crime worthy of death to give liberty to a vicious beast, how much greater is the crime of sanctioning the work of the liquor seller! — *Mrs. E. G. White.*

A Mother's Loss

A widow, with two noble young boys, traded her country home for a cottage in one of our towns. The cottage was near a little shoe shop, where the honest workman plied his honest trade to the hurt of nobody. These boys went and came in their daily toil, and were innocent and happy about the cottage door of their widowed mother. But a saloon took the place of the shoe shop, and the music in the saloon attracted these boys. For a while they stood on the outside and listened, and then they stood on the inside, and the saloon got on the inside of them, and you know the old story. The mother wept over her drunken boys. The oldest, intoxicated on the public square, picked a quarrel with a man, drew his knife, and started toward him, and was shot down on the street. They carried his bleeding body to his broken-hearted mother. It was but a short time until the other boy came to his death through the same saloon. And this widow joined the great army of suffering mothers who make contributions of their precious boys to this infernal traffic.

A little while after her last boy was buried, the saloon took fire at midnight, and from it her little cottage caught fire, and she barely escaped with her life. She sat upon a little pile of wood in her yard at the midnight hour, with her sad face in her wrinkled hands, while the dying embers of her little cottage threw their ghosts upon her pitiful form. The crowd that gathered was moved by the picture. A subscription was started, and soon a man stood by her, saying: "Don't cry any more; we have raised money enough to replace your home." Lifting her face from her hands, she said: "I wasn't crying about the little house; it wasn't much, anyway. I wasn't crying about the furniture; there was little of that. But that same old saloon burned up John and Willie; nobody got up a paper to save my boys; and if you can not bring back John, and bring back Willie, don't bother about the little house. My life is ruined anyway."

Reader, will you not save the boys? — *Selected*.

Charged With Murder

The following narrative illustrates only too truly the responsibility and the guilt resting upon those who sanction or in any way help to legalize and perpetuate the liquor traffic: —

A prisoner at the bar, charged with, and convicted of, the murder of his wife, was asked by the judge if he had anything to say why sentence of death should not be passed upon him.

A solemn hush fell over the crowded court room, and every person waited in almost breathless expectation for the answer.

After a moment's silence, the prisoner arose to his feet, and, in a low, firm, but distinct voice, said: —

"I *have*! Your honor, you have asked me a question,

and I now ask, as the last favor on earth, that you will not interrupt my answer until I am through.

"I stand here before this bar, convicted of the wilful murder of my wife. Truthful witnesses have testified to the fact that I was a loafer, a drunkard, and a wretch; that I returned from one of my prolonged debauches, and fired the fatal shot that killed the wife I had sworn to love, cherish, and protect. While I have no remembrance of committing the fearful deed, I have no right to complain or condemn the verdict of the twelve good men who have acted as jury in the case; for their verdict is in accordance with the evidence.

"But, may it please the court, I wish to *show that I am not alone responsible for the murder of my wife!*"

This startling statement created a tremendous sensation. The judge leaned over the desk, the lawyers wheeled around and faced the prisoner, and jurors looked at one another in amazement. The prisoner paused a few seconds, and then continued in the same firm, distinct voice: —

"I repeat, your honor, that I am not the only one guilty of the murder of my wife. The judge on this bench, the jury in the box, the lawyers within the bar, the most of the witnesses, including the pastor of the old church, are also guilty before Almighty God, and will have to stand with me before his judgment throne, where we shall all be righteously judged.

"If it had not been for the saloons of my town, I never would have become a drunkard; my wife would not have been murdered; I would not be here now, ready to be hurled into eternity. Had it not been for these human traps, I would have been a sober man, an industrious workman, a tender father, and a loving husband. But to-day my home is destroyed, my wife murdered, my children — God bless and care for them — cast out on the mercy of the world, while I am to be hanged by the strong arm of the state.

"God knows I tried to reform, but as long as the open

saloon was in my pathway, my weak, diseased will power was no match against the fearful, consuming, agonizing appetite for liquor.

"For one year our town was without a saloon. For one year I was a sober man. For one year my wife and children were happy, and our little home was a paradise.

"I was one of those who signed remonstrances against reopening the saloons of our town. One half of this jury, the prosecuting attorney on this case, and the judge who sits on this bench, all voted for the saloon. By their votes and influence saloons were reopened, and they have made me what I am."

The impassioned words of the prisoner fell like coals of fire upon the hearts of those present, and many of the spectators and some of the lawyers were moved to tears.

"I began my downward career at a saloon *bar* — legalized and protected by the voters of this town. After the saloons you allowed have made me a drunkard and a murderer, I am taken before another bar — the bar of justice, and now the law-power will conduct me to the place of execution, and hasten my soul into eternity. I shall appear before another bar,— the *judgment bar of God,*— and there you who have legalized the traffic will have to appear with me. Think you that the great Judge will hold me — the poor, weak, helpless victim of your traffic — alone responsible for the murder of my wife? Nay, I, in my drunken, frenzied, irresponsible condition, have murdered one; but you have deliberately voted for the saloons, which have murdered thousands, and they are in full operation to-day with your consent.

"All of you know in your hearts that these words of mine are not the ravings of an unsound mind, but the truth of the Almighty God.

"You legalized the saloons that made me a drunkard and a murderer, and you are guilty with me before God and man for the murder of my wife.

"Your honor, I am done. I am now ready to receive my sentence, and be led forth to the place of execution. You will close by asking the Lord to have mercy on my soul. I will close by solemnly asking God to open your blind eyes to your own individual responsibility, so that you will cease to give your support to this dreadful traffic."

Not only does the Bible declare that no drunkard shall inherit the kingdom of God (1 Cor. 6: 9, 10), but it says, "Woe unto him that *giveth* his neighbor drink, that *puttest thy bottle to him, and makest him drunken.*" Hab. 2: 15. This shows that not simply the drinker, but all who are instrumental in tempting or influencing him to drink, God holds responsible for the results. They are parties to the act, and sharers in the guilt of its consequences.

Personal Liberty

It is insisted by many that prohibitory liquor laws interfere with personal liberty; but the contention is false. No man has a right to do anything that needlessly places the life or property of others in jeopardy. No man has a right to domicile even his own family in an unsafe building. If he lives in a city, he has no right to maintain defective flues or use defective stovepipes. The law takes cognizance of these things for the reason that by occupying unsafe buildings and using defective flues one jeopardizes life and property. For a like reason, civil law may properly prohibit the sale, and

A FALSE PLEA

even the use, of intoxicating beverages, since every intoxicated man is a menace to the peace and safety of his neighbors, and a source of danger to their property.

It is not true that whisky does not hurt those who let it alone. It lays a heavy tribute of loss of property, of happiness, and even of life, upon thousands of innocent victims every year.

Have those who are taxed to support courts, jails, hospitals, and asylums no rights the saloon-keeper and the tippler are bound to respect? Has the sober workman no right of protection against the unsteady hand or the dizzy head of his intoxicated fellow workman? Have the men, women, and children who throng our streets or traverse our country roads no right of protection against the numerous accidents due not to their own personal indulgence, but to the indulgence of others, in intoxicating liquors? Have the wives and children of drinking men no right of protection against the drink demon?

Truly it is not only the right, but the bounden duty, of the state to extend protection to all these. As well claim personal liberty in justification of the reckless automobilist, the sneak-thief, the thug, the murderer, as for the drunkard and the saloon-keeper.— *C. P. Bollman.*

THE STORY IN RHYME

It Must Be Settled Right

However the battle is ended,
  Though proudly the victor comes,
With fluttering flags and prancing nags
  And echoing roll of drums,
Still truth proclaims this motto,
  In letters of living light:
No question is ever settled
  Until it is settled right.

Though the heel of the strongest oppressor
  May grind the weak in the dust,
And the voice of fame with loud acclaim
  May call him great and just,
Let those who applaud take warning,
  And keep their motto in sight:
No question is ever settled
  Until it is settled right.

Let those who have failed take courage,
  Though the enemy seems to have won,
Though his ranks are strong, if he be in the wrong,
  The battle is not yet done;
For sure as the morning follows
  The darkest hour of night,
No question is ever settled
  Until it is settled right.

— Selected.

The Song of the Rye

I was made to be eaten and not to be drank;
To be thrashed in the barn, not soaked in a tank.
I come as a blessing when put through a mill;
As a blight and a curse when run through a still.

Make me up into loaves, and your children are fed;
But if into drink, I'll starve them instead.
In bread I'm a servant, the eater shall rule;
In drink I am master, the drinker a fool.

— Selected.

The Law and the Liquor Traffic

The Cost of a License

Little Willie came in with a glowing face,
And his questioning eyes showed just a trace
Of excitement and, maybe, of envy, too,
In their sunny depths so sweet and blue,
And he said, as his curls from his brow he tossed,
"Auntie, what is a license, and what does it cost?
Ned Baker's father, he told me at play,
Was going to buy a license to-day.
Papa's as rich as the Bakers, I know,
Why couldn't we have a license too?"

O'er her soul there swept a cold, dread wave,
Such as we feel by a yawning grave.
A look of terror stole into her face,
She clasped the child in a close embrace,
As if she feared that he might be lost.
"I don't know just what licenses cost;
But the license that Baker will buy, I think,
Is a license to sell his neighbor drink.
Fifty dollars, I think, that Ephraim Stone
Paid for one in days that are gone;
I paid more, ten thousand times;
No, 'twas not all in dollars and dimes:
My husband, your grand-uncle, Cyrus Jones,
Used to go over to Ephraim Stone's,

"At first, just to pass an hour away,
And hear what others might have to say.
But by and by he began to drink;
O, my heart grows sick when I stop to think
How the dark storm gathered as time went by,
Till no light was left in my life's dull sky!
Slowly hope was crushed, for nevermore
Could I trust and believe as I did before.
But there were the children, Bessie and Jack,
And I hoped for a time that they might bring him back.
Sometimes remorse would o'er him sweep,
And he would promise, while I would weep,

That for the sake of those children and me
He would be the man he used to be;
And that meant much — never prouder wife
Than I till that license wrecked my life.
But the promise was broken, and day by day
The darkness grew denser about my way.
His love seemed a thing of the long ago,
And at last one day he struck me a blow.

"Years have passed since then, but on my brow
I seem to feel it burning now.
Joy and gladness were long since fled,
Hope in my heart lay crushed and dead,
And when he struck me that bitter blow,
The last faint spark of love died too.
He died very soon in a drunken spree;
I was almost glad, for it set me free.

" My very life was wrapped up in Jack —
Sure he could not follow in his father's track;
But, ere I knew it, my brave, bright son
Was a slave to that license of Ephraim Stone.
O Willie, my darling! I can not tell
How the night of horror over me fell,
And storm-clouds gathered thick and fast
O'er my helpless head, till they broke at last,
And my beautiful boy was brought home dead,
Slain by a comrade's hand they said.
Over there in the shadows dark and deep
He lies, while I still live and weep.

"And Bessie? you say. Well, there came to our place
A gay young man with a handsome face.
He was bright and pleasant and winning, too —
Such as girls are apt to fancy, you know.
I begged and pleaded; for it was known
He liked the tavern of Ephraim Stone.
'Twas all in vain — these tears will start:
She married him — and — he broke her heart.

Scarce two years and she lay at rest,
With my only grandchild on her breast.

"I'm childless and hopeless and all alone —
All for that license of Ephraim Stone.
All alone I live, and I sit and wonder
If, when I search the home over yonder,
I shall find even there all I've loved and lost —
God only knows what that license cost."

— *Miss A. A. Rolfe.*

Anti-Saloon Battle Hymn

(To the tune of "Columbia, the Gem of the Ocean")

The mighty are gathering for conflict;
   The right is arrayed against wrong;
The hosts of the righteous are singing,
   And this is the voice of their song:

CHORUS:

The saloon, it must go! Do you hear us?
   Repeat it again and again.
They strive to make millions of money;
   We strive to make millions of men!

The curse of the traffic is awful!
   No language can tell it; and then,
It makes millions of widows and orphans,
   And drunkards of millions of men.

The prison it crowds with its victims;
   Asylums are filled with its woes;
It curses and blights every being
   As far as its influence goes.

This awful, unspeakable monster
   Must be banished from out our bright land;
From its shackles, O God! do thou free us!
   And for freedom we ever will stand.

— *Rev. G. W. Dungan.*

The Fence or the Ambulance

A parable addressed to voters.

'Twas a dangerous cliff, as they freely confessed,
  Though to walk near its crest was so pleasant;
But over its terrible edge there had slipped
  A duke and full many a peasant.
So the people said something would have to be done,
  But their projects did not at all tally.
Some said, "Put a fence round the edge of the cliff;"
  Some, "An ambulance down in the valley."

"For the cliff is all right, if you're careful," they said,
  "And, if folks even slip and are dropping,
It isn't the slipping that hurts them so much
  As the shock down below — when they're stopping."
So day after day, as these mishaps occurred,
  Quick forth would these rescuers sally
To pick up the victims who fell off the cliff
  With their ambulance down in the valley.

But the cry for the ambulance carried the day,
  For it spread through the neighboring city.
A fence may be useful or not, it is true;
  But each here became brimful of pity
For those who slipped over that dangerous cliff;
  And the dwellers in highway and alley
Gave pounds or gave pence, not to put up a fence,
  But an ambulance down in the valley.

Then an old sage remarked: "It's a marvel to me
  That people give far more attention
To repairing results than to stopping the cause,
  When they'd much better aim at prevention.
Let us stop at its source all this mischief," cried he,
  "Come, neighbors and friends, let us rally!
If the cliff we will fence, we might almost dispense
  With the ambulance down in the valley."

"Oh, he's a fanatic," the others rejoined:
  "Dispense with the ambulance? Never!
He'd dispense with all charities, too, if he could:
  No, no! we'll support them forever!
Aren't we picking up folks just as fast as they fall?
  And shall this man dictate to us? Shall he?
Why should people of sense stop to put up a fence
  While their ambulance works in the valley?"

But a sensible few, who are practical, too,
  Will not bear with such nonsense much longer:
They believe that prevention is better than cure,
  And their party will soon be the stronger.
Encourage them, then, with your purse, voice, and pen,
  And (while other philanthropists dally),
They will scorn all pretense, and put a stout fence
  On the cliff that hangs over the valley.

Better guide well the young than reclaim them when old;
  For the voice of true wisdom is calling,
"To rescue the fallen is good, but 'tis best
  To prevent other people from falling."
Better close up the source of temptation and crime
  Than deliver from dungeon or galley;
Better put a strong fence round the top of the cliff
  Than an ambulance down in the valley.
— *Joseph Malins.*

# TILL PROHIBITION'S DAY.

(FOR MALE VOICES.)

"Wine is a mocker, whosoever is deceived thereby is not wise."—Prov. 20 : 1.

F. E. B.   F. E. BELDEN.

1. The heart has lost its feel-ing, The home has lost its joy;
2. The twi-light soft is fall-ing, The moonbeams kiss the sea;
3. The ho-ly shrine is la-den With rose and lil-y fair;
4. The midnight moon is keep-ing Her si-lent watch on high;

A lone-ly moth-er kneel-ing, Is pray-ing for her boy:
The night-in-gale is call-ing; Love whispers, "true to thee:"
And his the stain-less maid-en With blos-soms in her hair:
A lone-ly wife is weep-ing O'er flow'rs that bloom'd to die:

Pray-ing, pray-ing, While Rum's red sig-nals glow;
Whis-pers, whis-pers, While flow'rs are drink-ing dew;
Blos-soms, blos-soms, To tell her hap-py lot;
Weep-ing, weep-ing, In hun-ger's cheer-less home;

Stray-ing, stray-ing, Where poi-son fountains flow.
Whis-pers, whis-pers, "I live for (wine and) you."
Ros-es, ros-es, And sweet for-get-me-not.
Keep-ing, keep-ing, Watch till the drunkard come.

5 O song! this message carry
To maids before the shrine,—
Beware! nor dare to marry
The man in love with wine:
Ever, ever
He's drawn with unseen chain,
Never, never
To be your own again.

6 Next to Immanuel's story
Is heard the tale of Rum,
And veiling Calvary's glory,
His shadow haunts the home:
Haunting, haunting,
Till God the demon slay,
Veiling, veiling,
Till prohibition's day.

Copyright, 1894, by F. E. Belden. By permission.

[For slides illustrating this song, see page 248.]

THE CORNER-STONE OF TEMPERANCE

"One step in the wrong direction paves the way for another."

"Whether therefore ye eat, or drink, or whatsoever ye do, do all to the glory of God."

"As we near the close of time, we must rise higher and still higher upon the question of health reform and Christian temperance, presenting it in a more positive and decided manner. We must strive continually to educate the people, not only by word, but by our practise. Precept and practise have a telling influence."

BIBLE READING ON TEMPERANCE

1. Temperance a fruit of the Spirit. Gal. 5:22, 23.
2. A round in the Christian ladder. 2 Peter 1:5, 6.
3. An essential to success. 1 Cor. 9:25.
4. Paul practised temperance. Verse 27.
5. Daniel purposed to be temperate. Dan. 1:8.
6. John the Baptist drank neither wine nor strong drink. Luke 1:13-15.
7. Intemperance brings sorrow and trouble. Prov. 23:29, 30.
8. Robs one of reason. Prov. 31:4, 5.
9. Makes it impossible to choose between right and wrong. Lev. 10:8-10.
10. Shuts the gate to heaven. 1 Cor. 6:10.
11. Christ gained the victory on the point of appetite. Matt. 4:1-4.
12. This victory is for all who will come to him for help. Heb. 4:15, 16.
13. He can keep us from falling. Jude 24, 25.
14. Scriptural injunctions. Prov. 23:31, 32; Eph. 5:18; 1 Cor. 6:19, 20; 10:31.
15. Promise to the overcomer. Rev. 21:7.

CHRISTIAN TEMPERANCE

An Evil and Its Remedy

"But as the days of Noah were, so shall also the coming of the Son of man be." To-day is filling that measure to overflowing. Modern surfeiting is eclipsing that of the antediluvians. Eating and drinking bind society together. Everywhere seeds of intemperance are being sown, and everywhere aching hearts are reaping the unwelcome harvest. Few would challenge the statement that intemperance is the most terrible pestilence of the twentieth century; but perhaps equally few realize the sad truth that many so-called Christian homes are lubricating the plane upon which loved ones are sliding down to intemperate lives. Nor would Satan have us believe this alarming fact. For six thousand years he has been enslaving the world to appetite; for six thousand years he has been deceiving many of those who profess to be God's children.

Yet the Lord is not weary of trying to lead his people back to the path of self-control. Along the walks of everyday life he sets up guide-posts. These guide-posts are the principles of Christian temperance, in whose clear light it can be seen how Satan is often privileged to place on well-decked tables his bait for the deadly cup, the filthy weed, and the despicable drug. When one understands the principles of Christian temperance, he sees clearly that one step in the wrong direction prepares the way for another; and that "the least deviation from right principles will lead to a separation from God, and may end in destruction."

The little leaflet entitled "The Demons' Council" gives a sadly true word-picture of Satan's work. It represents him as saying, "I will make their tables a snare unto them. They shall eat for gluttony, and not for strength. Their tables shall be loaded with rich, highly seasoned foods — flesh-meats, fiery relishes, spices, condiments, tea, coffee, and brandy sauces — which will stimulate appetite and passion. I will cause mothers to teach lack of self-control by pandering to appetite in allowing children to spend freely for every whim of taste." In this way Satan is causing our peace-loving homes to serve in his destroying army.

Nor are homes alone in disregarding the principles of temperance. Too often the gospel preached touches neither the appetite nor the passions of men. Many of the popular churches are courting intemperance. Church festivals are made a means of moving members to acts of benevolence. Of such gatherings one writer says: " These gluttonous feasts strengthen morbid appetite and inflame passions, and in the same degree weaken the moral powers and benumb the finer sensibilities of the soul."

But there is a remedy for this evil that is ruining homes, demoralizing society, and robbing churches of their first love. That remedy is found in the principles of Christian temperance. As the lighthouse shows the channel, and warns of the dangerous rocky coast, so Christian temperance gives both light and admonition. Wherever Christian temperance is accepted, it lays the ax at the root of the tree. It subdues the appetite, which usually triumphs over reason, and bids the tyrannical servant be subject to man's intellectual and moral faculties. It removes from tables the bait for gross intemperance. In the daily struggles it helps the higher powers of life to vanquish the lower, and makes the motto for living, " Total abstinence from that which is hurtful, and a moderate use of that which is good."

Proof of Remedy

" Eat ye that which is good, and let your soul delight itself in fatness." This is God's advice to his children. When Israel lusted after the flesh-pots of Egypt, God granted their request; but that indulgence of appetite brought leanness to

The Corner-Stone of Temperance 181

their souls. God has always sought to reveal to man the law which is traced upon every fiber of the human frame. Experience has ever corroborated these divine messages; and as fast as science learns her lessons, she is heard lisping the warnings God has given.

Historical records and scientific writings furnish innumerable testimonials, but only a few can be given here: "Two hundred years ago the king of England prohibited tea taverns, because, he said, they threatened the peace and order of his kingdom; people gathered there, and drank tea until they became careless, and talked treason." More than two decades ago Geo. J. Webster prepared a little book called "The Seven Great Evils." The evils he discusses are tea, coffee, chocolate, opium, tobacco, alcoholic beverages, and impurity. Dr. Crowther asserts that the excessive use of tea and coffee may produce semidelirium, and great prostration. "Tea," says the London *Lancet,* "has undoubtedly its victims, as well as alcohol. Alcohol, of course, is a more insidious poison than tea, and its effects are more drastic and perceptible. Nevertheless, tea may be equally stealthy in disturbing functional equilibrium. When we know that tea is a drug, not a food, we need not hesitate to affirm that any use of it whatever is an abuse of our system." Add to this testimony the fact that coffee and chocolate contain the same active principle as does tea.

The matron of the South Newington Inebriates' Home for Women, testifies that flesh foods produce a craving for narcotics. Others join in this testimony. Canon Hone Lyttleton, head master of one of the great public schools in England and nephew of the late Mrs. Gladstone, is reported as saying that as the diet is changed from meat to vegetables, there is a diminution in animal lust. Every meal taken according to the modern menu is a direct stimulus to passion. One of the grand results of the Russo-Japanese War is that we are beginning to consider seriously about diet, because the Japanese eat no meat, and are proving their prowess plainly.[1] "The wise little Japanese," says Edward Bok, editor of the *Ladies' Home Journal,* " found out this truth centuries ago, and his endurance is marvelous. Some day the American man will find it out; and when he eats less meat, he will be the better for it." Many have already learned that lesson. General Booth, leader of the Salvation Army movement; Mrs. Lillian Stevens, president of the National W. C. T. U.; Miss Margaret Bilz, national W. C. T. U. lecturer; Mrs. Lovell, superintendent of one of the W. C. T. U. departments, are among the noted people who are vegetarians.

Thus science and experience blend their voices in declaring that the way of the transgressor is hard, and in teaching the world that God's ways are ways of pleasantness. The sound of these voices falls as a rebuke upon the ears of every Christian who sees the light of true temperance, but is " following afar off."

Christian Temperance as a Part of God's Message

As the prism reveals the hidden colors of the sunbeam, so the Spirit of God breaks up the light of the gospel into its spectrum, and the student of truth sees that Christian temperance is among the colors that blend in that shaft of heavenly light. It is one of the fruits of the Spirit. See Gal. 5:22, 23. It is one of the rounds in the Christian ladder. See 2 Peter 1:6. As we look back through the avenues of time, we find that Christian temperance has been an absolutely necessary qualification of the children of God who have had special work to do. Daniel was used of God in Israel's deliverance from Babylon. Of him we read that he " purposed in his heart that he would not defile himself with the portion of the king's meat." While John the Baptist was preparing " in the desert a highway for our God," his simple dress and his abstemious diet were a constant rebuke to the luxury-loving Pharisees. As Paul stood before Felix

---

[1] But the Japanese, as a result of scientific studies, are introducing more meat.

and Drusilla, he witnessed of righteousness, of temperance, and of judgment to come.

When God stretched forth his hand to deliver Israel from Egypt, he fed them upon food from heaven until their foolish hearts rebelled. Their disobedience brought sorrow and sickness; and more than that, many of those who started for the promised land, sold their right to it for a taste of the flesh-pots of Egypt.

God has not arbitrarily made Christian temperance a part of his message, a fruit of the Spirit, or a step in the Christian's ladder. But since every sinful gratification tends to benumb the faculties and deaden the mental and spiritual perceptions; and since only clear, sound minds can carry a pure gospel to the world, it is evident that temperance is an absolutely necessary qualification of Christians. Some may argue that Christian temperance is not a part of the ten commandments. But the past lifts its voice against such clamor, and declares that he who disregards the laws of health can not keep the precepts of the decalogue in spirit and in truth.

When Solomon built the temple, he did not pick up any kind of material that chanced to be lying around. God superintended that work; and when the building was completed, God's glory filled the house. Even so his glory should fill the human temple; but it never can fill the heart that is lorded over by a perverted appetite. "God has given us faculties and talents; and it is our duty, as sons and daughters, to make the best use of them. If we weaken these powers of body and mind by wrong habits, or by indulgence of perverted appetites, it will be impossible for us to honor God as we should."

Historical Notes

Fifty years ago Christian temperance received very little attention. Science and religion were strangers to it. But now, in the twilight hour of earth's history, when the almighty arm is stretched forth to lead the remnant people into the heavenly Canaan, it is seen that Christian temperance is one branch of the great work which is to fit a people for the coming of the Lord.

From time to time, individuals, coming forward, have advocated various phases of Christian temperance; but in 1863 the Seventh-day Adventists as a denomination began to agitate the subject. The instruction given through their periodicals proved to be scientifically correct, and was far in advance of what was then being taught. Three years later they opened their first health reform institution. This was the small beginning of a work whose sanitariums now encircle the globe and give employment to one hundred doctors, nine hundred nurses, and one thousand other helpers. It was the beginning of a work which, in addition to those just mentioned, has a large well-trained corps doing self-supporting missionary work. Through health magazines and other denominational periodicals, this people has given wide publicity to the principles of health and temperance. In their church, the use of liquor or tobacco is made a test of fellowship. Generally speaking, tea and coffee are discarded from their tables, and flesh foods rarely used. Their aim is to live upon a simple, unstimulating diet, and to return to what they understand from Gen. 1:29 to be the natural diet of man. While no other denomination has taken so decided a stand for Bible temperance, many individuals in other connections have been persuaded to make the rules of Christian temperance some of their "living principles."

The beneficent rays of Christian temperance have long been shining on our pathway, but some are still wandering in the dark wilderness of disobedience. In this, as in all other phases of Christian living, one must have a personal experience. Victories over temptations are not negotiable; but to that individual who follows every ray of light, the saving grace is sufficient. We can conquer, if we will.

"To the true and the faithful
Victory is promised through grace."

ALLIES OF INTEMPERANCE

Selections from "Ministry of Healing"

Mustard, pepper, spices, pickles, and other things of a like character, irritate the stomach and make the blood feverish and impure. The inflamed condition of the drunkard's stomach is often pictured as illustrating the effect of alcoholic liquors. A similarly inflamed condition is produced by the use of irritating condiments. Soon ordinary food does not satisfy the appetite. The system feels a want, a craving, for something more stimulating.— *Page 325*.

Tea and coffee do not nourish the system. Their effect is produced before there has been time for digestion and assimilation, and what seems to be strength is only nervous excitement. When the influence of the stimulant is gone, the unnatural force abates, and the result is a corresponding degree of languor and debility.

The continued use of these nerve irritants is followed by headache, wakefulness, palpitation of the heart, indigestion, trembling, and many other evils; for they wear away the life forces.— *Page 326*.

In relation to tea, coffee, tobacco, and alcoholic drinks, the only safe course is to touch not, taste not, handle not. The tendency of tea, coffee, and similar drinks is in the same direction as that of alcoholic liquor and tobacco, and in some cases the habit is as difficult to break as it is for the drunkard to give up intoxicants.—*Page 335.*

Flesh was never the best food; but its use is now doubly objectionable, since disease in animals is so rapidly increasing. Those who use flesh foods little know what they are eating. Often if they could see the animals when living, and know the quality of the meat they eat, they would turn from it with loathing. People are continually eating flesh that is filled with tuberculous and cancerous germs. Tuberculosis, cancer, and other fatal diseases are thus communicated.—*Page 313.*

It is a mistake to suppose that muscular strength depends on the use of animal food. The needs of the system can be better supplied, and more vigorous health can be enjoyed, without its use. The grains, with fruits, nuts, and vegetables, contain all the nutritive properties necessary to make good blood. These elements are not so well or so fully supplied by a flesh diet. Had the use of flesh been essential to health and strength, animal food would have been included in the diet appointed man in the beginning.—*Page 316.*

Often intemperance begins in the home. By the use of rich, unhealthful food the digestive organs are weakened, and a desire is created for food that is still more stimulating. Thus the appetite is educated to crave continually something stronger. The demand for stimulants becomes more frequent and more difficult to resist. The system becomes more or less filled with poison, and the more debilitated it becomes, the greater is the desire for these things. One step in the wrong direction prepares the way for another. Many who would not be guilty of placing on their table wine or liquor of any kind will load their table with food which creates such a thirst for strong drink that to resist the temptation is almost impossible. Wrong habits of eating and drinking destroy the health and prepare the way for drunkenness.—*Page 334.*

THE CURE FOR NATIONAL INTEMPERANCE

Dietetic Cause of Intemperance

An important cause of the desire for strong drink not infrequently is to be found at our tables. The quantity and quality of the food served is often of a nature to create a desire for narcotics. As long as people take stimulating, highly seasoned, and irritating foods, they will feel a craving for stimulating drinks, and will naturally resort to the use of the narcotic most convenient and against which there exists the least personal or public prejudice.

Does the saloon-keeper keep a lunch-counter in his saloon because he has compassion for the poor and starving? We know this is not the case. Is his lunch-table laden with luscious, juicy fruits? Invariably it is laden with highly seasoned meats of various kinds, and with pickles, mustard, and other irritants; for he knows that such foods lead the eater directly to the bar for a drink; that they create a thirst which water can not quench. To this extent the saloon-keeper can be said to create a demand for his wares.

It is more than a mere coincidence that men who use alcoholic beverages freely are fond of highly seasoned foods, and that in countries where highly seasoned foods are freely used, alcoholic drinks are also largely consumed as a beverage.

Not all who eat highly seasoned or stimulating foods become drunkards, but in every such case the desire for narcotics is created. The person may pass through life ignorant of what his system is craving. Should he, however, get one drink, whether at the sick bed, the communion table, or in the saloon, that drink might prove the first step to a life of intemperance. Having learned what his system craves, it would be natural for him to resort to it again and again. If, after taking the first drink, he is kept from becoming a drunkard, it is because he is aware of the evils resulting from the use of alcohol, and has inherited or acquired more will power than his more unfortunate brother, who, perchance, is so unequally balanced that anything of a stimulating nature will lead to a complete loss of self-control. Such instances are by no means uncommon. Help must come to these by the removal of that which destroys self-control. It is becoming more and more apparent that reformatory measures pertaining to diet must be set in motion in order to wipe out, or even to mitigate in an appreciable degree, the sale of alcoholic drinks. Our observations have led us to conclude that so long as people eat as they do, they will continue to drink as they do.

Prevention by Right Diet

The education of mothers, wives, and daughters in the art of preparing nutritious, wholesome, non-irritating foods from the simple, non-stimulating products of the earth, should supplement our prohibitory efforts, if we would arrest the manufacture and sale of alcohol.

In the beginning, a man was placed in a garden, surrounded with all manner of trees pleasant to the sight and good for food, and the command was given, "Of every tree thou mayest freely eat." On the free use of such foods it is impossible to cultivate a desire for drink. The almost universal departure from the free use of these foods is responsible for the general use of alcoholic drinks.

The free use of juicy fruits is one of the best means of overcoming the drink habit. If persevered in, it will in time cure the worst case of inebriety. The desire for fruit and the desire for alcoholic drink can not exist in the same person; for one desire will surely destroy the other. It is left for each person to choose which of these tastes, with its accompanying results, shall contribute to his character building.

On this point, some time ago, the editor of the London *Clarion* related his experience, in an editorial, as follows: —

"I have just turned vegetarian. My friends are surprised; so am I. But whereas they are surprised that I have adopted this diet, I am surprised that I did not do it years ago. In one way the effects of the diet have surprised me. I have been a heavy smoker for more than twenty years. If there was anything in life which I feared my will was too weak to conquer, it was the habit of smoking. Well, I have been a vegetarian for eight weeks, and I find that my passion for tobacco is weakening. . . . Again, I have found I can not drink wine. Several times I have tried a glass of hock or Burgundy; it is no use. It tastes like physic. Why do I write these confessions? — Because these things have come upon me as a revelation; because I begin to see that the great cure for the evil of national intemperance is not a teetotal propaganda, but vegetarianism."

For years we have successfully employed this diet in connection with other measures in treating alcoholics. Our experience is that upon a non-irritating, non-stimulating diet the craving for drink weakens or disappears, but reappears as soon as meat and irritating foods are again eaten. The Salvation Army in some of its homes for inebriates has also adopted this diet with marked results.

Flesh and Intemperance

The craving for stimulants is often due to a lack of energy, and something is called for by the system to liberate the little that is possessed. The vegetable kingdom stores up energy to supply man's needs. It appropriates, organizes, and vitalizes the innutritious elements found in the air and soil, preparing them for man's use. In the fruits, grains, nuts, and vegetables, energy-producing elements, unassociated with poisons or wastes, are stored. Man should get his supply of life and energy from the fountainhead in order to possess the natural buoyancy to which he is entitled. Just to the extent that people depart from these simple, energy-charged foods, and use stimulating foods, will they experience a lack of energy, and feel the need of stimulants.

The flushed face, the fevered head, the increased sociability, and the feeling of exhilaration and strength experienced immediately after taking a cup of beef tea or a dinner composed largely of meats, are due to the immediate absorption of the waste products they contain. These products stimulate the same as does alcohol. The excessive hunger experienced a few hours after partaking of a meal composed largely of flesh-meats and such stimulating drinks as tea and coffee, is not a hunger for food, but for stimulation; this calls for frequent meals to satisfy the craving. Sooner or later the person may discover that alcohol will satisfy the supposed hunger as effectively as will the ingestion of more urates obtained from the meat. Many have discovered this, and resort to alcoholic beverages when this feeling of weakness appears. For this reason, in countries where meat is freely used, we find that alcoholic beverages are also freely used. Meat and highly seasoned foods are almost as difficult to give up as is alcohol; but he who gives up the former will find it much easier to give up the latter; while many can not give up the latter without first giving up the former. The sure and permanent cure of national intemperance lies in diet reform.— *D. H. Kress, M. D.*

There is a growing accumulation of testimony showing that a properly selected vegetarian diet — accompanied by obedience to the other laws of health — naturally and without effort takes away all desire for alcoholic stimulants.— *Dr. MacNamara, of England.*

"Mr. Eustace Miles, a scientific writer and an athlete, who is strictly accurate and impartial in all his statements, says that with the practise of 'food reform' he found that 'the desire, or even the liking, for alcohol was departing,'— a thing he had 'never imagined possible.'"

FOUR LESSONS ON TEMPERANCE

Christian Temperance

What is wine?

"Wine is a mocker, strong drink is raging: and whosoever is deceived thereby is not wise." Prov. 20: 1.

For what should men eat and drink?

"Blessed art thou, O land, when thy king is the son of nobles, and thy princes eat in due season, for strength, and not for drunkenness." Eccl. 10: 17.

What is one of the evil results of drunkenness and overeating?

"Be not among winebibbers; among riotous eaters of flesh; for the drunkard and the glutton shall come to poverty." Prov. 23: 20, 21.

What effect does licentiousness and wine have upon the morals?

"Whoredom and wine and new wine take away the heart." Hosea 4: 11.

What are common accompaniments of intemperance?

"Who hath woe? who hath sorrow? who hath contentions? who hath babbling? who hath wounds without cause? who hath redness of eyes? They that tarry long at the wine; they that go to seek mixed wine." Prov. 23: 29, 30.

How do intoxicants serve one in the end?

"Look not thou upon the wine when it is red, when it giveth his color in the cup, when it moveth itself aright. At the last it biteth like a serpent, and stingeth like an adder." Verses 31, 32.

What will drunkards, with other workers of iniquity, never inherit?

"Neither fornicators, nor idolaters, . . . nor thieves,

nor covetous, nor drunkards, . . . shall inherit the kingdom of God." 1 Cor. 6:9, 10.

What does God say of those who are instrumental in making men drunk?

"Woe unto him that giveth his neighbor drink, that puttest thy bottle to him, and makest him drunken." Hab. 2:15.

What example on temperance did Daniel give the world?

"Daniel purposed in his heart that he would not defile himself with the portion of the king's meat, nor with the wine which he drank." Dan. 1:8.

For what food and drink did he ask?

"Let them give us pulse to eat, and water to drink." Dan. 1:12.

Concerning what did Paul reason before Felix?

"He reasoned of righteousness, temperance, and judgment to come." Acts 24:25.

What admonition did Christ give which is especially applicable to our time?

"And take heed to yourselves, lest at any time your hearts be overcharged with surfeiting, and drunkenness, and cares of this life, and so that day come upon you unawares." Luke 21:34.

How did Christ say matters would be just before his second coming?

"As the days of Noah were, so shall also the coming of the Son of man be. . . . They were eating and drinking, marrying and giving in marriage." Matt. 24:37, 38.

From all this it is but reasonable to expect that there would be a crying need in the closing days of this world's history for Christians and every lover of the race to put forth the most earnest efforts to stay the terrible tide of intemperance. Intemperance means bondage and lack of self-control. Liberty stands for freedom and good government in the individual, the State, and the nation.— *Liberty.*

Bible Study

TEMPERANCE FOR CHRIST'S SAKE.— 1 Cor. 6: 19, 20 (note 1); Ps. 139: 14; Rom. 12: 1 (note 2); 1 Cor. 3: 17.

TEMPERANCE FOR ONE'S OWN SAKE.— 1 Cor. 6: 19, 20 (notes 3 and 4); 2 Cor. 7: 1 (notes 5 and 6).

DUTY TO STUDY LAWS OF HEALTH.— Ps. 119: 73 (note 7); Hosea 4: 6; Deut. 6: 7, 24; Ps. 119: 92.

LAWS OF HEALTH ARE GOD'S LAWS.— Ex. 15: 26 (note 8); Rom. 6: 12, 13, 23.

NOTES

1. "By a misuse of any of our powers we rob God of the honor due him."

2. "The health should be guarded as sacredly as the character."

3. "God has pledged himself to keep this human machinery in healthful action, if the human agent will obey his laws and co-operate with God."

4. "Satan knows that he can not overcome man unless he can control his will. He can do this by deceiving man so that he will co-operate with him in transgressing the laws of nature."

5. "Eating, drinking, and dressing have all a direct bearing upon our spiritual advancement."

6. "The brain nerves which communicate to the entire system are the only medium through which heaven can communicate to man and affect his inmost life. Whatever disturbs the circulation of the electric currents in the nervous system, lessens the strength of the vital powers; and the result is a deadening of the sensibilities of the mind."

7. "God's law is written by his own finger upon every nerve, every muscle, every faculty which has been entrusted to man."

8. "God has formed laws to govern every part of our constitutions, and these laws he has placed in our being are divine."

A Temperance Catechism

1. What is temperance? — Self-control in all things, but especially with reference to appetite.

2. What are the requirements of true temperance? — Total abstinence from all things harmful, such as intoxicating liquors, tobacco, and poisonous drugs, and the moderate use of things wholesome.

3. What is the harmful element in spirituous liquors? — Alcohol, a deadly poison, a small quantity of which, undiluted, produces insensibility and even death.

4. What makes tobacco injurious? — The poison nicotine, which is found in it. There is enough of this poison in one cigar, if introduced directly into the blood, to kill two men.

5. Where is the foundation of intemperance often laid? — In the home — by giving children alcohol as a medicine, by eating of meat and highly seasoned foods, by using pepper and other condiments which produce irritation in the stomach and create a craving for something strong, by the eating of poorly cooked foods, by partaking of bad combinations of foods and of rich pastries, which create the demand for stimulants.

6. What does the Bible say of strong drink? — "Wine is a mocker, strong drink is raging: and whosoever is deceived thereby is not wise." Prov. 20: 1.

7. Who is a wise son? — "Hear thou, my son, and be wise." "Be not among winebibbers; among riotous eaters of flesh." Prov. 23: 19, 20.

8. Why should a young man or woman entering on life shun intemperance? — Because it weakens all the forces of manhood or womanhood, physical, intellectual, moral, and spiritual, destroying the prospects of success in this life, and blighting the hopes of the life to come. "Every man that striveth for the mastery is temperate in all things." 1 Cor. 9: 25.

The Corner-Stone of Temperance 195

9. In what way does intemperance disqualify one physically for success? — The first requisite of success is to be a good animal. These poisons weaken all the vital powers. They stimulate the vital processes and produce a feeling of vigor, but it is artificial, and the reaction is weakness. Those who perform great athletic feats and endure great physical tests find temperance absolutely essential to success.

10. How does intemperance affect the mind? — The brain and nervous system are greatly harmed by these poisons. The drunkard, who is really insane and irresponsible, is an exaggerated example of the condition of every one who uses tobacco, and poisonous drugs, and alcohol moderately, or suffers from alcohol created in the stomach as a result of improper eating. The mind is clouded and can not do its work properly. Great thinkers like Gladstone, great inventors like Edison, and all skilled workmen find temperance an essential to success. Many railroads now refuse to employ those who use liquor, and the cigarette fiend is recognized as incapable.

11. How are the moral and spiritual powers affected? — It dethrones the moral and spiritual faculties. Even on the cruel cross the Son of man refused the poisonous draft offered him, lest his perception should be deadened, and he should sin against God, and the world should be lost.

12. How many suffer from the curse of intemperance? — "No man lives to himself," and the worst of all is that the innocent suffer from the terrible ravages of intemperance. Others are robbed of their purity by the impure thoughts and acts of the intemperate; the innocent suffer the loss of property, peace, and life itself, at the hands of irresponsible drunkards, and drug users; peace and happiness flee from the homes of the intemperate, and wives and children suffer on account of business failure; society is robbed of the helpful influence of men who, except for drink, might be a blessing to humanity and an honor to God.

13. How does intemperance affect the prospects of the

life beyond?— This life is given to prepare for eternity. Misuse of the body is a sin against God, and no drunkard can enter the kingdom of God. 1 Cor. 3: 16, 17; 6: 10.

M. E. KERN.

NOTE.— Other exercises in the form of catechisms may be arranged, using information drawn from this book or elsewhere. The foregoing can be used as a dialogue.

Responsive Reading

" Woe unto them that rise up early in the morning, that they may follow strong drinks; that continue until night, till wine inflame them!" Isa. 5: 11.

" And the harp, and the viol, the tabret, and pipe, and wine, are in their feasts: but they regard not the work of the Lord, neither consider the operation of his hands." Verse 12.

" And the Lord spake unto Aaron, saying, Do not drink wine nor strong drink, thou nor thy sons with thee." Lev. 10: 8, 9.

" They shall not drink wine with a song; strong drink shall be bitter to them that drink it." Isa. 24: 9.

" It is not for kings, O Lemuel, it is not for kings to drink wine; nor for princes strong drink." Prov. 31: 4.

" Woe to the crown of pride, to the drunkards of Ephraim, whose glorious beauty is a fading flower." Isa. 28: 1.

" He that loveth pleasure shall be a poor man: he that loveth wine and oil shall not be rich." Prov. 21: 17.

" For the drunkard and the glutton shall come to poverty: and drowsiness shall clothe a man with rags." Prov. 23: 21.

" Woe unto him that giveth his neighbor strong drink, that puttest thy bottle to him, and makest him drunken also." Hab. 2: 15.

" Woe unto them that are mighty to drink wine, and men of strength to mingle strong drink." Isa. 5: 22.

" Be not drunk with wine, wherein is excess; but be filled with the Spirit." Eph. 5: 18.

The Corner-Stone of Temperance

"*Wine is a mocker, strong drink is raging: and whosoever is deceived thereby is not wise.*" Prov. 20:1.

"Who hath woe? who hath sorrow? who hath contentions? who hath babbling? who hath wounds without cause? who hath redness of eyes?" Prov. 23:29.

"*They that tarry long at the wine; they that go to seek mixed wine.*" Verse 30.

"Look not thou upon the wine when it is red, when it giveth his color in the cup, when it moveth itself aright." Verse 31.

"*At the last it biteth like a serpent, and stingeth like an adder.*" Verse 32.

"Be not deceived: Neither fornicators, nor idolaters, nor adulterers . . . nor thieves, nor covetous, nor drunkards, nor revilers, nor extortioners, shall inherit the kingdom of God." 1 Cor. 6:9, 10.

"*Now, therefore, beware, I pray thee, and drink not wine nor strong drink, and eat not any unclean thing.*" Judges 13:4.

"Know ye not that your body is the temple of the Holy Ghost which is in you, which ye have of God, and ye are not your own?" 1 Cor. 6:19.

"*For ye are bought with a price: therefore glorify God in your body, and in your spirit, which are God's.*" Verse 20.

"Whether therefore ye eat, or drink, or whatsover ye do, do all to the glory of God." 1 Cor. 10:30.

W. A. COLCORD.

SHORT SELECTIONS

Coffee — Its History

Persia, the home of delicious fruits, seems to have given birth to coffee. Thence it was carried into Arabia, where it was first used, not as a beverage, but for medicinal purposes. Coffee did not become an article of trade until the middle of the sixteenth century, when it was introduced into the markets of Constantinople. It was used so freely in Turkey that the government finally forbade its use, but being unable to suppress the sale, levied a heavy tax upon it. The Mohammedan priests complained that the mosques were neglected, while the coffee-houses were thronged.

All the coffee grown in the New World is said to have sprung from a single plant which a French naval officer carried to Martinique in 1720, depriving himself of water when suffering from thirst, in order to nourish his coffee plant. From this plant, it is said that Brazil, Mexico, and the West Indies obtained their seed.— *Youth's Instructor.*

Wasted Money

According to the latest estimates, the world's product of tea is about five hundred million pounds annually, valued at seventy-five million dollars. More than one half of this is used in the British empire, at a cost nearly twice as great as the amount given by all Christians for foreign missions. In a little over fifty years the world's product of coffee has increased eightfold. Of the more than two billion pounds now produced annually, about one third is used in the United States. This country spends about ten times as much annually for coffee as for the support of Christian missions. For tea, coffee, and cocoa, the world spends daily nearly a million dollars,— almost twenty times as much as for missions.— *Selected.*

Contents of a Cup of Tea

What does tea contain to make it such a well-nigh universal beverage? Following are the chief chemical constituents of two typical varieties of the plant:—

	BLACK TEA	GREEN TEA
Water	8.20	5.96
Caffeine	3.24	2.33
Alcoholic extract	6.79	7.05
Tannic acid	16.40	27.14
Cellulose	34.00	25.90

—"*School of Health,*" *page 230.*

Contents of Coffee

Coffee strongly resembles tea, containing a trifle more than one per cent of caffeine, eight to nine per cent of caffeic acids, four to six per cent alcoholic extracts, and some other unimportant ingredients. Its effect on the digestion seems to be less decisive than that of tea, there being no tannic acid; but the nervous system is affected by strong coffee in much the same way as by tea.

Effects of Tea on the Heart

Huchard, one of the most prominent physicians of Paris, a specialist in diseases of the heart, calls attention to the fact that distressing palpitation of the heart is often due to toxic causes which are overlooked. Illustrative of this, he gives the case of a fashionable young woman who had constant and painful palpitation of the heart, and was laboring under the impression that she had an organic disease of the heart. On examination he found no evidence of any disease of the valves or heart structures, and on inquiry found that the young lady was in the habit of spending her afternoons in calling, frequently making several stops, and at each taking a cup of tea, so that in the course of the afternoon she drank many cups. Following his urgent advice, the young lady renounced the use of tea, and in a short time was entirely relieved of her cardiac trouble.

Huchard calls attention to the fact that it has long been known that the use of tea produces functional disorders of the heart of a very pronounced character. Dyspepsia, insomnia, and neurasthenia have also been shown by Morton and Bullard, of Boston, to result from the use of tea. He also asserts that coffee frequently produces the same symptoms, with tremor of the limbs, pain in the region of the heart, nausea, and profuse sweating. Here is something for tea drinkers and coffee drinkers to think about.— *Medical Missionary.*

Do You Drink Cider?

Regarding sweet cider as harmless, many have no scruples in purchasing it freely. But it remains sweet for a short time only; then fermentation begins. The sharp taste which it then acquires makes it all the more acceptable to many palates, and the user is loath to admit that it has become hard, or fermented.

Intoxication is quite as truly produced by wine, beer, and cider as by strong drinks. The use of these drinks awakens the taste for those that are stronger, and thus the liquor habit is established. Moderate drinking is the school in which men are educated for the drunkard's career.— *Mrs. E. G. White.*

Dr. Woods, in the "United States Dispensatory," says: "Alcohol is the intoxicating ingredient in all spirituous liquors, including under this head all wines, porter, ale, beer, *cider, and every other liquid which has undergone vinous fermentation.*"

Dr. Wiley on a Vegetarian Diet

Dr. Wiley, of Washington, D. C., when recently before the House Committee on Expenditures for the Agricultural Department of the United States government, said, when questioned as to what he regarded the best food for man: —

"I think we eat too much meat for health. For the sustenance of physical exertion, if you have hard work to do,

The Corner-Stone of Temperance

there is nothing better than starch or sugar. The cereal-eating nations can endure more physical toil than the meat-eating nations. That is not the accepted view, but it is true. You can not tire out a Japanese, who eats rice. He will draw you all around the town on a pound of rice, and be as fresh at the close of the day as when he started. You could not do that on a pound of meat to save your life."

Vegetarianism and Alcoholism

Speaking upon the relation between vegetarianism and total abstinence, Hon. Edvard Wavrinsky, a member of the Swedish parliament, a very active worker in the temperance cause, holding the office of International Chief Templar, says: —

"It is time that the friends of total abstinence duly appreciate and resort to the powerful ally they have in vegetarianism. If a drunkard can be induced to embrace the mild, healthful vegetarian diet, his desire for alcohol will at once be considerably reduced, and finally wholly fall off. He will feel somewhat lax in the beginning, lacking the excitement caused by flesh and alcohol; but soon he will feel his vitality increase, his outer and inner buoyancy return; and he will understand that under normal circumstances no stimulants are needed to keep the machinery of the body running.

"Of course they who want to serve and elevate humanity must control themselves in food and drink. It does not suffice that we do not use the destructive, intoxicating liquors; we must go the whole length, and also work for the best food, since this stands in exceedingly close relation to temperance."

It Should Be Done

Parents should begin the crusade against intemperance in their own homes. Many mothers who deplore the intemperance which exists everywhere, do not look deep enough for the cause. They are daily preparing a variety of dishes and highly seasoned foods which tempt the appetite, encourage overeating, and pave the way for the indulgence of stronger stimulants in their children. Mothers need to be impressed with the sacredness of their obligation to God and to the world to furnish society with children that are temperate in their habits and have the power to control their appetites and passions.— *Bible Echo*.

"Let appetite wear reason's golden chain;
And find in due restraint its luxury."

"Plain and healthful living tends to long and happy lives."

"A knowledge of the laws by which health is secured and preserved is of pre-eminent importance."

"By overeating, the stomach becomes debilitated, the digestive organs are weakened, and disease, with all its train of evils, is brought on as the result."

"Simple grains, fruits, and vegetables have all the nutrient properties necessary to make good blood. This a flesh diet can not do."

"One of the strongest temptations that man has to meet is upon the point of appetite."

"Christ began this work of redemption by reforming the physical habits of man."

"As we near the close of time, Satan's temptation to indulge appetite will be more powerful and more difficult to overcome."

"Our habits of eating and drinking show whether we are of the world or among the number that the Lord by his mighty cleaver of truth has separated from the world."

TEMPERANCE EVANGELISM

"Intemperance is a foe against which all need to be guarded. The rapid increase of this terrible evil should arouse every lover of his race to warfare against it. The practise of giving instruction on temperance topics in the schools is a move in the right direction. Instruction in this line should be given in every school and in every home. The youth and children should understand the effect of alcohol, tobacco, and other like poisons, in breaking down the body, beclouding the mind, and sensualizing the soul. It should be made plain that no one who uses these things can long possess the full strength of his physical, mental, or moral faculties."

WHAT THE TIMES DEMAND

The temperance cause has advanced by means of two principal methods of attack, moral suasion and legislative enactments. "The first great temperance awakening, which occurred two generations ago, made its appeal to the individual conscience." The efforts of the temperance forces during the present generation have been almost wholly concentrated on legislative reform and constitutional prohibition. Gratifying progress is being made in this line, and victory is crowning the efforts put forth in many places.

But with the dangers of reaction, especially where drastic laws are going into effect, and with the necessity of a mighty forward movement before us, we need to institute anew the old-time temperance evangelism. There is need to-day of men like the apostle Paul, who will preach "righteousness, temperance, and judgment to come," and press the message home by the power of the Holy Spirit, till sinners are converted and wicked rulers tremble on their thrones. There is need of a mighty army of loyal Christian young people and other devoted laymen who will, by living the principles of Christian temperance and engaging in personal effort, spread the doctrine and make disciples.

Political effort is proper in itself, but needs to be carefully guarded. There is danger that we shall come to think that men can be made righteous by law, and that other so-called reform measures will be enacted which violate the rights of conscience. If we recognize that good laws to be effective must first be written on the hearts of the people, and if we forever keep temperance work free from religious legislation, political efforts are right and proper. This ought we to do, and not leave the evangelistic and educational work undone. Lincoln said: "The man who molds public sentiment is greater than he that enacts laws or enforces statutes. For without an enlightened public opinion, laws will never be enacted, nor will they be enforced."

M. E. KERN.

OUR DUTY AND RESPONSIBILITY

Intemperance and Missions

Temperance is one part of the glad tidings which are to be given to all the world. Consequently those who have identified themselves with the gospel of Jesus Christ must strive to have their own lives reflect the principles of true temperance, and must do all in their power to lead others back to the path of self-control. Such help is needed everywhere. The scalding tears, the gnawing hunger, the smothered hopes — these painful reminders of intemperance — plead with us to enter the crusade against the enemy of all that is noble and true. Those who have brothers or friends in the slavery of intemperance are wringing their hands in distress. He whose eyes behold all these scenes of suffering, and whose bosom heaves with sympathy, urges us to make the subject of temperance "a living issue."

The greatest work before Christians is to give the gospel of Jesus Christ to the world. One of the greatest obstacles to the progress of this work is the curse of intemperance. This is true in so-called Christian nations; true in heathen lands. Rev. W. Day, twenty-five years a missionary in Africa, declared that he was only waiting for some one to take his place to go home to wage war against the liquor traffic. Chief Khama of the Bamangwato, in his pathetic appeal to the British representative, said: "I dread the white man's drink more than all the assagais of the Matabele. These kill men's bodies, and it is quickly over; but drink puts devils into men, and destroys both their bodies and their souls forever. Its wounds never heal. I pray your honor never ask me to open a little door to drink." Miss Corinna Shattuck, of central Turkey, says: "The drink curse is the greatest we have to contend against." Drunkenness nearly destroyed the heathen Lapps. "The Hottentots have been nearly exterminated by brandy. The Basutos have perished in large numbers through liquor drinking, and the future of the Kafirs depends on drink being kept from them." "Missi," said the converted war-chief of the New Hebrides, "drink is killing my people. I weep over it. You bring us the good news from the Great Spirit in heaven, and we live; but why do your countrymen bring us death in the fire-water?" From China, from Japan, from India, from the Neglected Continent, and from the islands of the sea, come the same sorrowful tales.

The heathen lands are lying prostrate before the greed of civilized nations. In 1894 F. P. Noble said: "Since 1882 at least one hundred million gallons of spirits have flowed into Africa. From Boston, Liverpool, Hamburg, and Holland flow these streams of liquid damnation." Such conditions are thrusting a terrible reproach upon Christianity. "As drunk as a Christian," is a common proverb in heathen lands. "It is not enough," says Rev. Kingsbury, of Bulgaria, " for America to send out missionaries: the Christians of America must help to stop this soul-destroying flood of intoxicants that is pouring out of America into missionary lands." Truly, as another has said, "Temperance must become as much a part of the church work as missions."

"In our work more attention should be given to the temperance reform. Every duty that calls for reform, involves repentance, faith, and obedience. Thus every true reform has its place in the third angel's message. Especially does the temperance reform demand our attention and support." If the scenes of intemperance about us, the reports from heathen lands, and the direct words from the Lord do not arouse us to intense activity in opposing so terrible a curse, let us pray incessantly that our lives may be filled with that love which burned in the Saviour's bosom, and caused him to leave the courts of glory and come to this dark, sin-stricken world to rescue mankind from degradation and sin.

Working for the Intemperate

"Let him alone," said the man to his friend, who stopped to help up a drunken man, and to get him into a place of safety; "let him alone, he's only a swine anyway." "I know he is beastly," said the friend, "but he ought not to be; somewhere under this mass of filth and profanity a man is buried." The unfortunates who have fallen into the tempter's snare need the touch of a sympathetic hand. This hand, Christian workers should extend to them. They need to know that somebody cares for them; to know that there is a power at their disposal which can keep them from falling; and to know that He who can keep, also bids them come. These glad tidings some one should whisper to those who despair because of many failures.

It is hard to get up. "You talk about my drinking," says the drunkard, "but you say nothing about my thirst." That thirst is the scourge which drives the captive on to destruction. Here is a striking incident. During the Civil War a sutler's wagon with a barrel of whisky was broken down between the two lines within easy range of the sharp-shooters on both sides. The certainty of instant death did not deter men on both sides from attempting to reach the barrel. Finally it was destroyed by a cannon, and the temptation thus removed, but not until several men had been killed. Such is the terrible thirst that is robbing the world of sobriety. We must recognize the power of this craze, and be able to tell of the draft that quenches even such burning thirst.

"In dealing with the victims of intemperance, we must remember that we are not dealing with sane men, but with those who, for the time being, are under the power of a demon. Be patient and forbearing. Think not of the repulsive, forbidding appearance, but of the precious life that Christ died to redeem. As the drunkard awakens to a sense of his degradation, do all in your power to show that you are his friend. Speak no word of censure. Let no act or look express reproach or aversion. Very likely the poor soul curses himself. Help him to rise. Speak words that will encourage faith. Seek to strengthen every good trait in his character. Teach him how to reach upward; show him that it is possible for him to live so as to win the respect of his fellow men. Help him to see the value of the talents which God has given him, but which he has neglected to improve."

The work for those tempted ones merits our best endeavor. Grace is sufficient for them. They may arise and walk in newness of life. " One who is weakened and even degraded by sinful indulgence may become a son of God. It is in his power to be constantly doing good for others and helping them to overcome temptation; and in so doing he will reap benefit to himself. He ma ybe a bright and shining light in the world, and at last hear the benediction, ' Well done, thou good and faithful servant.' "

Working for the Youth

As a traveler passes through Switzerland, the guide says to him, " Be careful, don't touch anything like that. There is a pile of snow a thousand feet high, and possibly a loud word will turn it loose, and an avalanche will come." In journeying through the country of life, the Guide who knows that pathway best, bids the traveler, " Be careful." The least tampering with sin may fill the air with temptation, and bring down a snow-slide of woes. Many light-hearted youth are journeying in this path. They would shudder at the thought of bringing upon themselves or others the terrible avalanche which comes as a result of intemperance. Yet they venture to touch this or that, arguing that these little things can do no harm. But good intentions can not save them.

One temperance worker of wide experience has said that ninety-six per cent of those who trifle with the temptations of intemperance are lured on to the drunkard's doom.

Temperance Evangelism 209

Another tells us that nine tenths of the criminals were once Sunday-school children. Again, statistics inform us that the saloons in the United States turn out about six hundred thousand drunkards every year, and of this number one sixth, or one hundred thousand, are boys from sixteen to twenty years old.

Youth who are thus beset with temptations are all about us. The fallen ones should not be neglected; neither should those who have not yet tasted the bitter dregs of intemperance be forgotten. One former is worth many transformers.

WHAT SHALL IT PROFIT A COMMUNITY IF IT GAIN THE WHOLE WORLD AND LOSE ITS OWN BOYS

By permission of Y. M. C. A. Press.

John B. Gough said: "Prevention is better than cure. It is worth a life effort to lift a man from degradation. To prevent his fall is far better." "I have been working a good deal with drinking men," said Dwight L. Moody, "and I think the rest of my work will be with the young. Once in a while a drunkard may stand up for a time and keep away from the cup; but it takes all his strength and all his time to fight against the habit. It is a good deal better to begin when you are young, and never get the habit fostered in you." Help the youth! Help them to help themselves and others. Remember, the worker whose life reflects the principles of true temperance will accomplish most for the youth about him.

The importance of living the precepts we advocate is forcibly shown in the following incident: A young man had been sentenced to twenty years' imprisonment. He was given an opportunity to speak. Facing the crowded court room, he began: " Dr. Pickert, I took my first lesson in gambling from you! You said there was no harm if I did not go in ' too heavy.' I went in too heavy, it seems." The doctor's face grew crimson. Looking at another, he said, " I took my first lesson in forging from you, Mr. Wyatt." A sense of guilt caused the juror addressed to drop his head. The young man scanned the sea of faces before him, and fixed his gaze on a woman; then, choking with emotion, he continued, " I took my first glass of brandy from a lady — a lady who has young sons." Again and again his words sent arrows of conviction to guilty hearts. Finally, lifting his eyes to the gallery, he said: " Father, you had a great future planned for your only son. I'm sorry I've disappointed your hopes and darkened your home. Forgive me." Four months later the judge received the following letter: —

" Judge Morse, I've tried to escape, and am writing this from the hospital ward. I was not quite brave enough to bear the thought that I must pass twenty years in this tomb. I much prefer the one I am about to enter — the grave. I feel sure that if you had been sober the last day of the trial,[1] my sentence would not have been for twenty long years. I tried to escape, and the guard shot me; the doctor says I can not recover, so you see my term will soon end. Be careful of Clarence [the judge's son]; it is pretty hard for young men to resist the temptations that are sanctioned by law, and patronized by those in civil power. Be careful of Clarence; boys follow where men lead, and to be or do like some men is the highest ambition boys have. I followed the wrong kind of examples, but can not die without sending you this parting message: Be careful of Clarence.

" ALBERT RUSHWORTH,

" No. 187, Cell 18."

---

[1] The judge had not only himself been drinking, but had treated the jurors as well.

Temperance Evangelism

Signing the Pledge

"I am not a drunkard." "I can drink or let it alone." "I don't want to bind myself to a pledge." These and other objections temperance workers meet when they seek to secure signers to the pledge. However, "it is foolish egotism," says another, "to say you are too strong to be overcome by that mocker who has conquered such giants as Webster, Pitt, Burns, and Poe." Doubtless all admire Daniel for pledging himself not to defile his body, the Rechabites for their vow of total abstinence from wine, and Paul for putting restraint upon himself both for his own and for others' sake; yet how easy it is to fail to get from the records of ancient heroes the admonition they contain for modern sinners.

The pledge of itself can save no one from intemperance; but it is a constant reminder of Him who can keep the tempted one from yielding, and the very act of signing strengthens the will for its struggle against temptation. The Belgium public schools celebrate a pledge-taking day. During twenty-three years a certain Sunday-school in New York obtained thirteen hundred signers. It is claimed that without a known exception the signers have remained true to their vows, and become pronounced friends of temperance. The temperance pledge was first introduced into the United States in 1789, and thousands testify to its saving influence. It has many friends. Note the sentiment from the following paragraphs: —

The best savings-bank for a young man's money is the total abstinence pledge.— *T. L. Cuyler.*

The old-fashioned temperance pledge,— spread it. . . . There are thousands of persons who, having made a promise, will keep it till the day of Judgment.— *T. De Witt Talmage.*

The man who will not sign a temperance pledge to help a weak brother, though he may not need it himself, is not so much of a man as he thinks himself to be.— *John Wanamaker.*

For thirty years I have been a temperance man. Had it not been for my total abstinence principles in the early days of my temptation, I should probably have gone the same way so many of my companions went, who lived drunkards' lives and are filling drunkards' graves.— *Abraham Lincoln.*

In the first place, the dangers seem to me so real and great, the benefits so meager and doubtful, the bearings of the question so wide and deep, that I count it better definitely to face and decide the question of the use of liquor once for all; and to decide it in the line of abstinence. . . . A pledged total abstinence seems to me desirable because it is the most positive and definite way in which one's influence can be made effective for others.— *Henry Churchill King, President Oberlin College.*

Intemperance, licentiousness, and profanity are sisters. Let every God-fearing youth gird on the armor and press to the front. Put your names on every pledge presented, to give influence to temperance, and to induce others to sign the pledge. Let no feeble, weak excuse be offered as a reason for your refusing to put your name to the temperance pledge. Work for the good of your own souls and for the good of others.— *Mrs. E. G. White.*

Everywhere they [Christian workers] should present to the people the principles of true temperance, and call for signers to the temperance pledge.—*" Ministry of Healing."*

These quotations are sufficient argument, it would seem, to justify all efforts being put forth in behalf of pledge signing.

What Shall We Do?

Many seasons have come and gone since the lamp of true temperance was first placed in the hands of Christians. Many articles have been written on this subject, many periodicals published, many books printed, and many lectures given. What lack we yet? The efforts of voice and pen are to be seconded more heartily by personal example and personal effort. It was said of the scribes, " They say, and do not." This ought not so to be, yet we bow our heads as we confess that often there has been considerable discrepancy between precept and practise.

The call of the hour is to make temperance " a living issue." Not only are we to work for the advancement of what is generally understood as the temperance cause, but we should realize that " the light God has given us on health reform is for our salvation and for the salvation of the world." It must shine in our homes, and from our homes to other homes. It must be permitted to have its bearing upon the question of diet as well as on drink.

Then with the call of the hour comes this solemn warning, " God will not much longer bear with this intemperate generation." " The end of all things is at hand." Time for work is short. All have something to do. Some feel that because they can not join with other Christians in everything, they should unite with them in nothing. But the temperance cause is common ground. " We are not to stand aloof from them; but while there is to be no sacrifice of principle on our part, as far as possible we are to unite with them in laboring for temperance reforms." Circumstances will aid each in determining his specific duty. But for the benefit of those who consecrate their efforts to this work, who make their motto, " No compromise and no cessation of our efforts till victory is gained,"— for their benefit are here added some suggestive extracts: —

" Wherever you go, let your light shine forth. Hand our papers and pamphlets to those with whom you associate, when you are riding on the cars, visiting, conversing with your neighbors."

" Those who are struggling against the power of appetite should be instructed in the principles of healthful living."

" Those who are endeavoring to reform should be provided with employment."

" Open the Bible before the tempted, struggling one, and

over and over again read to him the promises of God."

To do the best work, we must go about it prayerfully, intelligently, and earnestly. We must pray to win, plan to win, and work to win. We should become so familiar with gospel temperance and with the entire gospel that we shall be able to "pass easily and courteously from subjects of a temporal nature to the spiritual and eternal." As we carefully study the temperance movement, let us strive to understand our relation to it just where we are.

> "Just where you stand in the conflict,
> There is your place;
> Just where you think you are useless,
> Hide not your face;
> God placed you there for a purpose,
> Whatever it be;
> Think! he has chosen it for you;
> Work loyally."

This work will require perseverance; but first, last, and always, let us remember that ministering angels precede, accompany, and follow the earnest worker on his mission. Finally, let no disappointments cause us to despair, but, consecrating our efforts daily for the salvation of souls, let us labor on unceasingly, and leave results with God.

> "Our human love and His divine
> Can bridge the chasm o'er;
> And when he bids them go in peace,
> We help them sin no more."

HINTS FOR TEMPERANCE WORKERS

1. Keep your eyes open for items in papers; keep and classify striking ones. Such will be good weapons in temperance warfare.

2. Keep yourself supplied with good temperance literature.

3. Do house-to-house work. Thus you may teach the principles of Christian temperance both by visiting and by handing out well-chosen literature. At the same time signers to the temperance pledge may be obtained.

4. Where possible, organize groups for the study of all phases of the temperance cause; such as, scientific, economic, and moral. A young woman who had once been a member of such a class, after spending some years in India as a missionary, wrote that she received some of her best training in that temperance class, for the greatest need she had found in India was something against intemperance.

5. When possible, organize cooking classes. Teach the principles of dietetic temperance.

6. Encourage all to read temperance literature.

7. Encourage students to write theses or essays on temperance topics.

8. Emphasize the positive side of temperance. Show its value to a life.

9. Attack the *liquor traffic,* not the *liquor-traffic dealer;* the sin, not the sinner.

10. Be kind and courteous in all your work.

How Shall We Treat the Saloon-Keeper?

It is the custom with some temperance workers to rail upon the saloon-keeper, to say hard things about him, and to treat him as though he were intentionally doing all the harm his business is doing.

While every one is and must be responsible, to a large degree at least, for the results of his acts, and while the liquor business is and ever must be an evil and a blighting curse, it is better, for the most part, to deal with the evil rather than to rail upon those who, through mercenary motives, are parties to it. Saloon-keepers are men, and should be treated as such, though engaged in a bad business. This was the policy pursued by Francis Murphy.

A case is related in which the children of a certain saloon-keeper were ostracized at school, and his family generally shunned in society; and yet, as the result of a kindly act on the part of a gospel minister, he was led to give up his business and become a Christian.

Though some are greater sinners than others, all have souls to save or lose; all need salvation. This fact the true Christian will ever recognize. W. A. COLCORD.

Tempt Not Others

The minister of a church was charged with "the excessive use of intoxicants," and when announcing his resignation from the pulpit, he told his congregation that "he had learned to drink in their homes. The first time he ever tasted wine, he said, was at the home of a member of the congregation, who was now one of his accusers."—*Present Truth.*

Pass It On

"Have you found the heavenly light; pass it on!
Souls are groping in the night; daylight gone!
Hold thy lighted lamp on high —
Be a star in some one's sky;
He may live who else would die; pass it on!
Be not selfish in thy greed; pass it on!
Look upon thy brother's need; pass it on!
Live for self, you live in vain;
Live for Christ, you live again;
Live for him, with him you reign; pass it on!"

THE TEMPERANCE PLEDGE

The temperance pledge is the Magna Charta of my liberty.— *George Dodds.*

Kaiser William recently pledged himself to total abstinence for life; so did Hon. William H. Taft, President of the United States of America.

What He Pledged

In replying to objections to signing the pledge, a reformed drunkard said: " Strong drink occasioned me to have more to do with pledging than ever teetotalism has done. When I used strong drink, I pledged my coat, I pledged my bed, I pledged, in short, everything that was pledgable, and was losing every hope and blessing, when a temperance friend met me, and convinced me of my folly. Then I pledged myself, and soon got other things out of pledge, and got more than my former property about me."

Lincoln's Temperance Pledge

Abraham Lincoln, when offered wine at a great banquet, publicly refused, and stated that he had been fifty years an abstainer. To the friend who persuaded him to sign the pledge, he said: " I owe more to you than to almost any one else of whom I can think."

Pledge Written, Signed, and Advocated by Abraham Lincoln

" *Whereas,* The use of intoxicating liquors as a beverage is productive of pauperism, degradation, and crime, and believing it is our duty to discourage that which produces more evil than good, we therefore pledge ourselves to abstain from the use of intoxicating liquors as a beverage."

TOTAL ABSTINENCE

I never took a teetotaler to York Castle [prison] in my life, nor to Wakefield House of Correction, either.— *New York Policeman.*

When the mind is paralyzed, the moral nature stands defenseless before the temptations to which it is most inclined. — *Dr. D. H. Kress.*

Never was there a person who regretted that he had never used tobacco or liquor.— *Selected.*

Only a clear brain can think God's thoughts after him. Only a steady hand can glorify the divine Carpenter. Only a heart unhurried by artificial stimulants can be loyal in its love to Christ and humanity.— *Frances E. Willard.*

Is there no middle way betwixt total abstinence and excess which kills you? For your sake, reader, and that you may never attain to my experience, with pain I must utter the dreadful truth, there is none.— *Charles Lamb, in "Confessions of a Drunkard."*

The only safe way of drinking . . . is "to leave off before you begin."— *Canon Farrar.*

A wine-glass is never *right side* up until it is *upside* down.— *Selected.*

Dr. Cartwright, of New Orleans, who served through the great yellow fever epidemic there, said, " About five thousand of them [the regular drinkers] died before the epidemic touched a single sober man so far as I can get at the facts."

Nansen, the Swedish explorer, when asked if he used liquor when traveling in the arctic regions, said: "No; if I had, I should never have returned alive."

Dr. Lorenz, one of the world's greatest surgeons, said, when wine was offered to him: " My success as a surgeon depends upon my brain being clear, my muscles firm, and my nerves steady. No one can take alcoholic liquors without blunting these physical powers, which I must keep always on edge. As a surgeon, I must not drink, as it would make me unfit for duty."

R. J. Newman, an Indian trader of Darlington, Oklahoma, says: " The Cheyenne and Arapahoe Indians are fine people. Most of them work hard, are prosperous, and own their own homes. They don't drink."

Thomas A. Edison, the great inventor and electrician, on being asked once by Miss Frances E. Willard what led him to become a total abstainer, said, " I think it was because I had better use for my head."

Cruikshank, the artist, offered five hundred dollars for proof of a violent crime committed by a total abstainer; and the money remains unclaimed to this day.

" Abraham Lincoln promised his mother, a few days before her death, that he would never drink intoxicating liquor. This promise, made when a boy, he ever faithfully kept. In the days when drinking was almost universal, he was regarded as peculiar."

I was born a teetotaler, and I signed the pledge very early, and I sign it again and again, every time I get a chance. I have two reasons for abstaining: First, I believe it is best for me, and, secondly, even if I imagined I was strong enough to withstand the temptations of drink, I am not willing that my example as a Christian should lead others astray.— *W. J. Bryan.*

SIGNAL LIGHTS

It comes in the issue to one of two things: either the body must conquer, or the soul must conquer.— JOSEPH PARKER.

A Loyal Temperance Lad

A little fellow, the son of poor parents, had been brought up to hate the drink evil and everything connected with it. It was hard for the father to feed so many mouths, so, at an age when most boys are in school, the lad was forced to become an apprentice. He was a stanch teetotaler, and he was fearless in his determination not to allow himself to be defiled by drunken associations.

The very first morning, the foreman of the shop offered him a glass of beer. "No, thank you," said the lad, "I never touch that stuff." "Look here, youngster," replied the foreman, "we have no teetotalers here." "If you have me, you'll have one," answered the boy, bravely, yet respectfully.

The foreman was irritated at this opposition to his wishes, and, holding up the glass of beer, he said: "Now, my boy, there's only one master here, and you'll have this drink either inside or outside."

The little fellow looked up brightly, yet with a resolute face that showed the purpose in his heart: "Well, sir, you can do as you please. I brought my clean jacket with me, and a good character. You may spoil my jacket, but you sha'n't spoil my character."

Of course such resolution won the day, and the lad was permitted to go his own way without further trouble with the foreman. In his heart, the man respected the brave loyalty to principle shown in the outset by so young a boy, and he proved a true friend. The men tried jibes and sneers, but the master forbade anything of the sort so emphatically that it ceased, and the lad soon made them all friends by his unselfish, obliging ways.— *Sophie Bronson Titterington.*

What the Reformed Drunkard Lost

" I have been thinking about the losses I have met with since I signed the temperance pledge. I tell you there is not a man in the society that has lost more by stopping drink than I have. Wait a bit till I tell you what I mean. There was a nice job of work to be done in the shop to-day, and the boss called for me.

"' Give it to Law,' says he; ' he's the best hand in the shop.'

" Well, I told my wife at supper time, and she says, ' Why, Laurie, he used to call you the worst! You've lost your bad name, haven't you?'

"' That's a fact, wife,' says I; ' and it ain't all I've lost in the last six months, either. I had poverty and wretchedness, and I've lost them. I had an old ragged coat and a shockin' bad hat, and some waterproof boots that let the wet out at the toes as fast as they took it in at the heels. I've lost *them*. I had a red face and a trembling hand, and a pair of shaky legs that gave me an awful tumble now and then. I had a habit of cursing and swearing, and I've got rid of *that*. I had an aching head and a heavy heart, and, worse than all the rest, a guilty conscience. I thank God I've lost them all!'

" Then I told my wife what *she* had lost. ' You had an old ragged gown, Mary,' says I, ' and you had trouble and sorrow, and a poor, wretched home and plenty of heartaches, for you had a miserable drunkard for a husband. Mary, Mary! thank the Lord for all that you and I have *lost* since I signed the Good Samaritan Pledge!'"

Freedom or Slavery?

A man said: " I won't sign the pledge because I won't sign away my liberty." " What liberty?" " Liberty to do as I please." Is that liberty? Any man who does as he pleases, independently of physical, moral, and divine law, is a mean, miserable slave. There is not so pitiful a slave that crawls on the face of this earth as the man who is the slave of evil habits and evil passions. What is it to be free? To be capable of self-government is to be free. To abandon every habit that you consider to be wrong, is to be free. To fight against that which holds you in bondage, is to be free. A man who overcomes an evil habit is a hero.

I knew a man who said he would give up the use of tobacco. He took his plug of tobacco out of his pocket and threw it away, and said, "That is the end of the job." But it was only the beginning. He found the very tip of his tongue clamoring for it. He said: "I will go and get another. I will buy another plug, and when I want it awfully, then I will take a little." And he did want it awfully, and took his knife and his piece of tobacco, and then he thought God's Spirit was striving with him. He held the tobacco in his hand and said: "I love you, and I want you. Are you my master, or am I yours? That is a question I am going to settle. You are a weed, and I am a man. You are a thing, and I am a man. I will master you if I die for it. It never shall be said of me again, 'There is a man mastered by a thing.' I want you, but I will just take care of you. I will fight you right through." He said it was six months before he could get over the desire for that tobacco; but he fought it right through.

That man was a hero. A hero has to battle against an enemy. Cocks can fight, and dogs can fight; but for a man to battle against himself, to conquer every evil desire and wicked passion in the sacred name of duty, that is to be brave.—*John B. Gough.*

"Take a Drop"

"Come in, Patrick, and take a drop of something," said one Irishman to another.

"No, Mike; I'm afraid of drops ever since Tim Flaherty died."

"Well, what about Tim?"

"He was one of the liveliest fellows in these parts. But he began the drop business in Barney Shannon's saloon. It was a drop of something out of a bottle at first. But in a little while Tim took a few drops too much, and then he dropped into the gutter. He dropped his place, he dropped his coat and hat, he dropped his money; he dropped everything but his thirst for strong drink. Poor Tim! But the worst is to come. He got crazy with drink one day, and killed a man. And the last time I saw him, he was taking his last drop, with a slip-noose around his neck. I have quit the dropping business, Mike. I have seen too many good fellows when whisky had the drop on them. They took just a drop from the bottle, then they dropped into the gutter, and then they dropped into the grave. No rumseller can get a drop in me any more, and if you don't drop him, Mike, he will drop you."

The whisky business is a lawless desperado. It tries to "get the drop" on boys and girls, on men and women, on politicians and officers. The train robber presents his pistol, with the demand, "Your money or your life." Rum gives no such alternative; its demand is, "*Your money and your life.*" — *Selected.*

The Courage of His Convictions

After Mr. Henry Wilson was elected to the United States Senate, he gave his friends a dinner at a noted Boston hotel. The table was set with not a wine-glass upon it.

"Where are the wine-glasses?" asked several, loud enough to remind their host that some of his guests did not like sitting down to a wineless dinner.

"Gentlemen," said Mr. Wilson, rising and speaking with a great deal of feeling, "you know my friendship for you and my obligations to you. Great as they are, they are not great enough to make me forget the rock whence I was hewn and the pit whence I was dug. Some of you know how the error of intemperance overshadowed my youth. That I might esscape, I fled from my early surroundings and changed my name. For what I am, I am indebted under God to my temperance vow and my adherence to it.

"Call for what you want to eat, and if this hotel can provide it, it shall be forthcoming. But wines and liquors can not come to this table with my consent, because I will not spread in the path of another the snare from which I escaped."

Three rousing cheers showed the brave senator that men admired the man who has the courage of his conviction.— *Selected*.

Sixteen Lost, One Saved

At a public dinner given to General Harrison, when he was a candidate for the office of president of the United States, one of the guests, rather conspicuously, "drank to his health." The general pledged his toast by drinking water. Another gentleman offered a toast, and said, " General, will you favor me by drinking a glass of wine?" The general, in a very gentlemanly way, begged to be excused. He was again urged to join in a glass of wine. This was too much. He rose from his seat, and said, in a most dignified manner: —

"Gentlemen, I have twice refused to partake of the winecup. I hope that will be sufficient. Though you press the matter ever so much, not a drop shall pass my lips. I made a resolve when I started in life that I would avoid strong drink. That vow I have never broken. I am one of a class of seventeen young men who were graduated at college together. The other sixteen members of my class now fill drunkards' graves — and all from the pernicious habit of wine drinking. I owe all my health, my happiness, and my prosperity to that resolution. Would you urge me to break it now?"

The effect on the company may be imagined.— *Selected*.

Poor Rosy

Jennie Williams and Kittie Bruce and Cora Mills had come to spend the afternoon with Nellie Evans.

It was a lovely place they had to play in, under the great old trees, with a swing and a hammock and a croquet ground, besides looking forward to tea in the summer-house.

They were in the full tide of play, having a splendid time, when Cora Mills exclaimed: "If there dosen't come Bessie Blynn, with that old red book that she is always poking in everybody's face, trying to get them to sign the pledge. I do wish she wouldn't come over here spoiling our fun. What do girls want to sign a pledge for, anyway? Ladies never drink. As if there was any danger of our getting so low! Don't let's sign it."

Cora thought herself a very wise little girl, though she was only ten.

"O girls!" said Bessie, as she came up the hill, "I'm glad I found so many of you together; you will all put your names in my temperance pledge-book, won't you? I'm trying to see how many names I can get before our next meeting."

The other little girls looked at Cora, expecting her to be spokesman, but she did not feel so brave about speaking out her mind now. Bessie was a tall girl of fourteen, and one of the best scholars in the school.

"Let's see how many names you have already," said Kittie Bruce. "Why, here's Raymie Albright's name; sweet little fellow! he's printed it himself; and here's Harry Winslow's, too; what a pretty writer he is!"

"Come, girls!" said Nellie, "let us go and talk to mother about it; I know she'll let me sign it, though. Mother is a great temperance woman."

The girls all followed Nellie up on the piazza, and Mrs. Evans welcomed them smilingly.

"Certainly you may sign it, Nellie," she said, after they

had talked the matter over a little. "I will put my name down too, because I want to help along this temperance society all I can."

"I'll sign it," said Jennie, "then maybe my brother Johnnie will. Some boys no bigger than he is go to saloons, they say, and drink beer. I mean to do everything in the world I can to make him a temperance boy. Boys have so many temptations." And Jennie looked troubled.

"That's right," said Mrs. Evans; "let us look out for these brothers."

"Well, I'll sign it," frank little Kittie said, "because I guess I'm in danger myself. I love cider so that I can't let it alone if there's a bit in the house. I'm just wild after it; somebody sent mama a pitcher full the other day, and I felt as if I could drink it all myself."

The girls laughed at this, except Cora. She said: "I'd be ashamed, Kittie Bruce. I shall not sign it, because I am not in danger. I don't think I shall ever get so low that I can't keep from doing anything that isn't genteel."

"Sit down, girls," said Mrs. Evans; "let me tell you a true story. You have all seen old Rosy, who drives the two dogs hitched to a cart, and goes about gathering up garbage, and looking scarcely human, with her hard, brown face, ragged dress, and bare feet. You must get Grandma Brown to tell you how, forty years ago, she was a beautiful young woman. She moved in the best society, and had a great many friends. Mrs. Brown says they went into company together a great deal, and Rosy was usually the belle of the evening. She said, too, that Rosy was the most beautiful bride she ever saw. She was dressed in white silk, with a long white veil, fastened with a white wreath, and her cheeks had such a soft, lovely color that Rose was the very name for her."

"Did old Rosy ever look like that?" the girls said, all in one voice.

"Yes, and she married a very fine young man. They

went to housekeeping in their new home, pretty as a bird's-nest; but something was wrong about that home. The husband and wife did not seem happy; the wife acted strangely, and some thought she was growing insane. But it all came out after a time. Rosy had formed the habit of drinking! She did it in quite a genteel way, Cora. She sipped small tastes of wine at first, from delicate little glasses, when she was out at evening parties. Then she grew so fond of it that she spent her pocket money on the choicest wines, and drank in secret. She had two sweet children, and her husband gave her plenty of money to dress them with, but they looked like beggar children; the money all went for wine and brandy. When her husband found out how it was, he tried to reform her; he took away all her money, and watched her closely. But it was all of no use; she contrived to get her brandy in some way or other.

"After a few years her husband died. What property she could get hold of she soon used up, and at last became very poor. Some kind people took her children from her and cared for them.

"Rosy would do any sort of work for money enough to get a drink. The mistress of the elegant home went out washing. Finally she sank so low that nobody wanted her even for that work, and now she is what you see her. One would never guess that old Rosy and Mrs. Edward Berkley were the same person. If only somebody had come to Rosy when she was a little girl, and asked her to sign the pledge, how different her life might have been!

"Perhaps girls are not so strongly tempted as boys, but, my dear little women, you will never regret it if you become firm teetotalers now; for then, as Jennie says, 'it will help Johnnie.'"

"Poor old Rosy!" said Kittie, "I shall never laugh at her again." She and Jennie put their names in the book, and Cora came down so much as to say that if it would help anybody else, she was willing to sign, but for herself she needed no pledge.— *Mrs. C. M. Livingston.*

RECITATIONS

What Came From Signing the Pledge

We have lots of nice things at our house these times,
    And lots of money, too;
So many nickels and so many dimes,
    We hardly know what to do.

For papa has changed his mind, you know,
    And instead of throwing away
A nickel here and a nickel there,
    A dozen times a day,

In those horrid saloons, as he used to do,
    He brings them every one home;
Dear mama has the most of them,
    But Susie and I have some.

We often used to be hungry and cold,
    And mama would cry all day,
And papa used to be naughty and cross,
    And we had to hide away;

But now he's as good as good can be,
    And seems to love us so;
He don't leave us alone at night any more,
    As he used to long ago.

He says it's all from signing the pledge —
    What a splendid thing it must be!
To bring again such happiness
    To mama and Susie and me!

                      — *Virginia J. Kent.*

Dare to Say "No"

Dare to say No when you're tempted to drink;
Pause for a moment, my brave boy, and think —
Think of the wrecks upon life's ocean tossed
For answering Yes without counting the cost;
Think of the mother who bore you in pain;
Think of the tears that will fall like the rain;
Think of her heart, and how cruel the blow;
Think of her love, and at once answer, "No."
Think of the hopes that are drowned in the bowl;
Think of the danger to body and soul;
Think of sad lives once as pure as the snow;
Look at them now, and at once answer, "No."
Think of manhood with rum-tainted breath;
Think how the glass leads to sorrow and death;
Think of the homes, that, now shadowed with woe,
Might have been heaven had the answer been No;
Think of lone graves both unwept and unknown,
Hiding fond hopes that were fair as your own;
Think of proud forms now forever laid low,
That still might be here had they learned to say No;
Think of the demon that lurks in the bowl,
Driving to ruin both body and soul,—
Think of all this as life's journey you go,
And when you're assailed by the tempter, say, "No."
— *Selected.*

Danger!

Write it on the workhouse gate;
Write it on the schoolboy's slate;
Write it on the copy-book,
That the young may often look:
 "Where there's drink, there's danger!"

Write it on the churchyard mound,
Where the rum-slain dead are found;
Write it on the gallows high;
Write it for all passers-by:
 "Where there's drink, there's danger!"

Write it in the nation's laws,
Blotting out the license clause;
Write it on each ballot white,
So it can be read aright:
  "Where there's drink, there's danger!"

Write it on the ships that sail,
Borne along by storm or gale;
Write it large in letters plain,
Over every land and main:
  "Where there's drink, there's danger!"

Write it over every gate,
On the church and halls of state,
In the heart of every band,
On the laws of every land:
  "Where there's drink, there's danger!"

—*Selected.*

Come, Sign the Pledge To-night

(To be sung to the tune of "The Son of God Goes Forth to War.")

To those enslaved by alcohol,
  Who wish to break the chain,
We come to give a helping hand,
  To make them free again.

CHORUS:

Come, sign the pledge; 'twill make you free;
  Have courage to do right!
A better time you'll never see:
  Then sign the pledge to-night.

A mother or a sister dear
  Will joy to see the sight;
A wife or child perchance 'twill cheer:
  Then come and sign to-night.

We say to those who never felt
  The power of appetite,
"A weaker brother needs your help:"
  Then come and sign to-night.

—*Will Scott.*

TEMPERANCE MEETINGS

"Be satisfied with nothing but your best."

"The surest way not to fail is to determine to succeed."

"Thy soul must overflow
 If thou another soul would reach !
It takes the overflow of heart
 To give the lips full speech."

WHAT TEMPERANCE WORKERS SHOULD TEACH

Temperance Workers Should Teach

1. History of intemperance.
2. Effect of liquor, tobacco, and other forms of intemperance on the human system. (Use experiments.)
3. Poverty, crime, insanity, immorality, and disease caused by intemperance.
4. Dangers of moderate use of liquor, tobacco, drugs, etc.
5. Subtility of liquor, drugs, and tobacco to create an appetite for themselves, and the great difficulty of breaking the habits when once formed.
6. Failure of alcohol and drugs to cure disease, or upbuild the system.
7. Waste of money.
8. Relation of diet to intemperance.
9. Intemperance as an obstacle to positions of trust.
10. Intemperance as an obstacle to the spread of the gospel.
11. History of temperance efforts.
12. Lives of temperance workers.
13. Duty of lawmakers.
14. Fallacy of high license.
15. Duty of Christians.
16. Value of total abstinence to a life.

SUGGESTIONS FOR PROGRAMS

The Central Theme

Make the temperance meeting a success. Plan to meet the actual needs about you, then work your plan. Do not try to tell your audience all that is known about temperance. Have a definite aim in view — a central theme. Have one or two strong papers or addresses bearing directly on that theme, and then see to it that all other exercises give convincing and appealing emphasis to it. Remember "sheet lightning is non-destructive, but when concentrated, it becomes a mighty power."

Prayer

"Let us advance upon our knees," will be a good motto for temperance meetings. Be not among those who will do everything to make their work a success except pray for it. Remember also that the shirking of him who prays, and the praying of him who shirks, are both an abomination unto the Lord. Pray for the children, the youth, the parents, the homes, the government. Pray for the enslaved and the free. Pray not because it is good form, but because God hears and answers prayer.

Music

Well-chosen hymns, sung with spirit and energy, carry conviction. The following are a few of the good gospel and temperance songs: "Dare to Do Right," "Yield Not to Temptation," "Dare to Be a Daniel," "Throw out the Life-Line," "Rescue the Perishing," "What Shall the Harvest Be?" "Where Is My Wandering Boy To-night?" "The Bird With the Broken Pinion."

Scripture Lessons

"The weapons of our warfare are not carnal, but mighty through God to the pulling down of strongholds;" therefore the Scripture lesson should be a part of the program. Claim the promise in Isa. 55:11. Vary the method of giving the Scripture lesson. Here are a few suggestions: —

1. Have a short Bible reading, given by one individual, on such subjects as —

    (*a*) Solomon on temperance.
    (*b*) Warnings of Isaiah.
    (*c*) Paul's attitude toward temperance.
    (*d*) Bible temperance.

2. Reading of one text followed by a few *pointed* remarks.

3. Responsive reading.

    (*a*) Leader and audience.
    (*b*) Young men and young women.

4. Questions and answers for responsive reading.

5. Bible temperance heroes.

    (*a*) Daniel (Daniel 1).
    (*b*) Rechabites (Jeremiah 35).
    (*c*) John the Baptist (Luke 1:13-17).

6. Bible temperance order — the Nazarites (Num. 6:1-21; Lam. 4:7).

Blackboard Exercise

1. Write upon the board these words: "Men whom we all want to be total abstainers." As the audience suggests names, write them on the board, such as judges, surgeons, teachers, preachers, engineers, sea captains.

2. Write the words: "This is the house that rum built." Place a brace after the sentence. Get suggestions, such as, poorhouse, jail, penitentiary, reform school, insane asylum.

3. Draw a bottle and place on it the words of Hab. 2:15. Draw a glass and write on it the words of Prov. 23:20.

4. Draw a barrel. On the top of it write "whisky." On its side write some results of drink, such as, hunger, sorrow, crime, poverty, tears, death, loss of home, loss of heaven.

Charts

On a large paper placard print neatly some striking statistics, as, for instance, how the amount of money used for liquor or tobacco compares with that expended for foreign missions, for food, etc. Show that liquor makes about one hundred thousand graves yearly in the United States, etc.

Mottoes

Display on a blackboard or wall statements or mottoes bearing on the temperance question. For example: "The saloon wants your boy. Can you spare him?" "Wanted: a nice cottage in exchange for a choice lot of liquors." "Every man that striveth for the mastery is temperate in all things." "Where there's drink, there's danger." "If sinners entice thee, consent thou not."

Miscellaneous

1. A little paper of current temperance news would be a beneficial feature of a temperance program. Make the items short, pithy, and spicy.

2. A question box often adds interest. Let no answers be drawn out into lengthy talks.

3. Select brief quotations, and copy on cards which are numbered. Distribute these, if possible, before meeting, as it may bring some who would otherwise be absent. At the meeting call for the reading of these by number.

4. Have a roll-call with responsive quotations on temperance from noted people.

5. Select individuals to give talks on various phases of temperance. Limit each speech to two minutes.

6. "Temperance Catechism," page 194, and "Saloon Catechism," page 47, can be used for dialogue.

7. Perform some simple experiment, with a talk.

8. Cartoons reproduced on larger scale are very good.

SUGGESTIONS FOR A YOUNG PEOPLE'S TEMPERANCE RALLY

1. Appoint a good strong committee to plan for work and to prepare the program.

2. Ask other young people's societies to help.

3. See that every number on your program bears on temperance.

4. Let your program be practical — adapted to help the local temperance workers.

5. Make your program an evidence that you stand for total abstinence and for the total abolition of the liquor traffic.

6. Have chalk talks, charts, mottoes, etc.

7. Have good music, good recitations, etc., and all well rendered.

8. Have pledges on hand, and invite all to sign.

9. Have an exhibit of the best temperance literature you have.

10. Arrange to receive strangers at the door and seat them, and see that all visitors are spoken to before they leave.

11. Insist on every part being thoroughly learned. Rehearse! Rehearse!

12. Let not your program be too long. Josh Billings says, " I do not care how much you say just so you say it in a few words."

TEMPERANCE RALLIES AT CAMP-MEETINGS

Experience has demonstrated that much good may be accomplished by holding temperance rallies at camp-meetings, and other like gatherings, where circumstances are favorable. When properly conducted, they bring blessings to the meetings themselves, make good impressions upon many, and materially advance the temperance cause. The fact that there is no time to be lost in rescuing those about to go over the great Niagara of intemperance should lead to the holding of many such rallies. The following are a few suggestions as to how to plan for these and conduct them: —

Arrange for a number of addresses and appropriate songs. Several short, clear-cut addresses on different phases of the question will generally be found to be more interesting and effective than one or two long ones.

Select some suitable person to act as chairman.

In arranging the program, take special care that the opening and closing addresses are made by those whose views are well known, and who will give the right turn and wind-up to the meeting.

Wisdom and caution should be exercised in securing outside speakers. Learn from good authority who are representative temperance workers in the community. Whether they are eloquent speakers is not of so much concern as is their standing and influence in the community, especially in the temperance cause. After learning who these are, let two or three representative individuals visit them, laying before them clearly the character of the rally to be held, and inviting them to take part. Have it understood that no points of difference in matters of faith are desired or expected in any of the addresses delivered, thus avoiding any embarrassment that might otherwise occur.

In one of the addresses a plain, straightforward statement can be made as to the province and limits of civil authority, to the effect that while religious legislation on the part of civil government is out of place, it is within the province of the state to prohibit crime, or that which breeds crime and disorder; that the state should prohibit the liquor traffic because it is a menace to society, a burden to the state, a despoiler of homes, and a breeder of crime and disorder generally. The state has no right to permit, much less to legalize, license, and receive a revenue from a traffic whose whole history shows that it produces such baleful results.

And do not let the personal, individual side, and the hopeful side, of temperance be overlooked.

Addresses can be given or papers read on such topics as, "The Evils of Intemperance," "The Curse of the Liquor Traffic," "Does Prohibition Prohibit?" "Does Prohibition Invade Personal Liberty?" "Revenue Versus the Cost of the Liquor Traffic," "Prevention Better Than Cure," "The Responsibility of Parents," "What Young People May Do," "Interesting Incidents," "Testimony of Eminent Men," and "Signing the Pledge."

It is well to have well-prepared resolutions ready to present at the conclusion of the addresses. The one on page 244 may be taken as a sample.

If the chairman feels confident of a practically unanimous approval, he can call for a rising vote.

At the close of the rally, have temperance pledges at hand, and invite the people to sign. Also have some good temperance literature ready to place in the hands of the people.

See that good reports of the meeting are prepared and furnished the local newspapers.

After the arrangements for the rally have been made, notices of it should be inserted in the newspapers, and announcements may be gotten out and circulated. These will help to secure a good attendance. W. A. COLCORD.

THIRTY TOPICS FOR TEMPERANCE PAPERS, ESSAYS, OR TALKS

1. Water the All-Sufficient Beverage of Man.
2. The Woman's Christian Temperance Union.
3. Tobacco Legislation.
4. Should Alcohol Be Used as a Medicine?
5. Curse of Intemperance in Heathen Lands.
6. Our Duty and Responsibility.
7. Which —" The Old Oaken Bucket " or " The Little Brown Jug "?
8. The Safety of Never Beginning.
9. Intemperance and Positions of Trust.
10. The Cost of the Liquor Traffic.
11. Personal Liberty and Prohibition.
12. The Value of Total Abstinence to a Life.
13. Why I Signed the Pledge.
14. The Cigarette Curse.
15. Tea and Coffee.
16. Foundation of Intemperance in the Kitchen.
17. Fruits of the Liquor Traffic.
18. The Great American Fraud (Patent Medicines).
19. Bible Temperance.
20. Progress of the Temperance Movement.
21. Temperance Education.
22. Relation of Vegetarianism to Temperance.
23. Autointoxication.
24. The Drug Habit.
25. Prohibition or High License, Which?
26. Does Prohibition Prohibit?
27. Noted Temperance Workers.
28. The Responsibility of Parents.
29. The Responsibility of the Church.
30. The Responsibility of the State.

SIMPLE EXPERIMENTS

Experiments will aid in holding attention and in securing facts in memory. Have all the things you will need ready for use — matches, a few dishes, lamp (filled), etc. See to it that no experiment be a failure.

1. Alcohol burns with blue flame and great heat. Pour a very little alcohol in a plate. Light a match to it. Notice the color of flame, also heat.

2. Sometimes when mixed with other substances, alcohol is hard to detect; but the peculiar blue flame always reveals it. When a substance contains more than forty per cent of alcohol, it will burn as in experiment No. 1, and will give a blue flame. Test whisky, paragoric, Jamaica ginger, etc. The burning of any alcoholic liquid on a plate proves that forty per cent or more of the liquid is alcohol.

3. If a liquid containing alcohol will not burn on a plate, try heating it. The vapor of alcohol will burn. However, if the liquid contains less than ten per cent of alcohol, it is hard to detect the presence of alcohol by means of these simple experiments. When the liquid is about to boil, hold a lighted match over it, and if sufficient alcohol is present, the escaping vapor will ignite.

4. Alcohol is not a natural product. It is the product of fermentation. Test fresh grape juice, or fresh fruit juice of any kind, by any of the foregoing methods, or by any method.

5. Alcohol affects albumen. Put the white of an egg into a glass. Pour over it some alcohol. Soon the egg becomes hardened. Remember the blood, the brain, and other tissues of the body contain albumen. Note the inevitable effect on these — hardening, shrinking, drying up.

6. Test the effect of alcohol upon meat. Put a piece of

Temperance Meetings 241

raw beef into a bottle of alcohol. Close it. Let it stand a few days. The meat hardens and shrinks, for alcohol coagulates the albumen, and draws the water out.

7. Place a small amount of whisky in a receptacle. An equal amount of Hostetter's Bitters in another. Light both. The one burning the longer and the more readily contains the larger proportion of alcohol.

Take some small crystals of potassium bichromate and

BURNING ALCOHOL IN PATENT MEDICINES

add some strong sulphuric acid. Shake or let it stand until the liquid turns to a very dark brown. This makes the test solution, which, being heavy, will drop to the bottom suspected alcoholic liquor, and add a drop or two of the test solution, which, being heavy, will drop to the bottom of the tube and give a deep-green color. If shaken, the whole liquid will become green. This is a very simple test, and will enable one to detect five or even as low as two and one-half per cent of alcohol.

NOTE.— By use of a simply made distilling apparatus any liquid containing alcohol may be distilled until it contains a large enough per cent of alcohol to burn. Such an apparatus may be made from an ordinary teapot, a wide-mouthed bottle, and a short piece of rubber tubing. Stand the bottle in a pan of cracked ice or icewater. Place the teapot over a fire. Put one end of the rubber tubing over the spout of the teapot and put the other into the bottle. Put the liquid to be distilled into the teapot, and cover it. As the liquid boils, the vapor will pass through the tube into the bottle, where it will be condensed.

SAMPLE PROGRAMS AND PLEDGES

An Hour With John B. Gough

Opening Exercises.

Roll-Call: Quotations from Gough.

Sketch: "The Greatest Leader of the Modern Temperance Reform."

Solo: "The Drunkard's Lament"— written by J. B. Gough (page 67).

Reading: "Freedom or Slavery" (page 221).

Short Talk: "How Gough's Life Helps Me."

Trial of King Alcohol

The evils of drink can be forcibly presented in the form of a trial of King Alcohol for deception, theft, immorality, murder, the wrecking of homes, and causing poverty, unhappiness, political corruption, disease, and death. Let the leader of the meeting, or some one specially appointed, make a statement of the accusation, and have different ones personifying science, etc., bear their testimony, while some one representing alcohol will present the defense, bringing in the usual arguments adduced in support of the liquor traffic. The judge should then instruct the jury, consisting of the audience, and call for the vote on "guilty" or "not guilty," after which he should pronounce the sentence in a well-prepared speech.

Opening Song.

Prayer.

Scripture Reading: Saloon-Keeper's Psalm (Ps. 10: 5-11).

Song: "Where There's Drink, There's Danger."

Reading: Statement of the Accusation.

Testimonies Against King Alcohol (three-minute talks or papers on): —

Experiences of a Drunkard; Science; Economy; Society; The Home; Religion; Morality.

King Alcohol's Defense (five-minute talk). Revenue, Social Function, etc.

Song: "Down in the Licensed Saloon."

Statement of Case to Jury.
Pronouncement of the Sentence (seven minutes).
Song: "Anti-Saloon Battle Hymn."

Petition Against the Manufacture and Sale of Liquors
To the Honorable [*Legislative Body*]:

We, the undersigned, adult residents of ——, believing the liquor traffic to be a menace to the peace and welfare of the community, a prolific source of crime, and therefore a matter which may properly be dealt with by civil legislation, respectfully but earnestly urge the passage of ——, entitled "A Bill to Prohibit the Manufacture and Sale of Intoxicating Liquors in ——."

A Resolution

Whereas, The liquor traffic is a menace to the peace and welfare of the home, a burden to the state, a curse to the community, and is sapping the moral foundation of society; therefore,—

Resolved, That we hereby express ourselves as unalterably opposed to the liquor traffic, and in favor of municipal, state, national, and world-wide prohibition.

Temperance Pledges

Realizing the importance of having my mind and body in the best possible condition, both for the happiness of myself and of those with whom I associate, I hereby solemnly promise, by God's help, to abstain from the use of tobacco, alcoholic drinks, and other narcotic poisons, and to do what I can for the cause of true temperance.

Realizing the importance of having my mind and body in the best possible condition to do God's service and to withstand the evil influences of these last days, I hereby solemnly promise, by God's help, to abstain from the use of tea, coffee, tobacco, alcoholic drinks, and other stimulants and narcotic poisons; to exercise temperance in all things according to the light which God has given me; and to do what I can for the cause of true temperance.

BIBLIOGRAPHY

Leaflets

1. Judge Morse's Reasons (100 for 25 cents).
2. A Thing to Cry Over, by Rev. John Hall (100 for 20 cents).
3. What a Christian Can Do, by Rev. R. S. Holmes (100 for 25 cents).
4. Battles Fought and Won, by Rev. Geo. C. Wilding (100 for 15 cents).
5. Drink Like a Gentleman (100 for 15 cents).
6. African Missions and the Liquor Traffic, by Robert E. Speer (100 for 15 cents).
7. A Boy's Determination, by Elbertine Robertson (100 for 15 cents).
8. The Temperance Pledge, by Rev. Francis J. Collier (100 for 25 cents).
9. The Draft That Quenches Thirst (100 for 20 cents).
10. Temperance Recitations (several numbers; 100 for $1).
11. Why Mark Never Became a Printer (50 for 15 cents).
12. Minister or a Saloon-Keeper — Which? (50 for 15 cents).
13. The Deacon and the Drunkard's Ditch, by Rev. Geo. M. Hammel (10 for 20 cents; 50 for 50 cents).
14. Christian Patriotism, by John G. Woolley (10 for 20 cents; 50 for 50 cents).
15. Gran'sir Saxon's Vote, by Mrs. O. W. Scott (5 or less for 3 cents each; 50 for 50 cents).
16. How the Dram-Shop Helps Business, by Prof. Geo. E. Foster (100 for 30 cents).
17. The Liquor Traffic and Foreign Missions, by Mrs. Marion Dunham (100 for 30 cents).
18. Prohibition Means Homes (50 for 15 cents).

19. Why I Am a Prohibitionist, by Frances E. Willard (50 for 15 cents).

20. Why I Pledge Against Cider, by Sallie B. Hoskins (50 for 20 cents).

21. What Can We Do? by Ada Melville Shaw (50 for 15 cents).

22. The Tobacco Habit and Its Effects Upon School Work, by H. H. Seerley (50 for 20 cents).

23. The Rights of Those Who Dislike Tobacco, by Anna Garlin Spencer (100 for 30 cents).

24. Restriction of Prohibition, by Neal Dow (100 for 30 cents).

25. How to Make Prohibition Prohibit, by Neal Dow (100 for 30 cents).

26. Fallacies of High License, by Frances E. Willard (100 for 30 cents).

27. On Which Side Are You? by Frances E. Willard (100 for 30 cents).

28. Alcohol and Disease (½ cent).

29. Liquor and Poverty (½ cent).

30. Counting the Cost of Alcohol (½ cent).

31. Is Alcohol a Food? (½ cent).

32. The Cure for National Intemperance (½ cent).

33. Patent Medicines (¾ cent).

34. Some Effects of Tobacco Using (½ cent).

35. Pointed Facts About Tobacco (¼ cent).

36. Tobacco Using (1½ cents).

37. The Tobacco Habit (5 cents).

38. Diet and Endurance (5 cents).

39. Medical Use of Alcohol (¾ cent).

40. The Liquor Traffic and Prohibition, by Mrs. E. G. White (100 for 25 cents).

41. Drunkenness and Crime, by Mrs. E. G. White (1 cent each).

42. Charged with Murder (¾ cent).

43. The Demons' Council, by D. E. Scoles (½ cent).

44. A Chat With My Tobacco-Using Brother, by R. W. Parmele (½ cent).

How to Order

Leaflets Nos. 1-10, from Rev. J. F. Hill, Cor. Sec., 72 Conestoga Bldg., Pittsburg, Pa.

Leaflets Nos. 11-27, from Ruby I. Gilbert, 915-131 Wabash Ave., Chicago, Ill.

Leaflets Nos. 28-44, from Review and Herald, Takoma Park Station, Washington, D. C.

Temperance Magazines

The Boy Magazine, edited by Lucy Page Gaston. Published monthly. 10 cents a copy, 50 cents per annum. Address, National Anti-Cigarette League, 1119 Woman's Temple, 184 La Salle St., Chicago, Ill.

The Union Signal, edited by Mrs. Lillian Stevens. Published weekly. $1 per annum. Address, Union Signal, Evanston, Ill.

Life and Health, edited by Dr. G. H. Heald. Published monthly. 10 cents a copy; $1 per annum. Address, Life and Health, Takoma Park Station, Washington, D. C.

Temperance Books

Prohibition Year Book. Lincoln Temperance Press, 92 La Salle St., Chicago. Paper, 25 cents; cloth, 50 cents.

Weapons for Temperance Warfare, by Belle M. Brain. United Society of Christian Endeavor, Boston and Chicago. Cloth, 35 cents.

Ministry of Healing, by Mrs. E. G. White. Review and Herald Publishing Assn., Takoma Park Station, Washington, D. C. Cloth, $1.50; postage, 15 cents.

Anti-Saloon League Year Book, thirty-five cents. Anti-Saloon League of America, 110 La Salle St., Chicago, Ill.

Social Welfare and the Liquor Problem, by Harry Warner. Fifty cents, in manilla cover. The Intercollegiate Prohibition Assn., Chicago, Illinois.

The Deadly Cigarette, by John Quincy Adams Henry. Thirty-five cents, in cloth. Richard J. James, 3 & 4 London House Yard, Paternoster Row, E. C., London, England.

Temperance Pledges

1. Total Abstinence, including tea and coffee.
2. Temperance, including tobacco and liquor.
3. Temperance, against liquor only.

Price of 1 and 2, 5 or more, 1 cent each; 3, 1 cent each, 75 cents a hundred.

Order from Review and Herald Publishing Association, Takoma Park Station, Washington, D. C.

Stereopticon Slides

The song, "Till Prohibition's Day," is illustrated by six beautiful stereopticon slides: "A lonely mother kneeling," "Straying where poison fountains flow," "I live for [wine and] you," "The holy shrine is laden," "A lonely wife is weeping," "Till prohibition day."

These and other temperance slides can be purchased or rented from the Medical Council of the General Conference, Takoma Park Station, Washington, D. C. Write for information.

INDEX

ABSINTHE, introduced into France, 124; use of prohibited in Belgium, 124; sale of forbidden on boats on Lake Geneva, 125.
Acrolein, produced by burning cigarette-paper, 82.
Abstinence, total, advocated by Daniel and Paul, 115; flag of total hoisted in 1836, 117; wave of total phenomenal, 146; represented by daily papers in Sweden and Norway, 152; relation of vegetarianism to, 201; testimonies in favor of, 218, 219.
Abyssinia, liquor traffic not allowed in, 125; prohibition in, 151.
Accidents, caused by drink, 22.
Acid, tannic, in cup of tea, 199.
Advertisement, an honest, for saloon, 54.
Alaska, temperance in, 123.
Alcohol, an evil genius, 13; causes ill-health, 22, 34; relative amount consumed per capita in different countries, 28; what science says about, 34, 35; antitheses between food and, 36, 37; causes degeneration of heart, liver, and kidneys, 39; paralyzing effect on brain, 41; charges enormous toll for its heat and energy, 42; list of things in which it is necessary, 42; food for lies, lust, idleness, dishonesty, 44; amount of consumed in patent medicines, 104.
Alcoholism, Twelfth International Congress on, 45.
Allies, powerful, of the liquor traffic, 147; of intemperance, 185.
Ambulance, The Fence and the (poetry), 174.
Americans, drunk, awaken disgust in Filipinos, 26.
Antitheses, between food and alcohol, 36, 37.
Appetite, for liquor, must be created, 31.
Army, the cold water, 117.
Attack, methods of used to advance temperance cause, 204.
Australia, temperance education compulsory in, 126.
Austria, temperance teaching forbidden to children in, 125.

BABE, the, cursed by saloon, 47. Baby, started on road to intemperance by soothing sirup, 110.
Badge, the Red Ribbon, 120.
Bar, the hotel, 60.

Barkeepers, no drunken, 155.
Bars, two kinds of, 54.
Bates, Joseph, founder of Fairhaven Temperance Society, 117.
Beecher, Lyman, aided temperance effort, 117.
Beer drinking, effects of noted in Germany, 35.
Beer drinker, how life insurance companies estimate life of, 20; incapable of recovering, 39; must be recreated, 39.
Beer, ship-loads followed Dewey's fleet, 26; the world's output of, 27; recommended by brewers, 32; drunk daily by New York City schoolchildren, 35; most injurious of all alcoholic drinks, 39; produces degeneration of all organs, 39; drank a gallon a day, 40; statement of Von Moltke concerning, 153.
Belgium, makes appropriation for teaching temperance in public schools, 124.
Beverages, alcoholic, cause of declining birth-rate, 40.
Bibliography, 245-248.
Bill, for drink, increase of in various countries, 16; Chicago's daily drink, 16; England's, 27; how to pay the household, 28.
Bills, ten-dollar, what became of, 23.
Biographies, short, 129-138.
Birth-rate, declining, facts concerning the, 40.
Blindness, caused by smoking, 80.
Blow, a, struck by drunken father, 52.
Boy, somebody's, will fill place in drunkards' line, 18.
Boys, needed by liquor dealers, 18; wanted for new customers, 18, 59; clubs organized to prepare to become saloon patrons, 19; convicted of burglary, assault, robbery, murder, 25; aged seven confesses drunkenness, 25; an open field for creation of liquor appetite, 31; under sixteen prohibited from smoking, 74; God wants, 76; don't smoke, 86; be careful what you sow, 96; number of, who become drunkards each year, 209.
Bohemia, temperance not taught to children, 125.
Bok, Edward, statement of against meat-eating, 182.
Books, temperance, 247, 248.

Index

Bottle, the, when to apply, 34.
Brewers, statement of, 32, 33.
Brewery, advance agent of American in Dewey's force, 26.
Bride, or beer, which? 50.
Business, selling patent medicines a profitable, 101; greed, the root of, 102; patent-medicine robbing America, 103; the liquor, not susceptible of reformation, 148; the liquor, costs millions to maintain, 162.
Bushmen, of Australia, destroyed by whisky, 15.
Burton, Sir Richard, on gunpowder and rum in South Africa, 15.

CAFFEINE, three grains of in glass of Coco-Cola, 108; amount of in cup of tea, 199.
Canada, local option in, 126.
Camp-meeting, suggestions for temperance rallies at, 237, 238.
Cancer, smoker's, causes death of General Grant, 79.
Casseday, Jennie, blessing of her life to the world, 132, 133.
Catechism, the saloon, 47; a temperance, 194.
Charity, a case for, 92.
Charts, suggested for temperance meetings, 235.
Children, of drinking parents, facts concerning, 35; of moderate drinkers, 36; defective in body and mind, 39; of hop-pickers, 79; must be instructed in temperance, 203; of saloon-keeper ostracized at school, 216.
China, ancient prohibition law in, 126.
Choice, General Sheridan's for his son, 45.
Church, the, and the liquor traffic, 147.
Churches, the popular, courting intemperance, 180.
Cigarette, first appearance of in United States, 74; laws passed against, 74; playing havoc in British army, 75; an outlaw in eight States, 77; nicotine contained in one, 78; made of drugged tobacco, 80; five poisons in, 80; the devil's device for killing young Americans, 82; as a mathematician, 84; the cure, 91; poem on the, 92; The Deadly (poetry), 97.
Cigarettes, ladies', 75; number of smoked in United States in one year, 77; cause expensive fires, 77; thousands sold to women in Philadelphia, 77; smokers of dangerous, 78; relation of to crime, 80; smoked two thousand boxes of, 81.
Cider, sweet, warning against, 200.
Cities, three hundred prohibition in United States, 152.
Clark, Dr. Billy, founder of first temperance society, 116.
Closing, Sunday, 160.
Cocaine, in catarrh remedies, 104; sold to schoolchildren in New Jersey, 111; remarkable increase of demand for, 111.
Coffee, an ally of intemperance, 185; home and history of, 198; contents of, 199.
Coffin, offered as premium, 81.
Column, of silver dollars, 23.
Congress, a temperance society of members of, 117.
Consideration, show none to liquor traffic, 158.
Corn, returns of one bushel used in liquor traffic, 17.
Corporation, determined stand taken against liquor by United States Steel, 154.
Cost, The, of a License, 171.
Council, The Demons', 179.
Courage, causes for, 120.
Course, the only safe, 185.
Court, effect of cigarettes seen in Kentucky, 78.
Courts, the, filled with criminals by saloon, 47.
Crime traced to grog-shops, 23; relation of cigarettes to, 80.
Crimes, shrinkage of in prohibition States, 144.
Cup, the social, 19.
Cure-alls, lure user to drug enslavement, 104.
Cure, the cigarette, 91; permanent for national intemperance, 190.
Cures, the drug-habit, 105.

DANGER, the cigarette a greater than drink, 76; the, of depending altogether on law, 204; poem, 229.
Day, Till Prohibition's (song), 176.
Dealers, patent-medicine, in prohibition territory, 110.
Decanter, song of the old, 14.
Declaration, of principles, adopted by United States Brewers' Association in 1908, 32.
Decree, a, issued in China against opium, 106.
Defense of man charged with murder, 165-168; of young man sentenced to imprisonment, 210.
Delirium tremens, number of cases of in Germany, 25.
Delusion, the alcohol-food, 41.
Den, opium, first building in an

Index

East India island, 110; inscription by opium smoker, 111.
Denmark, temperance taught in schools of, 125.
Dens, opium, luxurious, in London, 110.
Diet, better to depend on simple, 99; a correct, must supplement efforts for prohibition, 188; vegetarian employed in treating alcoholics, 189, 190.
Distilleries, established as result of Revolutionary War, 116.
Dividends, of the liquor traffic, 17, 18.
Divorce, one in five caused by drink, 30; frequency of, a danger-signal, 45.
Divorces, caused by drink, 25, 45; number of granted in 1903 in United States, 45.
Dogs, smoking not good for, 85.
Dow, Neal, efforts of in behalf of temperance, 130.
Drink, first the man takes a, etc., 15; harm done by among Pacific islanders, 15; wrecks homes, 30, 45; creation of appetite for, 31; demand for, world old, 32; the devil's way into a man, 44; why I oppose, 44.
Drinker, the moderate, in danger, 26; curses posterity, 36; the confirmed, no chance for success, 45.
Drinking, moderate, the ripe fruit of, 43, 56.
Drinks, advertised to relieve fatigue should be regarded with suspicion, 107; dangerous, sold in drug stores, etc., 107; contain cocaine and caffeine, 108.
Drop, Patrick refuses to take a, 223.
Drugs, better to discard, 99.
Drunkard, what the reformed lost, 221.
Drunkards, number of dying annually in Great Britain, 22; widows and orphans left by, 22; use tobacco, 84.

EATING and drinking, intemperance in, 110.
Education, stands or falls with temperance, 43; efforts in behalf of scientific temperance, 136.
Errands, God's, never fail, 12.
Exercise, blackboard, for temperance meeting, 234.
Experiments, simple, 240-242.
Extract, alcoholic, amount of in cup of tea, 199.
Evil, an, and its remedy, 179.
Evils, The Seven Great, 181.
Eyes, his, opened, 51.

FAT, morphine produces, 39.
Fee, result of doubling license in Chicago, 162; consumer pays, 162.
Fence, The, and the Ambulance (poetry), 174.
Finger, telltale mark on index carried by many girls, 75.
Finland, state-wide prohibition law in, 152.
Fires, caused by smoking, 77.
Fire-water, effects of, summed up by Indian chief, 44; appeal against by war-chief of New Hebrides, 206.
Firm, world's largest dry-goods, favors prohibition, 154.
Flame, light-blue, some patent medicines will burn with a, 104.
Flesh, never the best food, 186; eating of often causes craving for stimulants, 189.
Food, certain effects of, 36, 37; mistake to suppose muscular strength depends on animal, 186.
Forces, advance of temperance in 1908, 145.
Fortress, a well-nigh impregnable, 19; diligence of enemy in, 20.
France, the scourge of alcoholism in, 123.
Fraud, the great American, 99, 103.
Fiend, a, 93.
Fruits, the, of the saloon, 141; use of, an aid to temperance, 188.

GERMANY, temperance movement in, 123.
Gifts, table showing results of using God's in two ways, 38.
Ginger, Jamaica, an indictment of, 112.
Glass, the first, 19; what man is drinking from, 44; first given to Francis Murphy, 135.
Glasses, the two, 63.
Gordon, Anna A., work of, 133.
Gough, John B., labor of, 118; checkered career of, 132; last words of, 132; saying of, 209; an hour with, 243.
Grain, result of when made into bread or into beer, 38; bushels of distilled into whisky, 148.
Grape juice, deadly work of, 44.
Graves, drunkards', 17, 18.
Great Britain, early struggle of against liquor traffic, 123.
Greed, the, of civilized nations a reproach to Christianity, 206.

HABIT, evils of the tobacco, 72; connection of the cigarette with personal purity, 84; treating,

Index

evils of the, 86; the opium, 106; story of a man who tried to break his tobacco, 222.
Hawaii, license law in, 123.
Headache-powders, dangerous, 105.
Health, injured by small doses of alcohol, 34.
Heathen, the Melican, 50.
Heredity, weakened, cause of tuberculosis, 39.
Heritage, the, of intemperance, 35.
Heroine, made from morphine, 106; a dangerous toxic agent, 107.
Holland, temperance instruction in, 125.
Homes, our, in Satan's army, 180.
Hope, for the tempted, 11.
Hops, tons of used in beer, 28.
Hospital, a visit to Bellevue, 40.
Hungary, small consumer of intoxicants, 124.
Hunt, Mrs. Mary, efforts of in behalf of temperance education, 136.
Hymn, antisaloon battle, 173.
Hymns, list of temperance, 233.

I F, 58.
Illustrations: Rescue the Fallen, 8; The Old Decanter, 14; United States Drink Bill, 16; How My Boy Went Down, 19; The Real Black Hand, 24; Speaking of Vice, 48; A Timely Warning, 51; The Saloon Did It, 53; Wanted — A Bright Boy to Take This Man's Place, 59; The Career of a Cigarette Smoker, 70; To Oblivion, 86; Showing Relative Amount of Alcohol, 107; Founders and Home of First Temperance Society, 114; Neal Dow, 130; Anna A. Gordon, 133; Frances E. Willard, 134; Frances Murphy, 135; Mrs. Lillian M. N. Stevens, 137; Anti-Saloon Map of the United States, 140; Licenses in Various Cities, 142; Diagram, 145, 152; Tainted Money, 156; A False Plea, 168; The Fence and the Ambulance (illustrated poem), 174, 175; What Shall It Profit? 209; Burning Alcohol in Patent Medicines, 241.
India, religions of, prohibit intoxicants, 126.
Insanity, caused by drink, 23, 34; due to use of tobacco, 79.
Intemperance, began in Eden, 9; results of, 10, 11; a formidable agent of degeneration, 20; cause of poverty, 23; the heritage of, 35; in disguise, 103; most terrible pestilence of twentieth century, 179; allies of, 185; often begins in the home, 186, 194; dietetic cause of, 184, 185; why the young should shun, 195; how to deal with victims of, 207.
Intoxicants, annual bill for in United States, 16; occasion divorce, 45.
Issue, temperance a living, 205, 213.
It must be settled right (poetry), 170.
"I was drunk," brings death sentence to many, 23.

J APAN, temperance retreating in, 125.
Joints, opium, in London, 110.
Judges, juvenile court, deplore cigarette habit, 84.

K HAMA, Chief, appeal of, 205.
King Alcohol, societies formed by rebels of, 118; dethroned in nine States, 153; trial of, 243.

L ABELS, requirements concerning, 102.
Lad, story of a temperance, 220.
Lament, the drunkard's, 67.
Law, a novel cigarette, 78; the first American prohibition, 152; first on European soil, 152.
Laws, our, legalize drunkard making, 23; regulating patent-medicine business passed by several States, 103; Sunday, 160; prohibitory liquor do not interfere with personal liberty, 168.
Leaflets, temperance, 245-247.
League, the Anti-Cigarette, giving alarm, 76; the Anti-Saloon formed, 122.
Leaves, tobacco, stolen from Havana dock, 73.
Legion, Loyal Temperance, work of Anna A. Gordon for, 133.
Liberty, personal, a false contention, 168; not lost by signing pledge, 222.
License, definition of, 162; does not lessen liquor consumed, 162; does not meet cost of maintaining saloons, 162; cost of a, 171.
Lie, a, told by beer, 41.
Lincoln, Abraham, a temperance man, 212; temperance pledges signed by, 217.
Liquor, deaths caused by in Great Britain, 25; definitions of, 43; a near relative of tobacco, 73; condemned as a source of revenue, 156; destroys souls and bodies of men, 156; deciding the question of, 212.
Liquor dealers, boys needed by, 18;

Index

words from, 31, 32; varied methods of, 147; cultivate thirst for liquor, 147; seek to reach public through so-called religious publications, 147; allow no drunken barkeepers, 155.
Liquor drinking, increasing in United States, 26.
Liquors, intoxicating, per cent of crimes produced by, 21.
Literature, against opium circulated in Celestial Empire, 106; distributed by liquor dealers, 147.
Liver, affected by beer, 39; cirrhosis of caused by alcohol, 39.
Lord of hosts, the, is with us (song), 128.
Loss, a mother's, caused by drink, 164.

MAGAZINES, list of which insert no liquor advertisements, 153, 154; temperance, 247.
Malt, amount of used in one year's output of beer, 28.
Marriage, marred by intemperance, 11.
Match, no, for alcohol, 56.
Mathematician, the cigarette as a, 84.
Mathew, Father, efforts of for temperance in Ireland, 118.
Meat, not eaten by Japanese, 181.
Medicines, patent, branded worthless by Chicago druggist, 100; a formidable obstacle in path of temperance reform, 101; what they cost Americans annually, 101; worthless and dangerous, 103; contain so much alcohol they will burn with light-blue flame, 104.
Meetings, for temperance, 233; Scripture lessons for, 234; blackboard exercises for, 234; use of charts in, 235; mottoes for, 235; miscellaneous suggestions for, 235.
Menace, man who indulges in alcoholic drinks, a, 38.
Men, the saloon, not proud of finished product, 43.
Men, list of famous, who never smoked, 78.
Message, statement in Thanksgiving, 150; parting, of dying youth, 210.
Method, a short and easy, 34.
Mexico, scientific temperance taught in schools of, 126.
Minister, statement of a drinking, 216.
Ministry of Healing, selections from, 185, 186.
Mistakes, in freight office, made by cigarette smokers, 79.

Moody, Dwight L., testimony of, 209.
More gospel, less rum, a plea from the Kongo, 10.
Mortality, rate of among children of mothers employed in tobacco factories, 81.
Mortgages, expensive, 55.
Mother, sent to scrub by saloon, 47.
Mothers, responsibility of for forming habits of temperance, 202.
Motto, no compromise and no cessation, 12; the, of Red Ribbon movement, 120; a good, for temperance meetings, 233.
Mottoes, suggested for temperance meetings, 235.
Movement, the Red Ribbon, 118, 120; the Blue Ribbon, 118, 120.
Murder, narrative of man charged with, 165.
Murphy, Francis, founder of Blue Ribbon reform, 120; wonderful work of, 135; policy pursued by, 216.

NEED, the, of to-day in the temperance cause, 204.
Nicotine, acts on the heart, 72, 87; effects of seen in newsboys, 75; named by Jean Nicot, 78; enough in one cigarette to kill two toads, 78; first effect of on system, 87; produces anemia, 88; acts directly on nerve-centers, 87; enough in one cigar to kill two men, 194.
No, dare to say, 229.
Norway, every fifth person in, an abstainer, 125.
Notice, a, posted by manufacturing company against cigarettes, 74; issued by Rock Island Railroad against cigarette, 78.

OPIUM, men led to habit by smoking cigarettes, 80; not a new problem, 105; history of in China, 105; decree issued against in China, 106; use of increasing in America, 106; being supplanted by morphine in China, 106; has victims in all civilized lands, 107; large amount of consumed in New York City, 110; importation of forbidden except as medicine, 110; proscribed in Mohammedan lands, 110; Japan trying to rid Formosa of curse of, 110; use of increasing in London, 110; alarming increase of demand for, 111; trade in opposed by Polyglot Petition, 134.

Option, local, call for in Russia, 124; in provinces of Canada, 126.
Orphans, efforts of Mrs. Annie Wittenmyer in behalf of, 130.
Outlaw, the cigarette an, in eight States, 77.

PERIL, a universal, 57.
Peruna, per cent of alcohol contained in, 104; sale of prohibited to Indians, 110.
Petition, Polyglot, 134; a, against manufacture and sale of liquor, 244.
Plans, campaign of the liquor army, 147.
Pledge, the, that makes us free, 98; motto of the Blue Ribbon, 120; millions induced to sign by Francis Murphy, 136; value of signing the, 211; the temperance Magna Charta of liberty, 217; signed by kaiser and president, 217; the only valuable, 217; Lincoln's temperance, 217; written, signed, and advocated by Lincoln, 217; is liberty lost by signing the? 222; what came from signing the, 228; sign the to-night, 230; a model temperance, 244; temperance, 248.
Poison, tobacco a malignant, 69; cigarette (a conversation), 88; the glowing, 156.
Prayer, necessity of, in temperance meetings, 233.
Presidents, three assassinated by men on fire with whisky, 21.
Principles, declaration of, adopted by brewers in 1908, 32.
Prisoners, thirty-five boy, 80; work of Jennie Casseday for, 133.
Prisons, how to shut up nine tenths of, 21.
Problem, the saloon, 19.
Programs, several sample, 243, 244.
Progress, the march of, 122.
Prohibition, fought by saloon men, 32; opposed by Chicago Liquor Dealers' Association, 49; ancient law for in China, 126; efforts of Lillian M. N. Stevens in behalf of, 137, 138; does it prohibit? 143; what it does, 144; results of securing, 148, 149; some results of, 150, 151; favored by world's largest dry-goods firm, 154; why we favor, 156, 157; nine reasons for, 156; seven reasons for, 157; vote for, 158.
Property, beer-drinking engineers and switchmen cause million-dollar loss of, 21.
Proverb, a Japanese, 15.

Pulse-rate, increased by nicotine, 87.

QUESTION, a, of liquor organ well answered, 160.
Questions, seven weighty, 85.

RAILWAY lines, position of twenty-five in the United States, 132.
Rallies, suggestions for temperance, 237, 238.
Rally, suggestions for a young people's temperance, 236.
Reaction, in cause of temperance reform, 118.
Reading, responsive, 196.
Reasons, for prohibition, 156, 157.
Recruits, from enemy's ranks, 118.
Reform, saloon, 49; more attention should be given to the temperance, 206.
Reproach, a humiliating, 15.
Resolution, a, passed by Congress in 1777, 116; a strong, 155; against the liquor traffic, 244.
Resources, wasted in Chicago, 29.
Revenue, saloon fools men by talk of, 48; turned into United States treasury by liquor traffic, 141; nation pays too much for, 142; liquor not a proper source of, 156.
Reynolds, Dr., founder of Red Ribbon movement, 120.
Rights, the, of those who pay taxes, 169.
Rogers, Mrs., recovery of, 108.
Roll, the honor, eight States on, 77.
Rosy, story of poor, 225.
Rules, interesting set of adopted by Chicago Liquor Dealers' Association, 49.
Rum, in Africa, 15; statement of Philadelphia judge concerning, 21; tragedy of in Manila and Philippines, 26.
Rush, Dr. Benjamin, efforts of for temperance and free schools, 129.
Russia, the sale of spirits a government monopoly in, 124.
Rye, song of the, 170.

SACRIFICE, the license, 64.
Saloon, the American, a curse in the Philippines, 15, 25; what it brings in its train, 18; wants your boy, 19; careful count made in a Chicago, 24; according to the saloon-keeper, 33; list of, 49; the model, 54; down in the licensed, 68; going at the rate of thirty a day, 121; a legal of offenses of, 47, 48; reform institution, 141.

Saloon-keeper, how shall we treat the, 215.
Saloons, in United States, 16; daily patronage of in Boston, 16; recruiting stations of liquor traffic, 20; of Hillsboro, Ohio, entered by earnest women, 119; increase of in Salt Lake City, 163.
Satire, a, illustrating unreasonableness of license system, 159.
Savings-bank, pledge, the best, 211.
Scene, a court-room, 159.
Schools, Maine's proportion of population in, 151.
Shoes, baby's, 46; cigarette money for one year would buy a pair of for each child in United States, 75.
Sign, the saloon-keeper's, 52; a, hoisted by young men, 83; a, displayed in Chicago drug store, 100, 103.
Signboard, a, 60.
Sirups, soothing, contain alcohol and opium, 104.
Sixteen lost, one saved, 224.
Slaves, how Americans become to drugs, 107.
Slides, stereopticon, 248.
Smoke, tobacco, deadly ingredients of, 73; infants killed by, 73.
Smoking, cigarette, prohibited by Lowell manufacturer, 74; forbidden by Rock Island Railroad official, 78; leads to opium habit, 80; denounced, 81; leads to indulgence in alcoholic drinks, 83; increase of, 84.
Smoking, prohibited in schools and colleges of France, 81; not good for dogs, 85.
Snuff, tax paid on, 77; cocaine in, 111.
Society, the first temperance, 116; membership of the Total Abstinence in 1846, 117; Washingtonian Total Abstinence, 118.
Somerset, Lady Henry, earnest advocate of total abstinence, 131.
Something to you, 62; must be done, 76.
Song, the, of the rye (poetry), 170.
Spain, a great consumer of wines and liquors, 125.
Spices, an ally of intemperance, 185.
Spirits, ardent, let in cold, 34; sale of, government monopoly in Russia, 124.
Stimulants, use of forbidden in British camp, 146.
Stevens, Mrs. Lillian M. N., a well-trained leader, 137; leader in the cause of prohibition, 138.
Suggestions, miscellaneous, for temperance meetings, 235; for young people's temperance rally, 236; for temperance rallies at camp-meetings, 237.
Sweden, fighting for local veto of liquor traffic, 124; seven newspapers represent total abstinence in, 152.
Switzerland, state control of liquor traffic in, 125.
System, the Gothenburg in Sweden, 124; the license, 161; abolition of, the only remedy, 161; why I do not believe in, 162.

TAVERNS, tea, prohibited, 181.
Tax, paid on snuff, 77; on cigars and cigarettes, 77.
Tea, statement of London *Lancet* concerning, 181; an ally of intemperance, 185; money wasted in, 198; contents of a cup of black, 199; of green, 199; effects of on heart, 199.
Telegram, a, from Atlanta, Georgia, 144, 151.
Temperance, defined by United Brewers' Association, 32; education stands or falls with, 43; beginning of work of in America, 115; revival of led to religious awakening, 117; high-water mark in, 118; reaction in case of, brought about by Civil War, 118; in other lands, 123; cornerstone of, 177; Bible reading on, 178; Christian, guide-posts of, 179; principles of Christian, 180, 181; Christian, a part of God's message, 182; historical notes on Christian, 183; four lessons on, 191-197; Bible study on, 193; catechism, a, 194, 195; responsive reading on, 196; relation of missions to, 205; what shall we do for? 213; call of hour for, 213; hints for workers in cause of, 215; meetings for, 231; central theme of meetings for, 233.
Testimonials, bureau for patent medicine, 101; many forged, 102.
Testimony, an unconscious, against beer, 40.
Theme, the central of temperance meeting, 233.
Things, stubborn, 89.
Thirst, the, of the drunkard, 207; draft which will quench, 207.
Tide, the, heaves onward, 121, 152.
Tiger, the blind, in Chicago, 22.
Times, what the demand, 204.
Tipplers, six, charter-members of

Washingtonian Temperance Society, 118.
Tobacco, robbing the world, 10; an ally of the liquor traffic, 69; historical notes on, 71; habit, effects of the, 72, 87; depresses heart action, 73; revenue paid by consumers of, 77; one good use for, 82; the use of paves the way to dissipation, 83.
Toll, an enormous, 42.
Topics, list of thirty for temperance papers, essays, or talks, 239.
Traffic, the liquor, a curse in all lands, 15; fostered in civilized countries, 16; effects of in larger cities, 16; returns of, 17, 18; how guarded, 19, 20; a cause of poverty, 23; statistics concerning in *English Watchword*, 27; a cancer in society, 43; a universal peril, 57; early effort to regulate, 115; state control of in Switzerland, 125; checked in Holland, 125; not tolerated in Abyssinia, 125; Polyglot Petition against, 134; regulate by annihilation, 139; does it pay to support the? 141; revenue from, 141; a loss to the nation, 143; resources of the, 146, 147; powerful allies of, 147; regulation of, a failure, 148; voters for are responsible for consequences of, 149; revenue from in 1908, 153; relative of all evil, 159; inconsistency of licensing, 163.
Treating, evils of the habit of, 86.
Turkey, religion of forbids use of intoxicating liquors, 126.

USER, the tobacco, 95.
United States, increase of drink bill in, 16; dividend of liquor traffic in the, 17; murders and suicides in the, 17; money spent for drink in the, 22; money spent for whisky, tobacco, and opium in, 22; liquor-drinking in the, 26; use of money in the, 28; annual tobacco bill of the, 77.

VEGETARIAN, reasons for becoming one, 189.
Vegetarians, list of noted, 182.

Vegetarianism, recommended by Dr. Wiley, 200; relation between total abstinence and, 201.
Vice, capitalized by license system, 162.
Victims, the, of intemperance need gentleness, 207.
Victory, a, depends on thoroughness, 121.
Vinci, Leonardo da, incident in life of, 53.
Volunteers, crowd drunkards' line, 18.

WAR, temperance for independence, 129; incident in Civil, 207.
Warning, an ancient Egyptian, 12.
W. C. T. U., the, permanently organized, 119, 122; belts globe, 118; first president of the, 130.
Whisky, four gallons of from one bushel of corn, 17; what a barrel of contains, 58; five hundred barrels of used weekly by patent-medicine firm, 110; does not hurt those who let it alone, 169; barrel of between two lines of sharp-shooters, 207.
Willard, Frances E., America's uncrowned queen, 13; her service for humanity, 134; statue of in national Capitol, 135.
Wilson, Henry, showed courage of his convictions, 223.
Wine, ancient Egyptian warning against, 12; anciently offered to the dead, 12; well defined, 43; decrease in use of in Great Britain, 153.
Wine-jars, in ancient tombs, 12.
Wine shops, ancient Egyptian, warning against, 12.
Wittenmyer, Mrs. Annie, efforts of in behalf of temperance, 130.
Words, significant, of the National Liquor Dealers' Association, 145.
Work, beginning of the temperance, 115.
Workers, hints for temperance, 215.
What temperance should teach, 232.
Wreck, a, at twenty-eight, 51.

YOUTH, snares for, 19; sent to work by saloon, 47; selling their birthright, 75; working for the, 209.

www.ingramcontent.com/pod-product-compliance
Lightning Source LLC
Chambersburg PA
CBHW070246230426
43664CB00014B/2415